NAHB Economics & Housing Policy Group

SINGLE-FAMILY BUILDER COMPENSATION STUDY
2022 EDITION

NAHB®

National Association
of Home Builders

Single-Family Builder Compensation Study, 2022 Edition

BuilderBooks, a Service of the National Association of Home Builders

Patricia Potts	Senior Director
Design Central	Cover Design
Robert Brown	Composition
Gerald M. Howard	Chief Executive Officer
Robert Dietz	Senior Vice President and Chief Economist, Economics and Housing Policy
Paul Emrath	Vice President, Economics and Housing Policy
Rose Quint	Assistant Vice President, Survey Research, Economics and Housing Policy

Disclaimer

This publication provides accurate information on the subject matter covered. The publisher is selling it with the understanding that the publisher is not providing legal, accounting, or other professional service. If you need legal advice or other expert assistance, obtain the services of a qualified professional experienced in the subject matter involved. The NAHB has used commercially reasonable efforts to ensure that the contents of this volume are complete and appear without error; however, the NAHB makes no representations or warranties regarding the accuracy and completeness of this document's contents. The NAHB specifically disclaims any implied warranties of merchantability or fitness for a particular purpose. The NAHB shall not be liable for any loss of profit or any other commercial damages, including but not limited to incidental, special, consequential or other damages. Reference herein to any specific commercial products, process, or service by trade name, trademark, manufacturer, or otherwise does not necessarily constitute or imply its endorsement, recommendation, or favored status by the NAHB. The views and opinions of the author expressed in this publication do not necessarily state or reflect those of the NAHB, and they shall not be used to advertise or endorse a product.

Published in the United States of America

25 24 23 22   1 2 3 4 5

ISBN: 978-0-86718-800-4
eISBN: 978-0-86718-801-1

For further information, please contact:
National Association of Home Builders
1201 15th Street, NW
Washington, DC 20005-2800
BuilderBooks.com

Table of Contents

Executive Summary

- The *2022 Single-Family Builder Compensation Study* provides information on the average salary, bonus, and fringe benefits for 39 common positions at single-family home building companies. Results are broken down by region of the country and size of the builder (dollar volume, starts, and number of employees).

- Nearly all single-family builders (94%) responding to the survey have a full-time President/CEO; 50% have a full-time VP of Construction; 47% have a full-time Superintendent; and 29% have a full-time Bookkeeper. The remaining 35 positions exist as full-time jobs at less than 40% of the responding firms.

- Builders were asked to report the annual salary and bonus/commission (if any) of each position existing at their firm. To produce the average total compensation for each full-time position, its average annual salary and average bonus/commission (computed among all respondents reporting a salary for the position on a full-time basis) were combined.

- The top five highest average total compensation levels are:

President/CEO	$218,858
Head/Director of Land Acquisition	$181,628
VP of Construction	$161,362
CFO/Head of Finance	$151,030
Head/Director of Sales & Marketing	$146,290

- The lowest five average total compensation levels are:

Receptionist	$39,762
Administrative Assistant	$47,664
Customer Service Manager	$52,418
Executive Assistant	$53,621
Bookkeeper	$55,551

- Builders were also asked about which of a list of 13 fringe benefits (health insurance, dental insurance, vision program, prescription program, life insurance, short term disability, long term disability, flex spending, 401K plan, paid vacation leave, paid sick leave, tuition reimbursement, and training) they offered to each of the positions existing at the firm.

- The two most-commonly offered benefits to full-time employees at single-family home building companies are paid vacation leave and health insurance: at least 90% and 73% of builders, respectively, offer those benefits to all the positions for which data can be calculated.

- The two least likely benefits builders offer their full-time employees are tuition reimbursement and flex spending: at most 53% of builders offer those benefits to any of the positions for which data can be calculated.

Chapter 1

Profile of Study Respondents

Like most other sectors of the American economy, the residential construction industry has been severely affected by the turmoil brought about by COVID-19 to the labor market. Since the onset of the pandemic, builders have had to adapt to office employees increasingly working remotely and on a more flexible schedule. The pandemic also made an ongoing, chronic shortage of skilled labor significantly worse, marked by an indefatigable rise in the number of construction job openings. Throughout the economy and across all sectors, millions of people have quit their jobs looking for better work-life balance, benefits, location, or pay — a phenomenon now commonly referred to as the Great Resignation.

These serious challenges have rendered the recruitment and retention of human capital a pressing objective for most businesses, one that will help determine their success in the years ahead. For this reason, and in order to provide our members the tools they need to run successful businesses, the National Association of Home Builders has produced new industry standards on compensation and benefits for employees of single-family home building companies.

In late 2021, the NAHB Economics and Housing Policy Group conducted a nationwide survey of single-family builders covering the most common 39 positions at these companies, with the objective of producing industry benchmarks for salaries, bonuses/commissions, and benefits. The survey was sent to a sample of 4,685 single-family builder members, appropriately stratified to represent builders of different size categories (based on number of starts) and across the four Census regions of the country. A total of 338 responses were received, for a response rate of 7.2%.

Chapters 1 through 4 will present a profile of the study respondents as well as in-depth analysis of the compensation and benefit structure for each of the 39 jobs. Five appendixes of detailed tables are also included, showing aggregate findings across all respondents and also breakdowns by Census region, 2021 dollar volume, 2021 single-family starts, and the number of employees on payroll. A distribution of responses across these categories are shown in Exhibit 1-1, along with the regional distribution of single-family starts in 2021.

Exhibit 1-1. Distribution of Responses		
Category	% of Respondents	% of Single-family Starts in 2021
Region		
Northeast	7	6
Midwest	21	13
South	50	57
West	22	24
2021 Dollar Volume		
Less than $1 million	7	
$1 million to $4,999,999	31	
$5 million to $9,999,999	20	
$10 million to $14,999,999	12	
$15 million or more	29	
2021 Single-Family Starts		
Zero	1	
1 to 10	43	
11 to 25	20	
26 to 99	19	
100 or more	17	
Number of Employees		
Zero	2	
1 to 2	12	
3 to 4	17	
5 to 9	34	
10 or more	35	

PRINCIPAL OPERATION

Exactly half of the study respondents are single-family custom builders. Another 34% are single-family spec/tract builders and 15% are single-family general contractors (Exhibit 1-2).

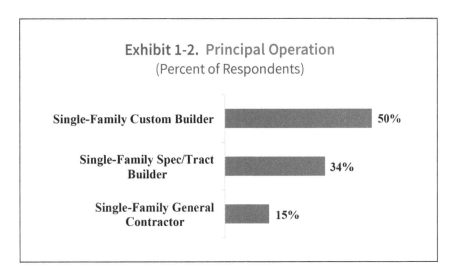

Exhibit 1-2. Principal Operation
(Percent of Respondents)

Single-Family Custom Builder — 50%
Single-Family Spec/Tract Builder — 34%
Single-Family General Contractor — 15%

SINGLE-FAMILY STARTS IN 2021

Builders who participated in the study expected to start an average of 64 single-family units and a median of 15 units in 2021. A plurality — 43% — expected to start 1 to 10 single-family units, 20% 11 to 25 units, 19% 26 to 99 units, and 17% had expectations they would start 100 or more single-family units in 2021 (Exhibit 1-3).

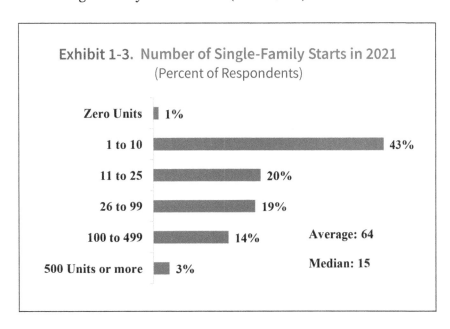

Exhibit 1-3. Number of Single-Family Starts in 2021
(Percent of Respondents)

Zero Units — 1%
1 to 10 — 43%
11 to 25 — 20%
26 to 99 — 19%
100 to 499 — 14%
500 Units or more — 3%

Average: 64
Median: 15

DOLLAR VOLUME OF BUSINESS IN 2021

The typical builder in the study reported a median dollar volume of business of $7.7 million in 2021. The plurality — 31% — expected to end 2021 with $1.0 to $4.9 million in volume, followed closely by 29% who expected to surpass $15 million. Only a small minority of 7% expected their dollar volume to fall below $1 million (Exhibit 1-4).

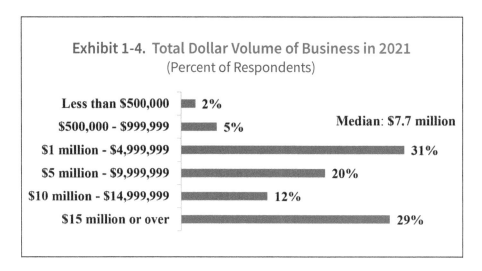

Exhibit 1-4. Total Dollar Volume of Business in 2021
(Percent of Respondents)

Less than $500,000	2%
$500,000 - $999,999	5%
$1 million - $4,999,999	31%
$5 million - $9,999,999	20%
$10 million - $14,999,999	12%
$15 million or over	29%

Median: $7.7 million

YEARS COMPANY HAS BEEN IN BUSINESS

More than half of the builders (56%) have been in business for more than 20 years, while a small minority (4%) have been in operation for less than 5 years. On average, single-family builders taking part in the study have been in business for 25 years (Exhibit 1-5).

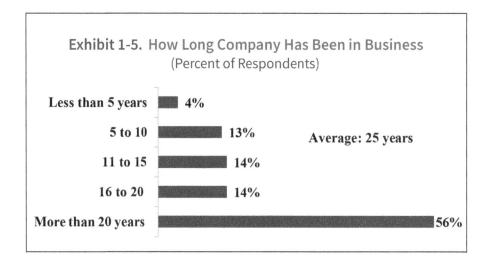

Exhibit 1-5. How Long Company Has Been in Business
(Percent of Respondents)

Less than 5 years	4%
5 to 10	13%
11 to 15	14%
16 to 20	14%
More than 20 years	56%

Average: 25 years

NUMBER OF EMPLOYEES

Thirty-five percent of the builders had at least 10 employees on the company payroll as of September 30, 2021. About the same share — 34% — had 5 to 9 employees, 17% had 3 to 4 employees, 12% only 1 to 2, and 2% had no employees at all. The average number of employees was 18 and the median 7 (Exhibit 1-6).

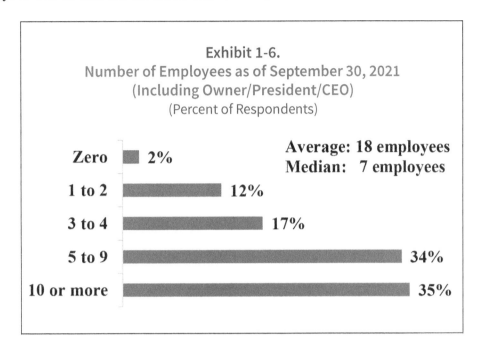

Exhibit 1-6.
Number of Employees as of September 30, 2021
(Including Owner/President/CEO)
(Percent of Respondents)

Average: 18 employees
Median: 7 employees

Zero	2%
1 to 2	12%
3 to 4	17%
5 to 9	34%
10 or more	35%

TOTAL PAYROLL

Fifty-seven percent of builders in the study chose to disclose their total annual payroll as of September 30, 2021. Of that group, nearly half (48%) had a total payroll of $100,000 to $499,999; for 22%, it ranged from $500,000 to $999,999; for 13%, from $1 million to $1.9 million; and for 9%, payroll exceeded $2 million a year. The average annual payroll was $727,314 and the median $432,000 (Exhibit 1-7).

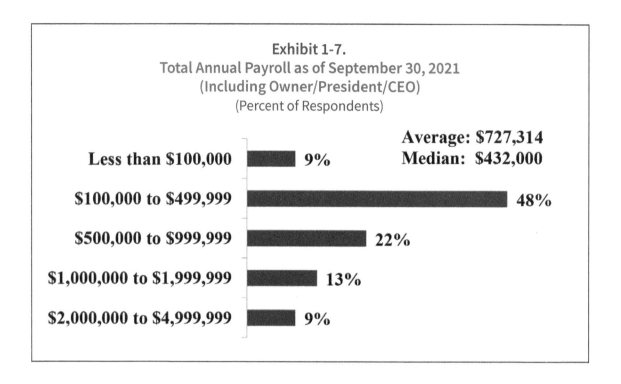

Exhibit 1-7.
Total Annual Payroll as of September 30, 2021
(Including Owner/President/CEO)
(Percent of Respondents)

ORGANIZATION OF THE STUDY

Chapter 2 provides an overview of the prevalence of each of the 39 positions at single-family building companies as well as average total compensation levels for each position, grouped by job family. In this study, average total compensation is defined as the sum of the average salary plus the average bonus/commission among all those reporting a salary. For brevity, the term "bonus" is used throughout this report to refer to either a bonus and/or a commission.

Chapter 3 provides an overview of the incidence of 13 fringe benefits across the 39 positions. The analysis shows that in the single-family home building industry, some fringe benefits to full-time employees are significantly more common than others. In this study, the calculation of the average incidence of a particular benefit for a specific job only considers the builders where that job exists on a full-time basis.

Chapter 4 provides a fuller, more detailed view of each of the position's existence on a full- or part-time basis, its average salary, bonus and total compensation as well as the likelihood of receiving fringe benefits by those who hold it on a full-time basis. The chapter also shows how compensation can vary across firms of different size.

Appendix A shows combined results for all single-family builders in the survey, but also detailed breakdowns by Census region, 2021 dollar volume, 2021 single-family starts, and number of employees on payroll.

Appendix B summarizes the incidence of each job (full-time), its average salary, bonus, and total compensation, grouped by job family.

Appendix C provides complete detail on the nature of each job (full-time vs. part-time), requirement for construction experience, average salary, bonus, and benefits, grouped by job family.

Appendix D highlights the incidence of each job (full-time) and its average total compensation, broken down (when available) by the number of single-family starts in 2021.

Appendix E lists other benefits not listed in the survey received by each of the 39 positions.

Chapter 2

Jobs & Compensation

MOST COMMON CONSTRUCTION COMPANY POSITIONS

The top four most common positions at single-family home building companies in this study are the President/CEO (94% report it as a full time position and 3% as part time), VP of Construction (50% full time, 2% part time), Superintendent (47% full time, 1% part time), and Bookkeeper (29% full time, 16% part time) (Exhibit 2-1).

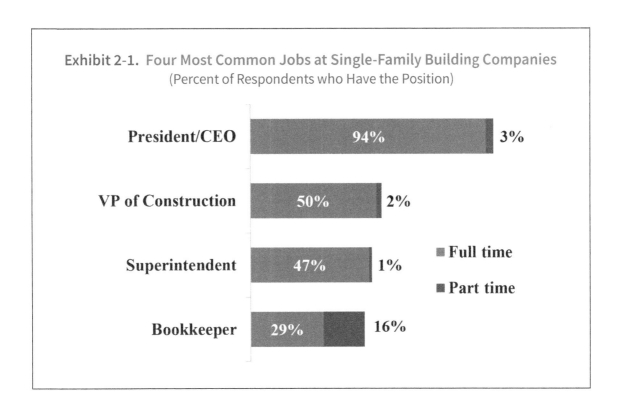

Exhibit 2-1. Four Most Common Jobs at Single-Family Building Companies
(Percent of Respondents who Have the Position)

Less than 40% of builders have any of the remaining 35 positions in their companies (Exhibit 2-2). In fact, in addition to the four shown in Exhibit 2-1, only 7 other positions exist (either on a full-time or part-time basis) at more than 20% of respondents' companies: Project Manager (35%), CFO/Head of Finance (32%), Head/Director of Sales & Marketing (26%), Production Manager (24%), Home Services/Warranty Manager (23%), Head/Director of Purchasing (22%), and Controller (22%).

Another 13 positions exist at 10% to 20% of builders' companies: Office Manager (18%), Salesperson (17%), Sales Manager (16%), Estimator (16%), Staff Accountant (16%), Administrative Assistant (16%), Selections Coordinator (15%), Head/Director of Production (14%), Receptionist (14%), Head/Director of Land Acquisition (13%), Executive Assistant (12%), Payroll Manager (12%), and Architect (10%).

The largest group of positions — 15 out of 39 — exist at fewer than 10% of the companies in the study, either as full-time or part-time jobs: Purchasing Manager (9%), Design Center Manager (8%), Settlement Coordinator (8%), Director of Human Resources (7%), Customer Service Manager (6%), Model Home Host (6%), CIO/Head of IT (5%), Web Design Specialist (5%), Contract Manager (4%), Land Manager (4%), Director of IT (4%), In-house Legal Counsel (2%), Head/Director of Development & Training (2%), Recruiter (1%), and Network Engineer (<1%).

TOTAL COMPENSATION BY JOB FAMILY

Builders were asked to report the annual salary and bonus (if any) of each of the positions existing at their companies. The rest of this chapter will present the average total compensation for full-time positions, grouped by job families. Average total compensation is calculated as the sum of the average annual salary and the average bonus amount. The average bonus for a position is calculated including zero bonuses. In other words, those who received a salary, but not a bonus, were included in the bonus calculation using a value of 0.

When comparing average compensation levels across jobs, *keep in mind that each average is calculated only among the builders who have that job as a full-time position.* For example, average compensation for the CEO is based on data from the 94% of respondents where that job exists as a full-time position. In contrast, average compensation for the Director of Human Resources is based on data from the 5% where that job exists as a full-time position. Results could not be produced for certain positions because insufficient responses made any estimates statistically unreliable.

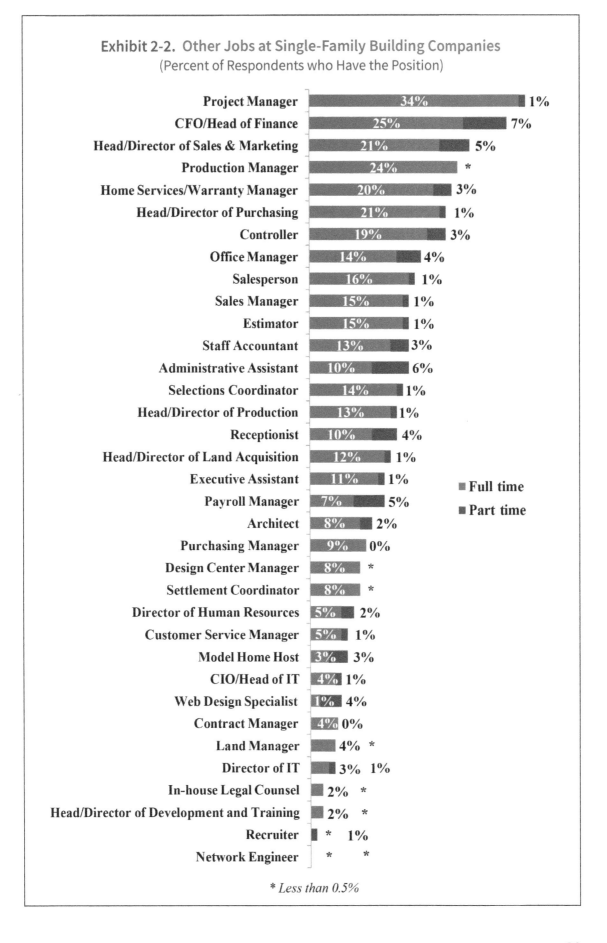

Exhibit 2-2. Other Jobs at Single-Family Building Companies
(Percent of Respondents who Have the Position)

Position	Full time	Part time
Project Manager	34%	1%
CFO/Head of Finance	25%	7%
Head/Director of Sales & Marketing	21%	5%
Production Manager	24%	*
Home Services/Warranty Manager	20%	3%
Head/Director of Purchasing	21%	1%
Controller	19%	3%
Office Manager	14%	4%
Salesperson	16%	1%
Sales Manager	15%	1%
Estimator	15%	1%
Staff Accountant	13%	3%
Administrative Assistant	10%	6%
Selections Coordinator	14%	1%
Head/Director of Production	13%	1%
Receptionist	10%	4%
Head/Director of Land Acquisition	12%	1%
Executive Assistant	11%	1%
Payroll Manager	7%	5%
Architect	8%	2%
Purchasing Manager	9%	0%
Design Center Manager	8%	*
Settlement Coordinator	8%	*
Director of Human Resources	5%	2%
Customer Service Manager	5%	1%
Model Home Host	3%	3%
CIO/Head of IT	4%	1%
Web Design Specialist	1%	4%
Contract Manager	4%	0%
Land Manager	4%	*
Director of IT	3%	1%
In-house Legal Counsel	2%	*
Head/Director of Development and Training	2%	*
Recruiter	*	1%
Network Engineer	*	*

Less than 0.5%

Executive Jobs

Builders report that Presidents/CEOs at single-family home building companies have an average annual salary of $150,426 and an average bonus (across all those who got a salary) of $68,432. This gives the President/CEO an average total compensation of $218,858. The VP of Construction has an average total compensation of $161,362 ($113,007 salary and $48,355 bonus), followed by the CFO/Head of Finance with an average total compensation of $151,030 ($118,159 salary and $32,871 bonus). Not enough responses were received for CIO/Head of IT to produce reliable compensation estimates for that position (Exhibit 2-3).

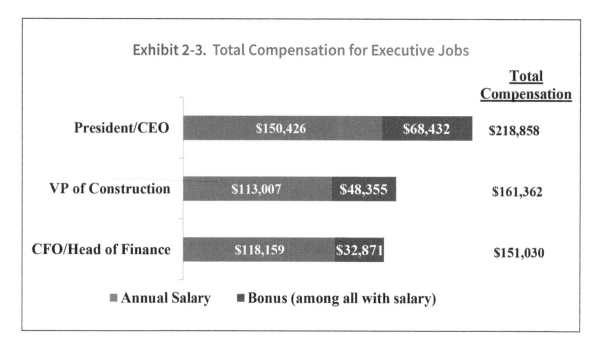

Exhibit 2-3. Total Compensation for Executive Jobs

	Annual Salary	Bonus (among all with salary)	Total Compensation
President/CEO	$150,426	$68,432	$218,858
VP of Construction	$113,007	$48,355	$161,362
CFO/Head of Finance	$118,159	$32,871	$151,030

Operations Jobs

The Head/Director of Land Acquisition has an average annual salary of $127,210 and a bonus (averaged among all those with a salary) of $54,418, for a total compensation of $181,628. The Head/Director of Sales & Marketing has an average total compensation of $146,290 ($101,913 salary and $44,377 bonus), the Head/Director of Production receives on average a total of $120,230 ($92,406 salary and $27,824 bonus), while the Head/Director of Purchasing receives on average a total of $103,524 ($86,601 salary and $16,923 bonus). Not enough responses were received for the Head/Director of Development and Training to produce reliable compensation estimates for that position (Exhibit 2-4).

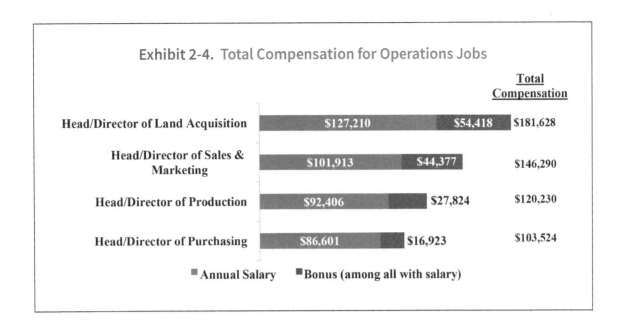

Exhibit 2-4. Total Compensation for Operations Jobs

Finance Jobs

The Controller has an average annual salary of $92,182 and a bonus (averaged among all those with a salary) of $20,344, for a total compensation of $112,526. The Staff Accountant has an average total compensation of $76,721 ($67,488 salary and $9,233 bonus), the Payroll Manager has an average total compensation of $71,102 ($64,763 salary and $6,339 bonus), and the Bookkeeper has an average total compensation of $55,551 ($49,693 salary and $5,858 bonus) (Exhibit 2-5).

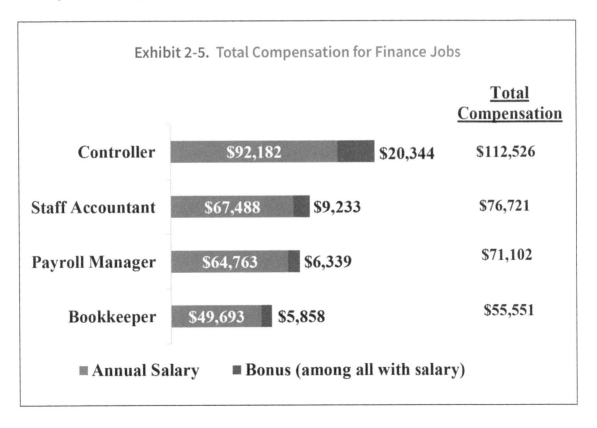

Exhibit 2-5. Total Compensation for Finance Jobs

Human Resources Jobs

The Director of Human Resources has an average annual salary of $89,567 and a bonus (averaged among all those with a salary) of $17,008, for a total compensation of $106,575. Not enough responses were received for Recruiter or In-House Legal Counsel to produce reliable compensation estimates for those positions (Exhibit 2-6).

IT Jobs

None of the three IT positions received enough responses to report reliable compensation estimates for salary or bonus.

Administrative Jobs

The Settlement Coordinator has an average annual salary of $56,838 and a bonus (averaged among those with a salary) of $8,915, for a total compensation of $65,753. The Office Manager has an average total compensation of $64,568 ($58,348 salary and $6,220 bonus), the Executive Assistant has an average total compensation of $53,621 ($49,394 salary and $4,227 bonus), the Administrative Assistant has an average total compensation of $47,664 ($44,956 salary and $2,708 bonus), and the Receptionist has an average total compensation of $39,762 ($35,971 salary and $3,791 bonus) (Exhibit 2-7).

Production Jobs

Production Managers receive an average annual salary of $80,842 and a bonus (averaged among all those with a salary) of $18,050, for a total compensation of $98,892. Architects have an average total compensation of $96,453 ($81,618 salary and $14,835 bonus), the Project Manager has an average total compensation of $92,018 ($78,294 salary and $13,724 bonus), the Superintendent has an average total compensation of $80,406 ($69,361 salary and $11,045 bonus), the Purchasing Manager has an average total compensation of $77,043 ($69,567 salary and $7,476 bonus), the Home Services/Warranty Manager has an average total compensation of $73,057 ($64,239 salary and $8,818 bonus), and the Estimator has an average total compensation of $71,450 ($62,155 salary and $9,295 bonus). Not enough responses were received for Contract Manager or Land Manager to produce reliable compensation estimates for those positions (Exhibit 2-8).

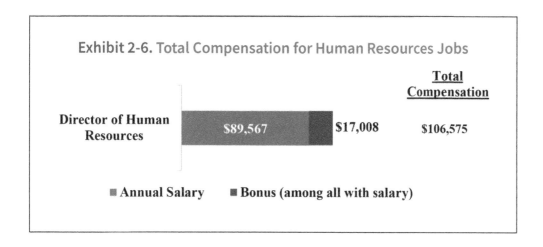

Exhibit 2-6. Total Compensation for Human Resources Jobs

	Annual Salary	Bonus (among all with salary)	Total Compensation
Director of Human Resources	$89,567	$17,008	$106,575

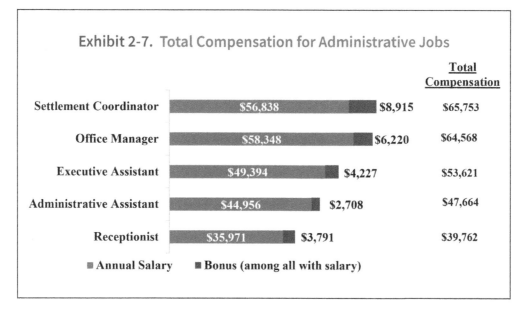

Exhibit 2-7. Total Compensation for Administrative Jobs

	Annual Salary	Bonus (among all with salary)	Total Compensation
Settlement Coordinator	$56,838	$8,915	$65,753
Office Manager	$58,348	$6,220	$64,568
Executive Assistant	$49,394	$4,227	$53,621
Administrative Assistant	$44,956	$2,708	$47,664
Receptionist	$35,971	$3,791	$39,762

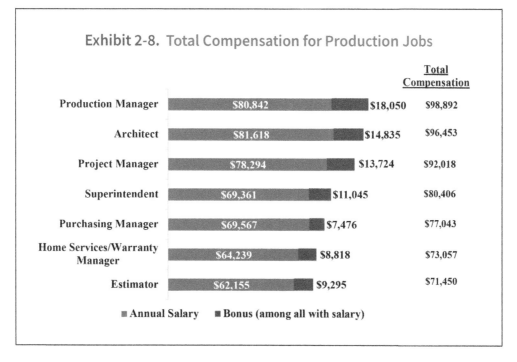

Exhibit 2-8. Total Compensation for Production Jobs

	Annual Salary	Bonus (among all with salary)	Total Compensation
Production Manager	$80,842	$18,050	$98,892
Architect	$81,618	$14,835	$96,453
Project Manager	$78,294	$13,724	$92,018
Superintendent	$69,361	$11,045	$80,406
Purchasing Manager	$69,567	$7,476	$77,043
Home Services/Warranty Manager	$64,239	$8,818	$73,057
Estimator	$62,155	$9,295	$71,450

Sales & Marketing Jobs

Salespeople receive an average annual salary of $36,199 and a bonus (averaged among all those with a salary) of $95,928 — the only position whose bonus exceeds its salary, for a total compensation of $132,127. The Sales Manager has an average total compensation of $115,980 ($69,133 salary and $46,847 bonus), the Design Center Manager has an average total compensation of $83,449 ($65,819 salary and $17,630 bonus), the Selection Coordinator has an average total compensation of $62,515 ($53,930 salary and $8,585 bonus), and the Customer Service Manager has an average total compensation of $52,418 ($47,109 salary and $5,309 bonus). Not enough responses were received for Model Home Host to produce reliable compensation estimates for that position (Exhibit 2-9).

Appendix B lists all positions and the share of builders where they exist as full-time jobs (column A) as well as their average total compensation (column D). In addition, a second bonus calculation is presented (column E) where only those who actually reported a bonus were averaged out (no "zero bonuses" were included). This calculation is helpful in determining what the average bonus was among full-time employees who actually received a bonus for any given position.

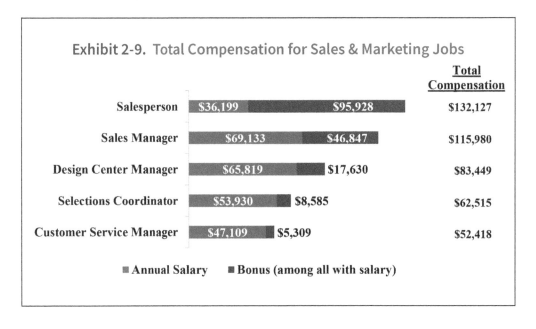

Exhibit 2-9. Total Compensation for Sales & Marketing Jobs

	Annual Salary	Bonus (among all with salary)	Total Compensation
Salesperson	$36,199	$95,928	$132,127
Sales Manager	$69,133	$46,847	$115,980
Design Center Manager	$65,819	$17,630	$83,449
Selections Coordinator	$53,930	$8,585	$62,515
Customer Service Manager	$47,109	$5,309	$52,418

Chapter 3
Employee Fringe Benefits

INCIDENCE OF BENEFITS ACROSS JOBS

In the single-family home building industry, some fringe benefits to full-time employees are significantly more common than others. Health insurance, for example, is offered by more than 70% of builders in the study to those who hold full-time jobs. In contrast, flexible spending is typically offered by only around 30% of builders. When comparing the incidence of any particular benefit across different jobs, however, it is important to remember that not all positions exist (at all or as full-time jobs) at any one respondent's company. Thus, the average share of builders offering health insurance to Project Managers, for instance, only takes into account builders where that position actually exists on a full-time basis.

Not enough builders provided information on fringe benefits for the following 10 positions, and therefore this study does not include benefit results for them: CIO/Head of IT, Head/Director of Development & Training, Recruiter, In-house Legal Counsel, Director of IT, Network Engineer, Web Design Specialist, Land Manager, Contract Manager, and Model Home Host. This chapter compares the incidence of each of the 13 fringe benefits listed in the survey across the remaining 29 positions.

Health Insurance

All 29 positions are offered health insurance by more than 70% of the single-family building companies where they exist as full-time jobs. In fact, at least 90% of builders who have the first six positions shown on Exhibit 3-1 offer them health insurance, from Director of Human Resources (100%) down to Controller (90%). Another 13 full-time positions are offered health insurance by 80% to 89% of builders who report they exist, from Home Services/Warranty Manager (89%) down to Production Manager (81%). Between 70% and 79% of builders provide health insurance to the remaining 10 positions, starting from Superintendent (79%) down to Bookkeeper (73%).

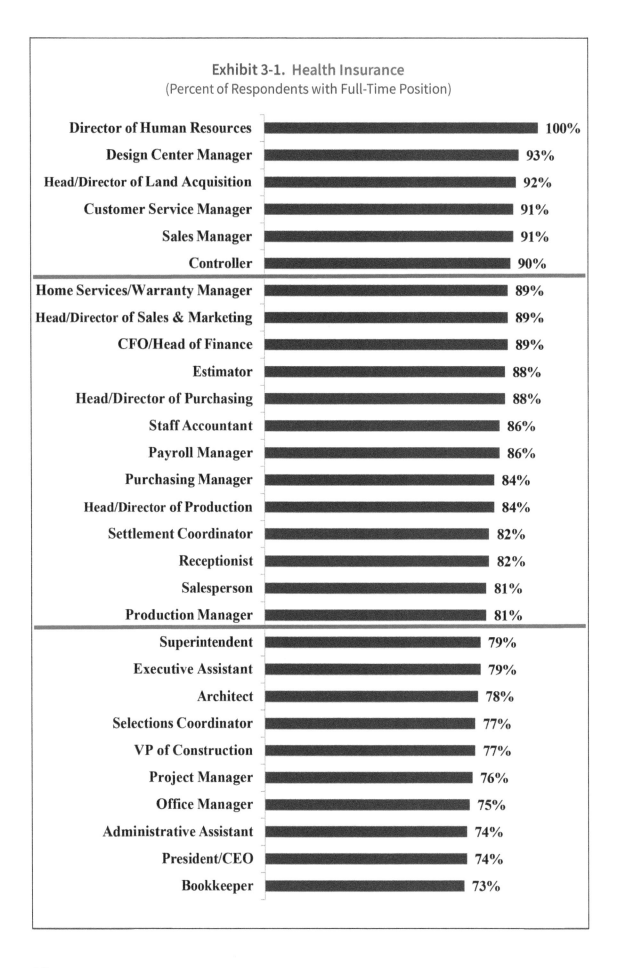

Exhibit 3-1. Health Insurance
(Percent of Respondents with Full-Time Position)

Position	Percent
Director of Human Resources	100%
Design Center Manager	93%
Head/Director of Land Acquisition	92%
Customer Service Manager	91%
Sales Manager	91%
Controller	90%
Home Services/Warranty Manager	89%
Head/Director of Sales & Marketing	89%
CFO/Head of Finance	89%
Estimator	88%
Head/Director of Purchasing	88%
Staff Accountant	86%
Payroll Manager	86%
Purchasing Manager	84%
Head/Director of Production	84%
Settlement Coordinator	82%
Receptionist	82%
Salesperson	81%
Production Manager	81%
Superintendent	79%
Executive Assistant	79%
Architect	78%
Selections Coordinator	77%
VP of Construction	77%
Project Manager	76%
Office Manager	75%
Administrative Assistant	74%
President/CEO	74%
Bookkeeper	73%

Dental Insurance

Dental insurance is somewhat less common than health insurance. In fact, only one position is offered dental insurance by more than 90% of builders where it exists as a full-time job: Customer Service Manager (91%). In another five cases, 83% to 88% of builders offer it, from Receptionist down to Director of Human Resources on Exhibit 3-2. Eighteen positions are offered dental insurance by somewhere between 50% and 80% of the builders who report they exist as full-time jobs, from Purchasing Manager (79%) down to Project Manager (50%). The remaining five positions are offered dental insurance by less than half of builders where they exist, with the least likely being the President/CEO (42%).

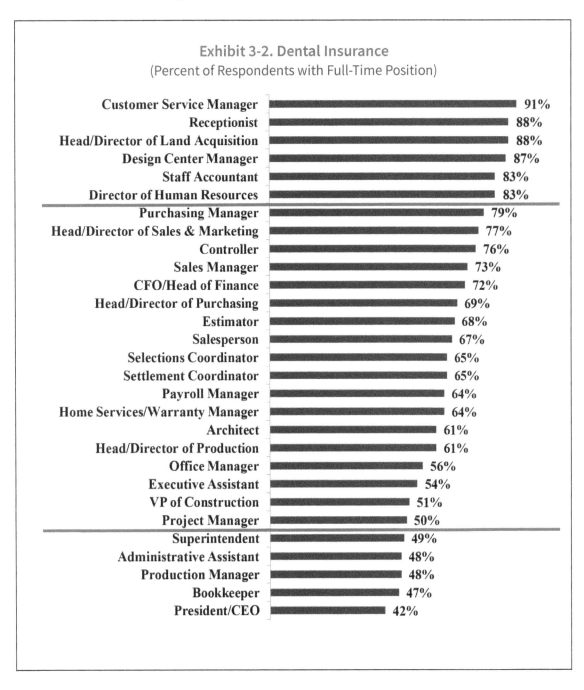

Exhibit 3-2. Dental Insurance
(Percent of Respondents with Full-Time Position)

Position	Percent
Customer Service Manager	91%
Receptionist	88%
Head/Director of Land Acquisition	88%
Design Center Manager	87%
Staff Accountant	83%
Director of Human Resources	83%
Purchasing Manager	79%
Head/Director of Sales & Marketing	77%
Controller	76%
Sales Manager	73%
CFO/Head of Finance	72%
Head/Director of Purchasing	69%
Estimator	68%
Salesperson	67%
Selections Coordinator	65%
Settlement Coordinator	65%
Payroll Manager	64%
Home Services/Warranty Manager	64%
Architect	61%
Head/Director of Production	61%
Office Manager	56%
Executive Assistant	54%
VP of Construction	51%
Project Manager	50%
Superintendent	49%
Administrative Assistant	48%
Production Manager	48%
Bookkeeper	47%
President/CEO	42%

Vision Program

Only two full-time positions are offered a vision program by more than 80% of builders who have them in their companies: Customer Service Manager (91%) and Purchasing Manager (84%). In the majority of cases, 19 positions to be precise, a vision benefit is offered by 50% to 67% of builders where they exist, from Design Center Manager (67%) down to Executive Assistant (50%) on Exhibit 3-3. The remaining eight positions are offered a vision program by less than half of the builders who have them in their companies, with the two least likely being President/CEO (33%) and Bookkeeper (39%).

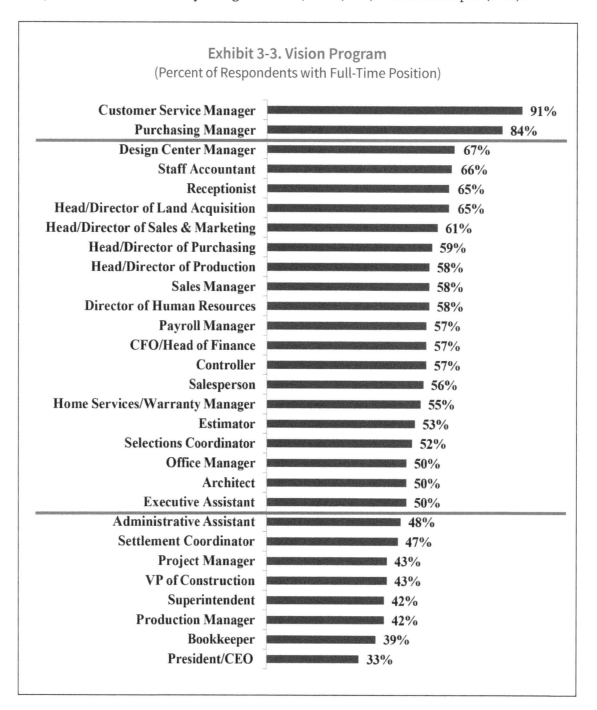

Exhibit 3-3. Vision Program
(Percent of Respondents with Full-Time Position)

Position	Percent
Customer Service Manager	91%
Purchasing Manager	84%
Design Center Manager	67%
Staff Accountant	66%
Receptionist	65%
Head/Director of Land Acquisition	65%
Head/Director of Sales & Marketing	61%
Head/Director of Purchasing	59%
Head/Director of Production	58%
Sales Manager	58%
Director of Human Resources	58%
Payroll Manager	57%
CFO/Head of Finance	57%
Controller	57%
Salesperson	56%
Home Services/Warranty Manager	55%
Estimator	53%
Selections Coordinator	52%
Office Manager	50%
Architect	50%
Executive Assistant	50%
Administrative Assistant	48%
Settlement Coordinator	47%
Project Manager	43%
VP of Construction	43%
Superintendent	42%
Production Manager	42%
Bookkeeper	39%
President/CEO	33%

Prescription Program

At best, 75% of builders who have a full-time Director of Human Resources offer a prescription program. Another six full-time positions are offered this benefit by 60% or more of the builders who have them in their companies, from Purchasing Manager to Controller on Exhibit 3-4. Between 50% and 59% of builders offer a prescription program to nine other full-time positions, from Receptionist (59%) up to CFO/Head of Finance (51%). In the plurality of cases — 13 positions from VP of Construction to the bottom of Exhibit 3-4 — less than half of builders provide a prescription program. The three least likely positions to be offered this benefit are President/CEO (31%), Executive Assistant (33%), and Bookkeeper (34%).

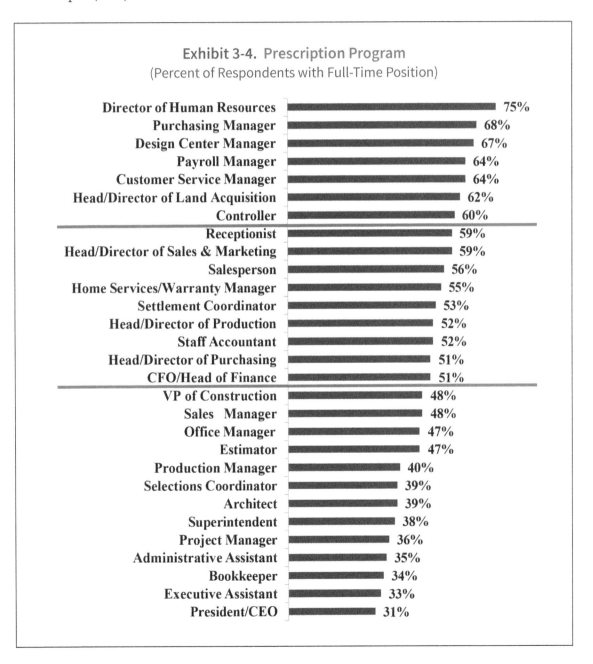

Exhibit 3-4. Prescription Program
(Percent of Respondents with Full-Time Position)

Position	Percent
Director of Human Resources	75%
Purchasing Manager	68%
Design Center Manager	67%
Payroll Manager	64%
Customer Service Manager	64%
Head/Director of Land Acquisition	62%
Controller	60%
Receptionist	59%
Head/Director of Sales & Marketing	59%
Salesperson	56%
Home Services/Warranty Manager	55%
Settlement Coordinator	53%
Head/Director of Production	52%
Staff Accountant	52%
Head/Director of Purchasing	51%
CFO/Head of Finance	51%
VP of Construction	48%
Sales Manager	48%
Office Manager	47%
Estimator	47%
Production Manager	40%
Selections Coordinator	39%
Architect	39%
Superintendent	38%
Project Manager	36%
Administrative Assistant	35%
Bookkeeper	34%
Executive Assistant	33%
President/CEO	31%

Life Insurance

Of the 29 full-time positions for which enough data are available to produce results on the prevalence of benefits, six are offered life insurance by more than 60% of the builders where they exist: from Director of Human Resources (83%) to Head/Director of Sales & Marketing (61%) on Exhibit 3-5. Another eight positions are offered life insurance by 50% to 59% of builders, from Settlement Coordinator (59%) to Estimator (50%). The remaining 15 positions are offered life insurance by less than half but more than a quarter of builders who have them on staff. The two least likely to be offered this benefit are Administrative Assistant (26%) and Production Manager (29%).

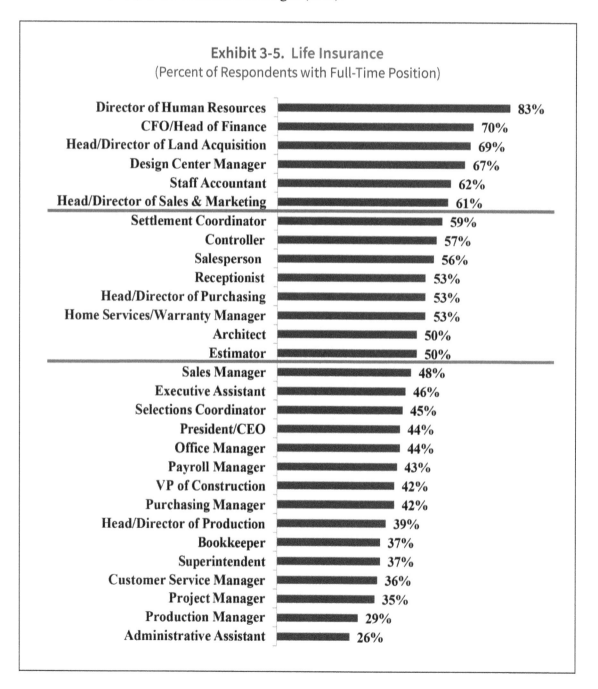

Exhibit 3-5. Life Insurance
(Percent of Respondents with Full-Time Position)

Position	Percent
Director of Human Resources	83%
CFO/Head of Finance	70%
Head/Director of Land Acquisition	69%
Design Center Manager	67%
Staff Accountant	62%
Head/Director of Sales & Marketing	61%
Settlement Coordinator	59%
Controller	57%
Salesperson	56%
Receptionist	53%
Head/Director of Purchasing	53%
Home Services/Warranty Manager	53%
Architect	50%
Estimator	50%
Sales Manager	48%
Executive Assistant	46%
Selections Coordinator	45%
President/CEO	44%
Office Manager	44%
Payroll Manager	43%
VP of Construction	42%
Purchasing Manager	42%
Head/Director of Production	39%
Bookkeeper	37%
Superintendent	37%
Customer Service Manager	36%
Project Manager	35%
Production Manager	29%
Administrative Assistant	26%

Short Term Disability

Only four full-time positions are offered short term disability by half or more of the builders that have them in their companies, from Design Center Manager (60%) to Director of Human Resources (50%) on Exhibit 3-6. Another 17 positions are offered this benefit at 30% to 49% of the companies where they exist, from Salesperson (47%) to Sales Manager (30%). Eight positions get short term disability from 20% to 29% of builders who report them, starting with Head/Director of Production (29%). The two least likely to receive this benefit are the President/CEO (20%) and the Bookkeeper (21%).

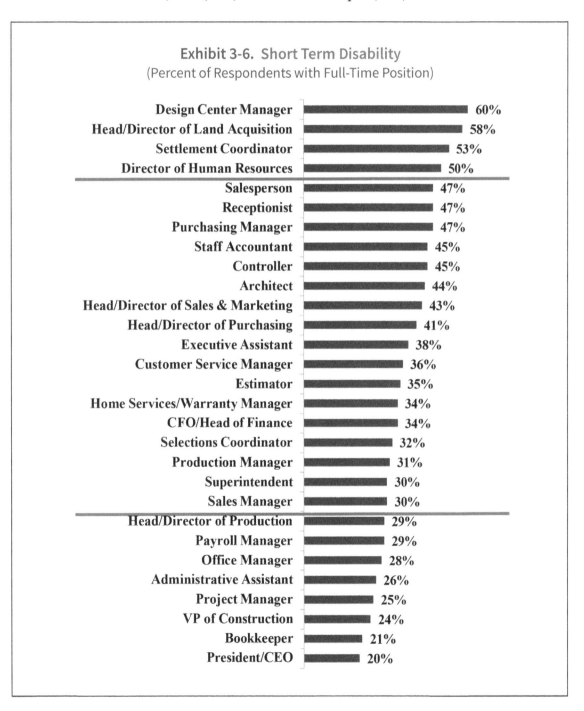

Exhibit 3-6. Short Term Disability
(Percent of Respondents with Full-Time Position)

Position	Percent
Design Center Manager	60%
Head/Director of Land Acquisition	58%
Settlement Coordinator	53%
Director of Human Resources	50%
Salesperson	47%
Receptionist	47%
Purchasing Manager	47%
Staff Accountant	45%
Controller	45%
Architect	44%
Head/Director of Sales & Marketing	43%
Head/Director of Purchasing	41%
Executive Assistant	38%
Customer Service Manager	36%
Estimator	35%
Home Services/Warranty Manager	34%
CFO/Head of Finance	34%
Selections Coordinator	32%
Production Manager	31%
Superintendent	30%
Sales Manager	30%
Head/Director of Production	29%
Payroll Manager	29%
Office Manager	28%
Administrative Assistant	26%
Project Manager	25%
VP of Construction	24%
Bookkeeper	21%
President/CEO	20%

Long Term Disability

Only three full-time positions are offered long term disability by half or more of the builders that have them at their companies: Director of Human Services (67%), Head/Director of Land Acquisition (62%), and Design Center Manager (60%). Another 17 positions are offered long term disability by less than half, but at least 30% of builders: from Staff Accountant (48%) to Sales Manager (30%) on Exhibit 3-7. The remaining nine positions are offered long term disability by less than 30% of builders where they exist, starting with Head/Director of Production (29%). The two least likely to receive this benefit are Project Manager and President/CEO (both at 22%).

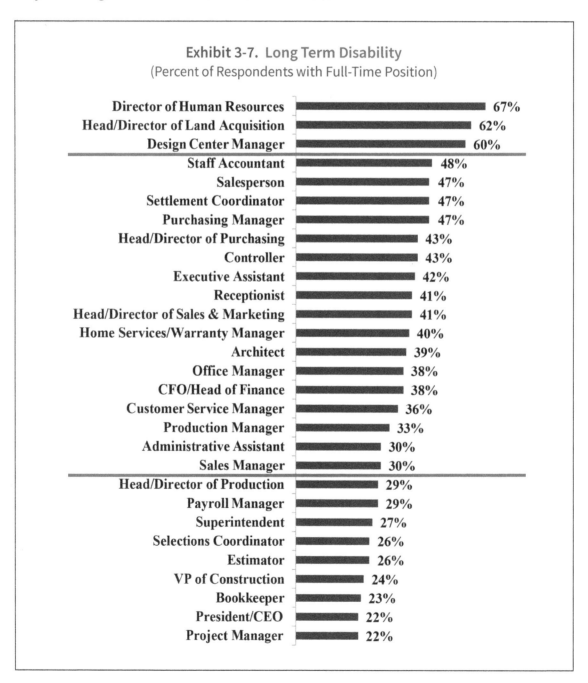

Exhibit 3-7. Long Term Disability
(Percent of Respondents with Full-Time Position)

Position	Percent
Director of Human Resources	67%
Head/Director of Land Acquisition	62%
Design Center Manager	60%
Staff Accountant	48%
Salesperson	47%
Settlement Coordinator	47%
Purchasing Manager	47%
Head/Director of Purchasing	43%
Controller	43%
Executive Assistant	42%
Receptionist	41%
Head/Director of Sales & Marketing	41%
Home Services/Warranty Manager	40%
Architect	39%
Office Manager	38%
CFO/Head of Finance	38%
Customer Service Manager	36%
Production Manager	33%
Administrative Assistant	30%
Sales Manager	30%
Head/Director of Production	29%
Payroll Manager	29%
Superintendent	27%
Selections Coordinator	26%
Estimator	26%
VP of Construction	24%
Bookkeeper	23%
President/CEO	22%
Project Manager	22%

Flex Spending

Flex spending is not a common benefit at single-family home building companies. In fact, only two positions are offered this benefit by at least half of the builders who have this position: Design Center Manager (53%) and Director of Human Resources (50%). Less than half, but at least 30% of builders offer flex spending to another 14 positions: from Head/Director of Land Acquisition (46%) to Head/Director of Purchasing (31%) on Exhibit 3-8. The remaining 13 positions are offered flex spending by less than 30% of builders who have them on staff, starting with Office Manager (28%) down to Bookkeeper (16%).

Exhibit 3-8. Flex Spending
(Percent of Respondents with Full-Time Position)

Position	Percent
Design Center Manager	53%
Director of Human Resources	50%
Head/Director of Land Acquisition	46%
Executive Assistant	42%
Staff Accountant	41%
Head/Director of Sales & Marketing	41%
Head/Director of Production	39%
Purchasing Manager	37%
Salesperson	36%
Payroll Manager	36%
CFO/Head of Finance	36%
Controller	36%
Customer Service Manager	36%
Settlement Coordinator	35%
Home Services/Warranty Manager	34%
Head/Director of Purchasing	31%
Office Manager	28%
Production Manager	27%
Sales Manager	27%
VP of Construction	26%
Receptionist	24%
Estimator	24%
Selections Coordinator	23%
Superintendent	22%
President/CEO	18%
Project Manager	18%
Administrative Assistant	17%
Architect	17%
Bookkeeper	16%

401K

Every one of the 29 positions in this analysis is offered access to a 401k retirement plan by more than 60% of the builders who have this position. At least 90% of builders provide this benefit to four full- time positions, from Design Center Manager (93%) to Head/Director of Production (90%) (Exhibit 3-9). Between 80% and 89% also offer it to another 10 positions: from Receptionist (88%) to Head/Director of Sales & Marketing (80%). Most positions — 15 of 29 — get the benefit of a 401k plan from 60% to 79% of builders where they exist, starting with Staff Accountant (79%) down to President/CEO (63%).

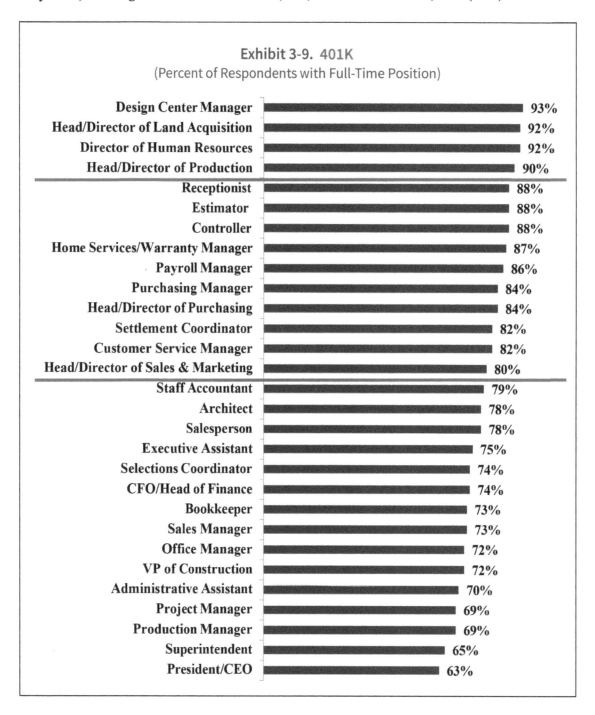

Exhibit 3-9. 401K
(Percent of Respondents with Full-Time Position)

Position	Percent
Design Center Manager	93%
Head/Director of Land Acquisition	92%
Director of Human Resources	92%
Head/Director of Production	90%
Receptionist	88%
Estimator	88%
Controller	88%
Home Services/Warranty Manager	87%
Payroll Manager	86%
Purchasing Manager	84%
Head/Director of Purchasing	84%
Settlement Coordinator	82%
Customer Service Manager	82%
Head/Director of Sales & Marketing	80%
Staff Accountant	79%
Architect	78%
Salesperson	78%
Executive Assistant	75%
Selections Coordinator	74%
CFO/Head of Finance	74%
Bookkeeper	73%
Sales Manager	73%
Office Manager	72%
VP of Construction	72%
Administrative Assistant	70%
Project Manager	69%
Production Manager	69%
Superintendent	65%
President/CEO	63%

Paid Vacation Leave

Paid vacation leave is the fringe benefit most commonly offered by single-family home building companies. Every full-time position is offered paid vacation by at least 90% of the builders where they exist. In fact, 12 positions are offered paid vacation leave by 100% of builders who have these positions, from Administrative Assistant to Director of Human Resources on Exhibit 3-10. The remaining 17 positions receive this benefit from 90% to 98% of builders who report they exist at their companies.

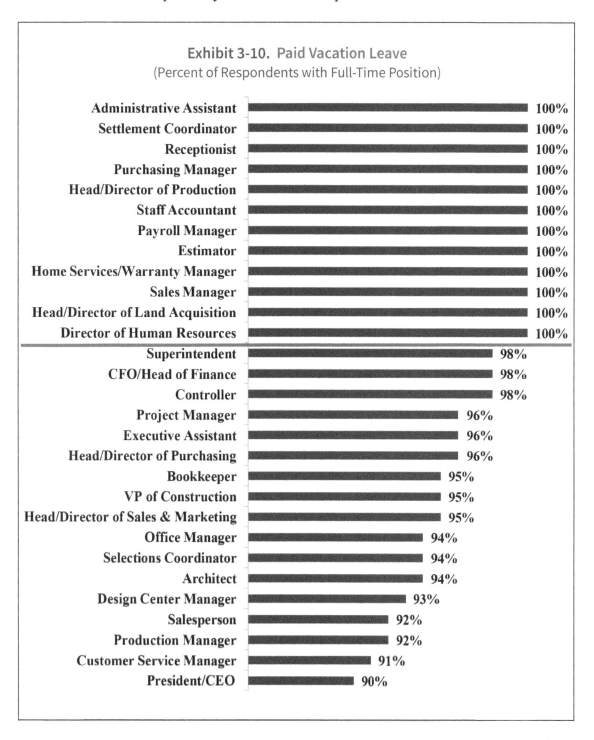

Exhibit 3-10. Paid Vacation Leave
(Percent of Respondents with Full-Time Position)

Position	Percent
Administrative Assistant	100%
Settlement Coordinator	100%
Receptionist	100%
Purchasing Manager	100%
Head/Director of Production	100%
Staff Accountant	100%
Payroll Manager	100%
Estimator	100%
Home Services/Warranty Manager	100%
Sales Manager	100%
Head/Director of Land Acquisition	100%
Director of Human Resources	100%
Superintendent	98%
CFO/Head of Finance	98%
Controller	98%
Project Manager	96%
Executive Assistant	96%
Head/Director of Purchasing	96%
Bookkeeper	95%
VP of Construction	95%
Head/Director of Sales & Marketing	95%
Office Manager	94%
Selections Coordinator	94%
Architect	94%
Design Center Manager	93%
Salesperson	92%
Production Manager	92%
Customer Service Manager	91%
President/CEO	90%

Paid Sick Leave

Over 60% of builders who have each of the 29 full-time positions on staff offer them paid sick leave. In two cases, the share exceeds 90%: namely, Receptionist (94%) and Director of Human Resources (92%). Between 70% and 90% of builders offer paid sick leave to 25 of the 29 positions in this analysis, from Administrative Assistant (87%) to Office Manager (72%) on Exhibit 3-11. Salespersons and Selection Coordinators are the least likely to receive paid sick leave, but even in those cases, 64% and 68% of builders offer it, respectively.

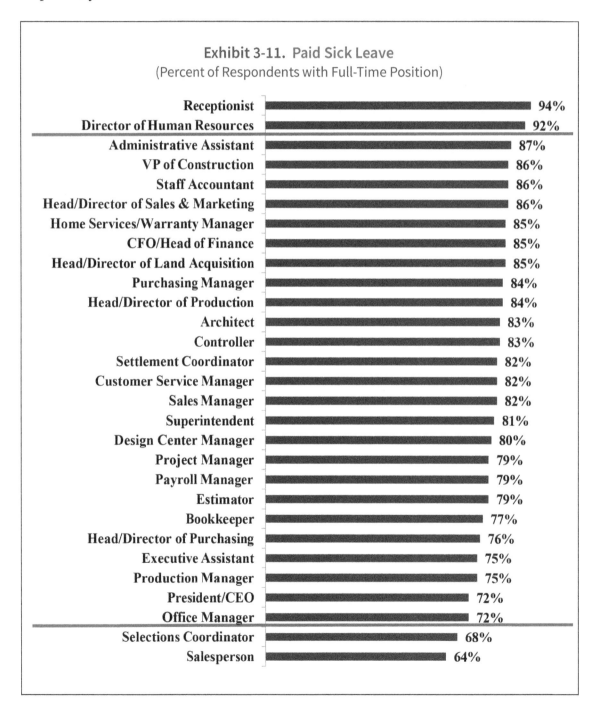

Exhibit 3-11. Paid Sick Leave
(Percent of Respondents with Full-Time Position)

Position	Percent
Receptionist	94%
Director of Human Resources	92%
Administrative Assistant	87%
VP of Construction	86%
Staff Accountant	86%
Head/Director of Sales & Marketing	86%
Home Services/Warranty Manager	85%
CFO/Head of Finance	85%
Head/Director of Land Acquisition	85%
Purchasing Manager	84%
Head/Director of Production	84%
Architect	83%
Controller	83%
Settlement Coordinator	82%
Customer Service Manager	82%
Sales Manager	82%
Superintendent	81%
Design Center Manager	80%
Project Manager	79%
Payroll Manager	79%
Estimator	79%
Bookkeeper	77%
Head/Director of Purchasing	76%
Executive Assistant	75%
Production Manager	75%
President/CEO	72%
Office Manager	72%
Selections Coordinator	68%
Salesperson	64%

Tuition Reimbursement

Only four positions are offered tuition reimbursement by more than 40% of the builders who report having them in their firm: Design Center Manager (53%), Head/Director of Land Acquisition (42%), Director of Human Resources (42%), and Settlement Coordinator (41%). In most cases (19 of 29 positions), however, only 20% to 40% of builders offer this benefit: from Executive Assistant (38%) to CFO/Head of Finance (21%) (Exhibit 3-12). The remaining six positions are much more unlikely to receive tuition reimbursement, as fewer than 20% of builders offer it to them. For instance, only 14% of builders who have a full-time Payroll Manager provide them with tuition reimbursement.

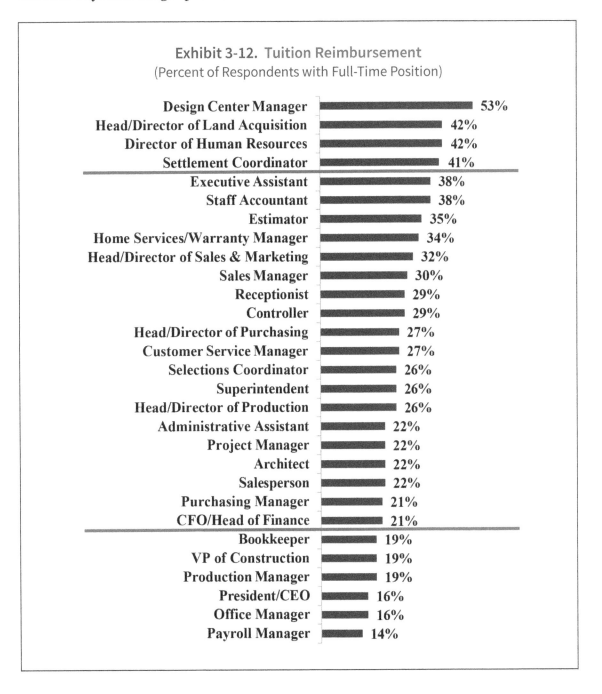

Exhibit 3-12. Tuition Reimbursement
(Percent of Respondents with Full-Time Position)

Position	Percent
Design Center Manager	53%
Head/Director of Land Acquisition	42%
Director of Human Resources	42%
Settlement Coordinator	41%
Executive Assistant	38%
Staff Accountant	38%
Estimator	35%
Home Services/Warranty Manager	34%
Head/Director of Sales & Marketing	32%
Sales Manager	30%
Receptionist	29%
Controller	29%
Head/Director of Purchasing	27%
Customer Service Manager	27%
Selections Coordinator	26%
Superintendent	26%
Head/Director of Production	26%
Administrative Assistant	22%
Project Manager	22%
Architect	22%
Salesperson	22%
Purchasing Manager	21%
CFO/Head of Finance	21%
Bookkeeper	19%
VP of Construction	19%
Production Manager	19%
President/CEO	16%
Office Manager	16%
Payroll Manager	14%

Training

Eighty percent of builders who have a full-time Design Center Manager on staff provide him/her with training. On the other hand, the majority of positions (the next 19 on Exhibit 3-13) are offered training by 50% to 70% of builders who have these positions: from Architect (67%) to Payroll Manager (50%). Another 9 positions are offered this benefit by fewer than half of the builders who have them on staff, from VP of Construction (49%) to Administrative Assistant (30%).

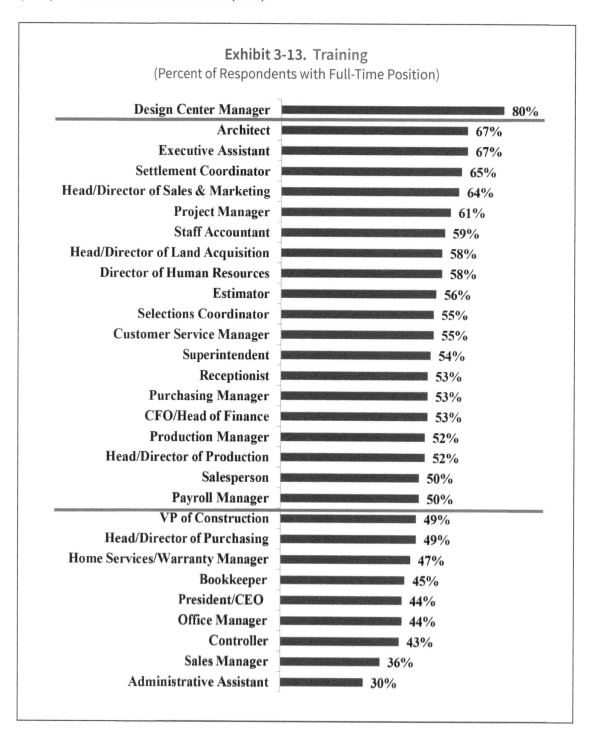

Exhibit 3-13. Training
(Percent of Respondents with Full-Time Position)

Position	Percent
Design Center Manager	80%
Architect	67%
Executive Assistant	67%
Settlement Coordinator	65%
Head/Director of Sales & Marketing	64%
Project Manager	61%
Staff Accountant	59%
Head/Director of Land Acquisition	58%
Director of Human Resources	58%
Estimator	56%
Selections Coordinator	55%
Customer Service Manager	55%
Superintendent	54%
Receptionist	53%
Purchasing Manager	53%
CFO/Head of Finance	53%
Production Manager	52%
Head/Director of Production	52%
Salesperson	50%
Payroll Manager	50%
VP of Construction	49%
Head/Director of Purchasing	49%
Home Services/Warranty Manager	47%
Bookkeeper	45%
President/CEO	44%
Office Manager	44%
Controller	43%
Sales Manager	36%
Administrative Assistant	30%

Other

Beyond the 13 benefits enumerated in this chapter, the survey also asked builders if they offered other benefits to any of their full-time positions. A minority of builders do offer additional benefits to most positions. In fact, 20% to 35% report that six positions receive other benefits, from Design Center Manager (33%) to Head/Director of Finance (21%) (Exhibit 3-14). Some of the other benefits mentioned are vehicle/gas allowance, profit sharing, paid parental leave, and volunteer time off (See Appendix E for complete list).

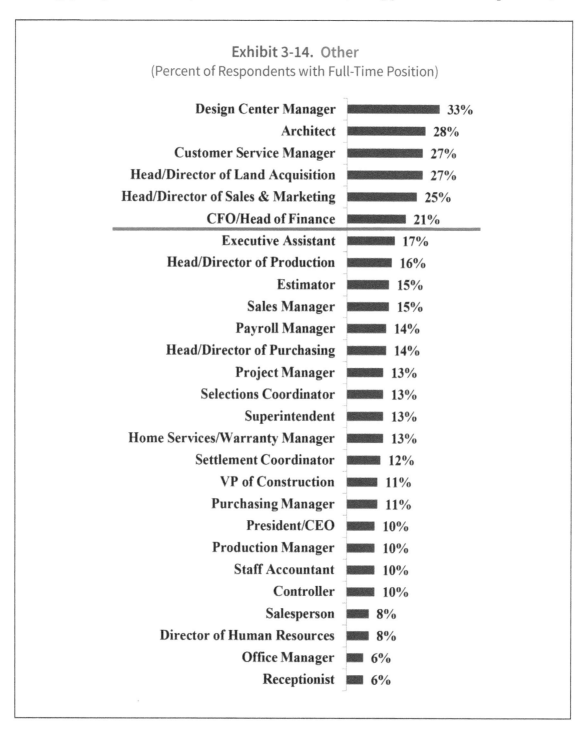

Exhibit 3-14. Other
(Percent of Respondents with Full-Time Position)

Position	Percent
Design Center Manager	33%
Architect	28%
Customer Service Manager	27%
Head/Director of Land Acquisition	27%
Head/Director of Sales & Marketing	25%
CFO/Head of Finance	21%
Executive Assistant	17%
Head/Director of Production	16%
Estimator	15%
Sales Manager	15%
Payroll Manager	14%
Head/Director of Purchasing	14%
Project Manager	13%
Selections Coordinator	13%
Superintendent	13%
Home Services/Warranty Manager	13%
Settlement Coordinator	12%
VP of Construction	11%
Purchasing Manager	11%
President/CEO	10%
Production Manager	10%
Staff Accountant	10%
Controller	10%
Salesperson	8%
Director of Human Resources	8%
Office Manager	6%
Receptionist	6%

Chapter 4

Compensation & Benefits by Position

This chapter provides detailed analysis of the incidence, compensation, and benefits for each of the 39 positions in the study individually. Positions are not organized alphabetically, but instead are grouped by job category, namely Executive, Operations, Finance, Human Resources, IT, Administrative, Production, and Sales & Marketing jobs (Appendix C). The analysis also highlights how compensation for the same position can vary across companies of different sizes, measured by the number of single-family units started in 2021 (Appendix D).

EXECUTIVE JOBS

President/CEO

Nearly all single-family builders responding to the survey have someone serving as President/CEO: 94% report the job exists as a full-time position and another 3% as part-time (Exhibit 4-1). Ninety percent report the person in this job "always" has experience in the construction trades, while 6% said "sometimes," and 4% "never or almost never" (Exhibit 4-2).

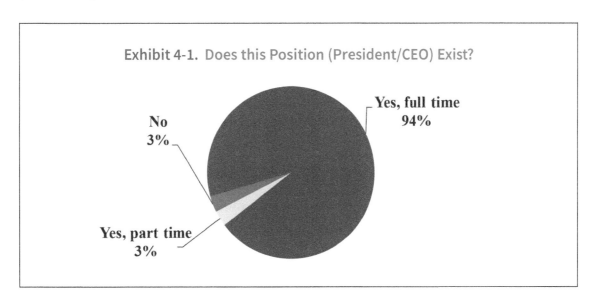

Exhibit 4-1. Does this Position (President/CEO) Exist?

No
3%

Yes, full time
94%

Yes, part time
3%

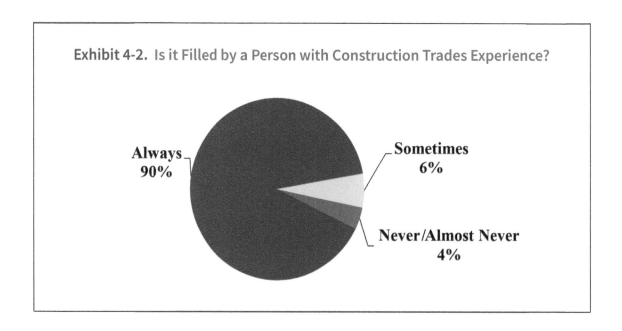

Exhibit 4-2. Is it Filled by a Person with Construction Trades Experience?

Always
90%

Sometimes
6%

Never/Almost Never
4%

Among those firms that have the position full-time, 6% report that the President/CEO has an annual salary of less than $50,000, 27% between $50,000 and $99,999, and 67% report it at $100,000 or more. The average annual salary for the President/CEO is $150,426, and the average bonus among all those reporting a salary is $68,432 (averaging in zero bonuses), for an average total compensation of $218,858 (Exhibit 4-3). Fifty-five percent of companies reporting a salary for this position also pay a bonus/commission. The average bonus among those who received a bonus is $124,963 (Appendix B).

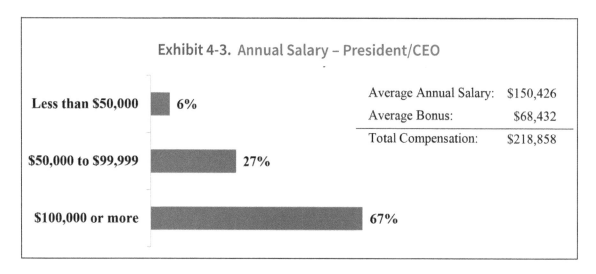

Exhibit 4-3. Annual Salary – President/CEO

Less than $50,000	6%
$50,000 to $99,999	27%
$100,000 or more	67%

Average Annual Salary:	$150,426
Average Bonus:	$68,432
Total Compensation:	$218,858

The President/CEO's total compensation and the size of the company are strongly correlated. Among those who started 1 to 10 single-family units in 2021, the average compensation for this position is $132,160. In contrast, at companies with 100+ starts, the average compensation for the President/CEO is $437,149 (Exhibit 4-4).

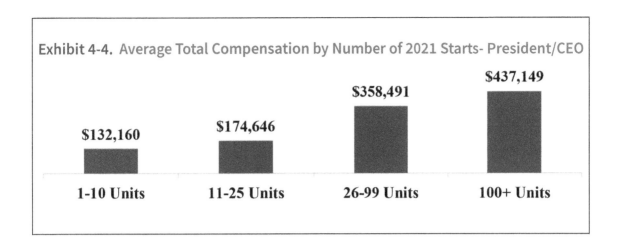

Exhibit 4-4. Average Total Compensation by Number of 2021 Starts- President/CEO

$132,160	$174,646	$358,491	$437,149
1-10 Units	11-25 Units	26-99 Units	100+ Units

The most common benefit offered to full-time Presidents/CEOs is paid vacation leave — 90% of builders who report the position exists at their companies offer this benefit to them. In addition, 74% offer health insurance, 72% paid sick leave, and 63% offer a 401K plan. Fewer than half offer the following benefits to their full-time President/CEO: training (44%), life insurance (44%), dental insurance (42%), vision program (33%), prescription program (31%), long term disability (22%), short term disability (20%), flex spending (18%), and tuition reimbursement (16%). Ten percent offer some other type of benefit to their President/CEO, the most common of which are a vehicle and profit sharing (Exhibit 4-5).

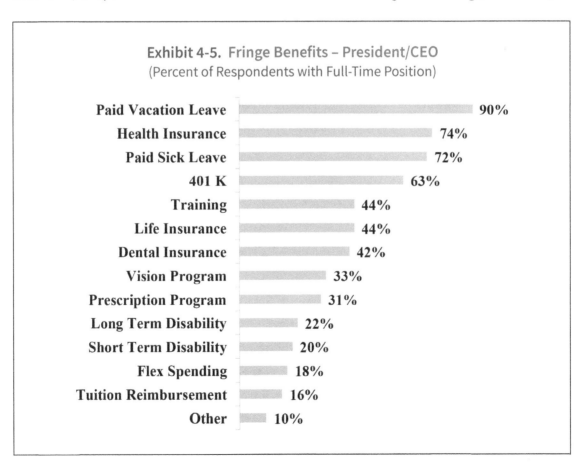

Exhibit 4-5. Fringe Benefits – President/CEO
(Percent of Respondents with Full-Time Position)

Benefit	Percent
Paid Vacation Leave	90%
Health Insurance	74%
Paid Sick Leave	72%
401 K	63%
Training	44%
Life Insurance	44%
Dental Insurance	42%
Vision Program	33%
Prescription Program	31%
Long Term Disability	22%
Short Term Disability	20%
Flex Spending	18%
Tuition Reimbursement	16%
Other	10%

VP of Construction

Fifty percent of the builders responding to the survey report the position of VP of Construction exists in their firm on a full-time basis, while 2% report it exists only on a part-time basis (Exhibit 4-6). Nearly all — 92% — of those who have this position report it is "always" filled by someone with experience in the construction trades. Only 7% say "sometimes" and 1% "never/almost never" (Exhibit 4-7).

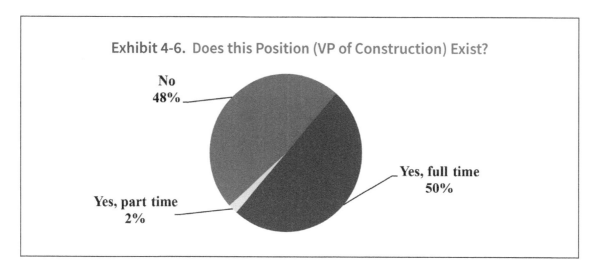

Exhibit 4-6. Does this Position (VP of Construction) Exist?

No
48%

Yes, full time
50%

Yes, part time
2%

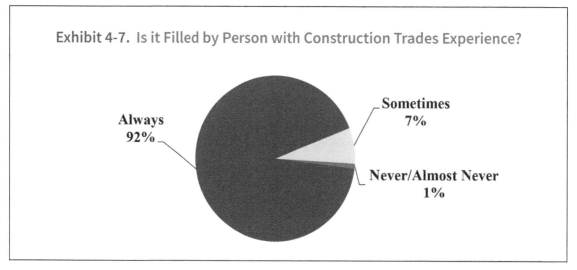

Exhibit 4-7. Is it Filled by Person with Construction Trades Experience?

Sometimes
7%

Always
92%

Never/Almost Never
1%

Among firms that have the position full time, 4% report an annual salary of less than $50,000, 34% between $50,000 and $99,999, and 62% report it at $100,000 or more. The average annual salary for the VP of Construction is $113,007 and the average bonus among all those reporting a salary is $48,355 (averaging in zero bonuses), for an average total compensation of $161,362 (Exhibit 4-8). Seventy-six percent of companies reporting a salary for this position also pay a bonus/commission. The average bonus among only those who reported a bonus (not averaging in zeroes) is $63,234 (Appendix B).

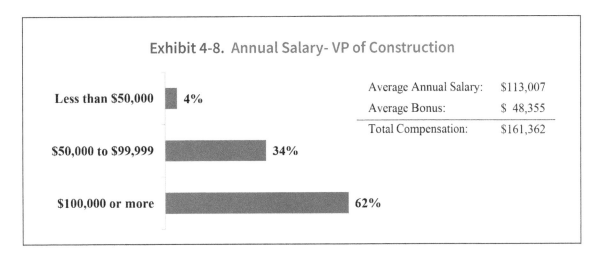

Exhibit 4-8. Annual Salary- VP of Construction

Average Annual Salary:	$113,007
Average Bonus:	$ 48,355
Total Compensation:	$161,362

Less than $50,000 — 4%

$50,000 to $99,999 — 34%

$100,000 or more — 62%

The likelihood that a builder employs a full-time VP of Construction increases with the size of the company: likelihood 30% of those with 1 to 10 starts in 2021 report this position, compared to 53% of those with 11 to 25 starts, 72% of those with 26 to 99 starts, and 80% of those with 100 or more units started in 2021 (Exhibit 4-9). Similarly, average total compensation for this position rises steadily with the number of units started: from $109,786 at companies with 1-10 starts, to $135,920 at those with 11 to 25 starts, $174,985 at those with 26 to 99 starts, up to $236,653 at companies with 100 or more single-family units started in 2021 (Exhibit 4-10).

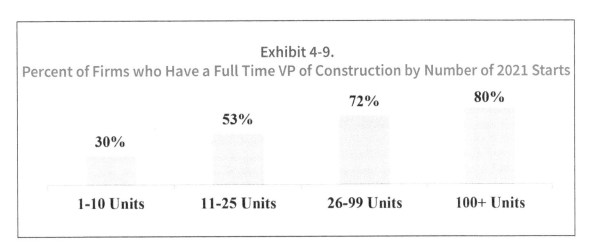

Exhibit 4-9.
Percent of Firms who Have a Full Time VP of Construction by Number of 2021 Starts

1-10 Units	11-25 Units	26-99 Units	100+ Units
30%	53%	72%	80%

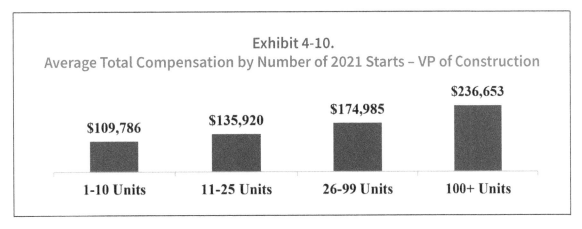

Exhibit 4-10.
Average Total Compensation by Number of 2021 Starts – VP of Construction

1-10 Units	11-25 Units	26-99 Units	100+ Units
$109,786	$135,920	$174,985	$236,653

The most common benefit offered to the VP of Construction is paid vacation leave — 95% of builders who have a full-time VP of Construction offer this benefit to them. More than 50% of builders also offer the following benefits: paid sick leave (86%), health insurance (77%), 401K (72%), and dental insurance (51%). On the other hand, less than half offer these benefits to their VP of Construction: training (49%), prescription program (48%), vision program (43%), life insurance (42%), flex spending (26%), long term disability (24%), short term disability (24%), and tuition reimbursement (19%). Eleven percent offer some other type of benefit, including a vehicle and profit sharing (Exhibit 4-11).

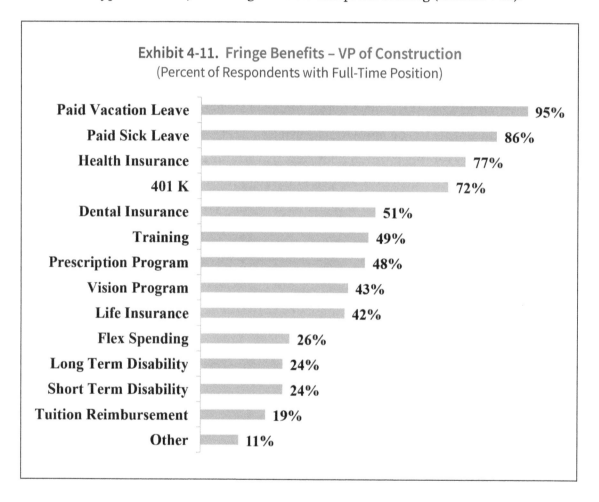

Exhibit 4-11. Fringe Benefits – VP of Construction
(Percent of Respondents with Full-Time Position)

Paid Vacation Leave	95%
Paid Sick Leave	86%
Health Insurance	77%
401 K	72%
Dental Insurance	51%
Training	49%
Prescription Program	48%
Vision Program	43%
Life Insurance	42%
Flex Spending	26%
Long Term Disability	24%
Short Term Disability	24%
Tuition Reimbursement	19%
Other	11%

CFO/Head of Finance

Around two-thirds (68%) of builders in the study do not have a CFO/Head of Finance. Of the remaining one-third, 25% have it as a full-time job and 7% as part-time (Exhibit 4-12). Among firms that have the position full-time, 33% report that the CFO/Head of Finance has an annual salary between $50,000 and $99,999 and 67% report it at $100,000 or more. The average annual salary is $118,159 and the average bonus among all those reporting a salary is $32,271 (averaging in zero bonuses), for an average total compensation of $151,030 (Exhibit 4-13). Sixty-five percent of companies reporting a salary for this position also pay a bonus/commission. The average bonus among only those who actually received a bonus is $50,801 (Appendix B).

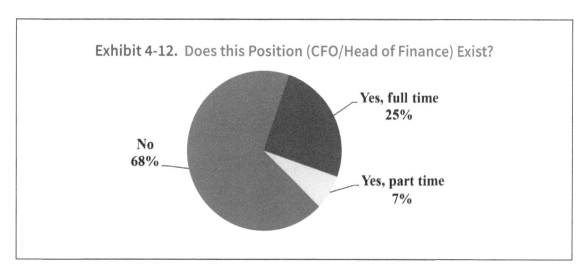

Exhibit 4-12. Does this Position (CFO/Head of Finance) Exist?

- Yes, full time 25%
- Yes, part time 7%
- No 68%

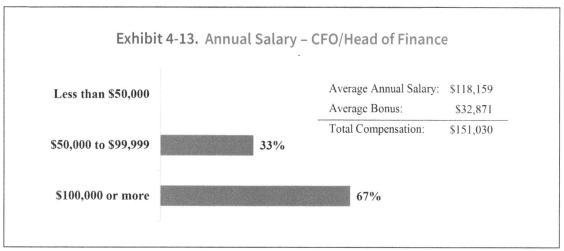

Exhibit 4-13. Annual Salary – CFO/Head of Finance

Less than $50,000	
$50,000 to $99,999	33%
$100,000 or more	67%

Average Annual Salary:	$118,159
Average Bonus:	$32,871
Total Compensation:	$151,030

The existence of a full-time CFO/Head of Finance and his/her total compensation are directly correlated with the company's size. While only 7% of builders with 1 to 10 starts in 2021 have a CFO/Head of Finance, the share grows to 31% of builders with 11 to 25 starts, 41% of those with 26 to 99 starts, and up to 63% of builders who started at least 100 single-family units in 2021 (Exhibit 4-14). Likewise, total compensation for the CFO/Head of Finance increases from $89,200 at companies with 11 to 25 starts to $199,345 at those with 100+ starts (Exhibit 4-15).

Exhibit 4-14.
Percent of Firms who Have a Full-Time CFO/Head of Finance by Number of 2021 Starts

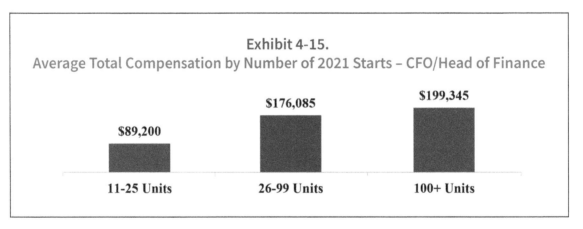

Exhibit 4-15.
Average Total Compensation by Number of 2021 Starts – CFO/Head of Finance

The most common benefits offered to full-time CFOs/Head of Finance are paid vacation leave (98%), health insurance (89%), and paid sick leave (85%). More than half of the builders who report this position also offer a 401K plan (74%), dental insurance (72%), life insurance (70%), a vision program (57%), training (53%), and a prescription program (51%). The remaining benefits are offered to the CFO/Head of Finance by fewer than 40% of builders where the position exists: long term disability (38%), flex spending (36%), short term disability (34%), and tuition reimbursement (21%). Twenty-one percent offer some other type of benefit, including a vehicle and profit sharing (Exhibit 4-16).

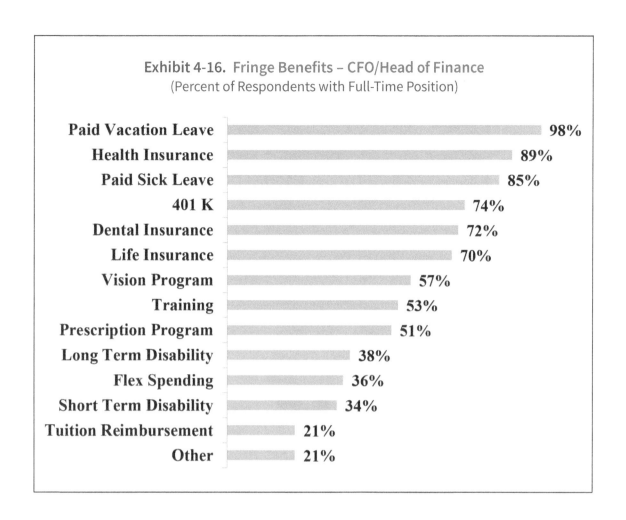

Exhibit 4-16. Fringe Benefits – CFO/Head of Finance
(Percent of Respondents with Full-Time Position)

Benefit	Percent
Paid Vacation Leave	98%
Health Insurance	89%
Paid Sick Leave	85%
401 K	74%
Dental Insurance	72%
Life Insurance	70%
Vision Program	57%
Training	53%
Prescription Program	51%
Long Term Disability	38%
Flex Spending	36%
Short Term Disability	34%
Tuition Reimbursement	21%
Other	21%

CIO/Head of IT

The position of CIO/Head of IT is uncommon at single-family home building companies. In fact, only 4% of builders in this study have a full-time CIO/Head of IT, while 1% have it only on a part-time basis (Exhibit 4-17). The salary, bonus, and benefits for this position cannot be reported due to its low incidence among builders responding to the survey (i.e., fewer than 10 builders reported information on compensation and benefits for this position).

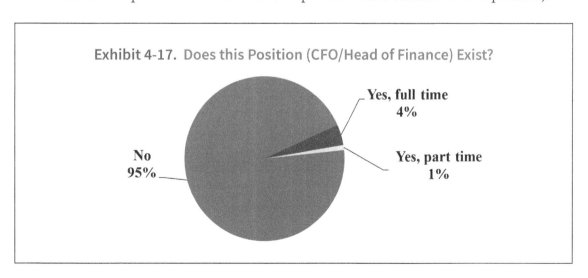

Exhibit 4-17. Does this Position (CFO/Head of Finance) Exist?

Yes, full time 4%

Yes, part time 1%

No 95%

Head/Director of Purchasing

Twenty-one percent of builders report that the position of Head/Director of Purchasing exists in their firm on a full-time basis, while 1% report it as a part-time job (Exhibit 4-18). In the majority of cases where position exists (79%), it is "always" filled by someone with experience in the construction trades, "sometimes" in another 17%, and "never/almost never" in just 4% (Exhibit 4-19).

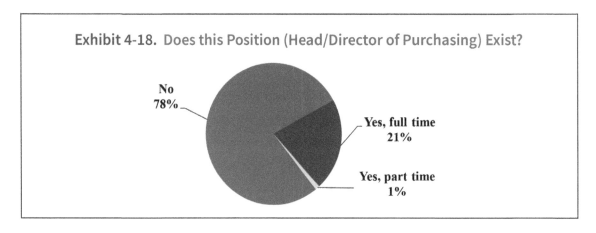

Exhibit 4-18. Does this Position (Head/Director of Purchasing) Exist?

No 78%

Yes, full time 21%

Yes, part time 1%

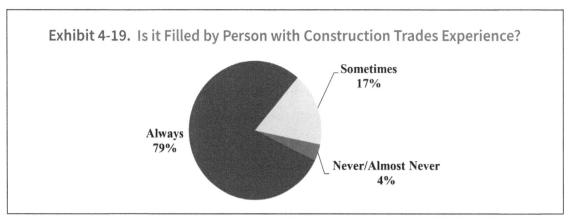

Exhibit 4-19. Is it Filled by Person with Construction Trades Experience?

Sometimes 17%

Always 79%

Never/Almost Never 4%

Among firms that have the position full-time, 6% report that their Head/Director of Purchasing has an annual salary of less than $50,000, 64% between $50,000 and $99,999, and 30% report it at $100,000 or more. The average annual salary is $86,601 and the average bonus among all those reporting a salary is $16,923 (averaging in zero bonuses), for an average total compensation of $103,524 (Exhibit 4-20).

Seventy-eight percent of companies reporting a salary for this position also pay a bonus/commission. The average bonus among only those who reported a bonus (not averaging in zeroes) is $21,697 (Appendix B).

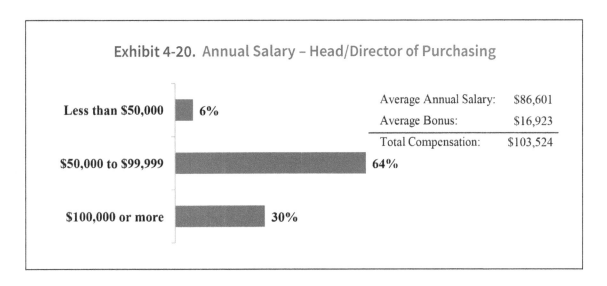

Exhibit 4-20. Annual Salary – Head/Director of Purchasing

Average Annual Salary:	$86,601
Average Bonus:	$16,923
Total Compensation:	$103,524

Less than $50,000 — 6%

$50,000 to $99,999 — 64%

$100,000 or more — 30%

The more single-family units a firm had in 2021, the more likely it was to have a Head/ Director of Purchasing. The share grows from 4% among those with 1 to 10 starts, to 17% of those with 11 to 25 starts, 31% of those with 26 to 99 starts, and to 70% among those with 100+ starts (Exhibit 4-21). Average total compensation for this job is $112,805 at builders with 26 to 99 starts and $121,224 at builders with 100+ starts (Exhibit 4-22).

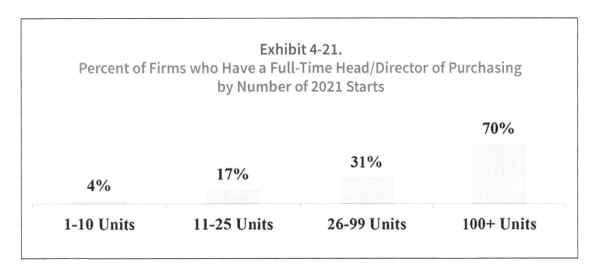

Exhibit 4-21.
Percent of Firms who Have a Full-Time Head/Director of Purchasing by Number of 2021 Starts

1-10 Units	11-25 Units	26-99 Units	100+ Units
4%	17%	31%	70%

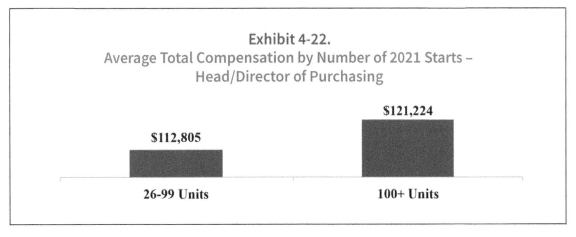

Exhibit 4-22.
Average Total Compensation by Number of 2021 Starts – Head/Director of Purchasing

26-99 Units	100+ Units
$112,805	$121,224

The three most common benefits offered to the Head/Director of Purchasing are paid vacation leave (96%), health insurance (88%), and a 401K plan (84%). Paid sick leave is offered by 76% of builders where position exists full-time, dental insurance by 69%, a vision program by 59%, life insurance by 53%, and a prescription program by 51%. Less than half of builders that have a Head/Director of Purchasing position offer it the remaining benefits: training (49%), long term disability (43%), short term disability (41%), flex spending (31%), and tuition reimbursement (27%). Fourteen percent offer 'other' benefits, such as childcare and a vehicle (Exhibit 4-23).

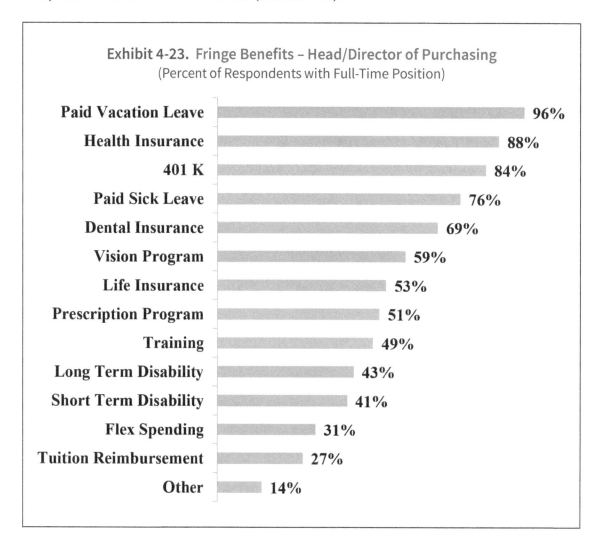

Exhibit 4-23. Fringe Benefits – Head/Director of Purchasing
(Percent of Respondents with Full-Time Position)

Benefit	Percent
Paid Vacation Leave	96%
Health Insurance	88%
401 K	84%
Paid Sick Leave	76%
Dental Insurance	69%
Vision Program	59%
Life Insurance	53%
Prescription Program	51%
Training	49%
Long Term Disability	43%
Short Term Disability	41%
Flex Spending	31%
Tuition Reimbursement	27%
Other	14%

Head/Director of Land Acquisition

A full-time Head/Director of Land Acquisition position exists for 12% of the builders who responded to the survey (Exhibit 4-24). Another 1% report having the position on a part-time basis. The majority (73%) report it is "always" filled by a person with experience in the construction trades and only "sometimes" by the other 27% (Exhibit 4-25).

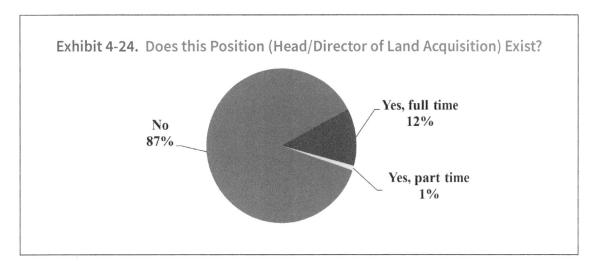

Exhibit 4-24. Does this Position (Head/Director of Land Acquisition) Exist?

No
87%

Yes, full time
12%

Yes, part time
1%

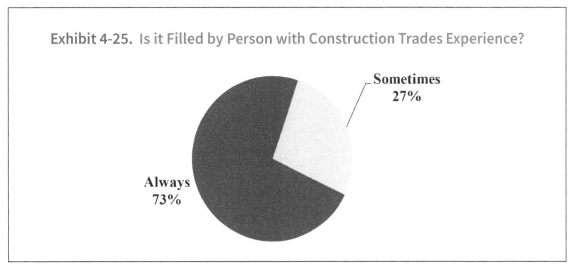

Exhibit 4-25. Is it Filled by Person with Construction Trades Experience?

Sometimes
27%

Always
73%

Among firms that have the position, 4% report that their Head/Director of Land Acquisition has an annual salary of less than $50,000, 19% between $50,000 and $99,999, and the other 77% report it at $100,000 or more. The average annual salary is $127,210, and the average bonus among all those reporting a salary is $54,418 (averaging in zero bonuses), for an average total compensation of $181,628 (Exhibit 4-26). Eighty-five percent of companies reporting a salary for this position also pay a bonus/commission. The average bonus among only those who reported a bonus (not averaging in zeroes) is $64,312 (Appendix B).

Having a full-time Head/Director of Land Acquisition is rare among small builders. None of the respondents with 1 to 10 starts and only a mere 6% of those with 11 to 25 starts have this position. In contrast, the share rises to 19% of those with 26 to 99 starts and to 57% among builders with 100+ single-family starts (Exhibit 4-27). Because of insufficient responses, average total compensation cannot be reported for this position for builders with fewer than 100 starts. At companies that start 100+ units, the job's annual compensation averages $172,831 (Appendix D).

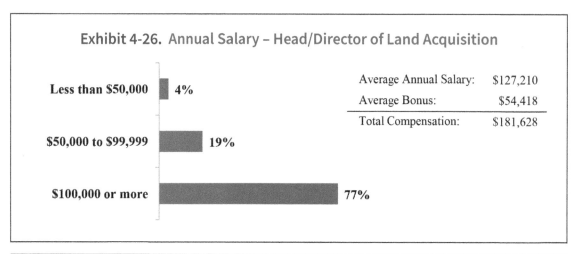

Exhibit 4-26. Annual Salary – Head/Director of Land Acquisition

Average Annual Salary:	$127,210
Average Bonus:	$54,418
Total Compensation:	$181,628

Less than $50,000 — 4%

$50,000 to $99,999 — 19%

$100,000 or more — 77%

Exhibit 4-27.
Percent of Firms who Have a Full-Time Head/Director of Land Acquisition by Number of 2021 Starts

1-10 Units	11-25 Units	26-99 Units	100+ Units
0%	6%	19%	57%

All firms who report having a full-time Head/Director of Land Acquisition offer this position paid vacation leave as a fringe benefit. Most builders where a position exists also offer the following benefits: a 401K plan (92%), health insurance (92%), dental insurance (88%), paid sick leave (85%), life insurance (69%), a vision program (65%), long term disability (62%), a prescription program (62%), training (58%), and short term disability (58%). Fewer than half offer the following benefits to their Head/Director of Land Acquisition: flex spending (46%) and tuition reimbursement (42%). Twenty-seven percent offer some other type of benefit, such as paid parental leave and a company vehicle (Exhibit 4-28).

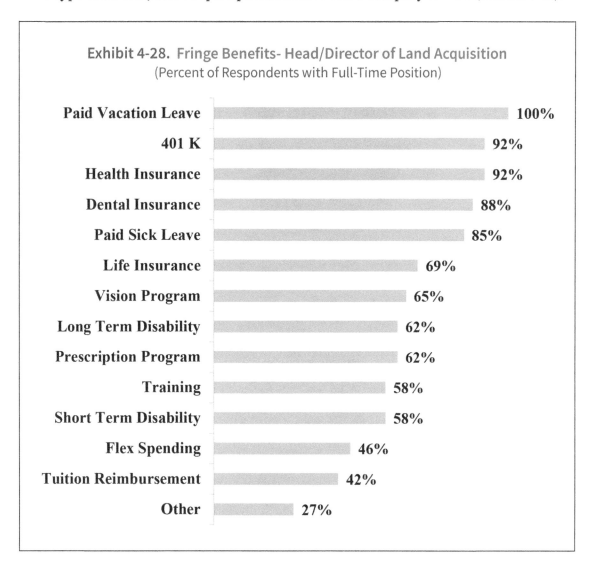

Exhibit 4-28. Fringe Benefits- Head/Director of Land Acquisition
(Percent of Respondents with Full-Time Position)

Paid Vacation Leave	100%
401 K	92%
Health Insurance	92%
Dental Insurance	88%
Paid Sick Leave	85%
Life Insurance	69%
Vision Program	65%
Long Term Disability	62%
Prescription Program	62%
Training	58%
Short Term Disability	58%
Flex Spending	46%
Tuition Reimbursement	42%
Other	27%

Head/Director of Production

Thirteen percent of single-family builders responding to the survey have a full-time Head/Director of Production on staff. One percent have it on a part-time basis (Exhibit 4-29). Having prior experience in the construction trades is important for this position, as 86% of builders where it exists say it is "always" filled by a person with such experience, compared to 14% who say only "sometimes," and none who say "never/almost never" (Exhibit 4-30).

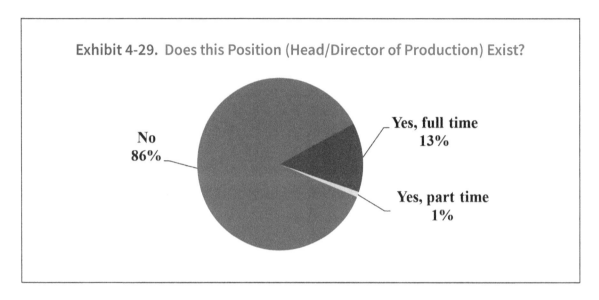

Exhibit 4-29. Does this Position (Head/Director of Production) Exist?

No
86%

Yes, full time
13%

Yes, part time
1%

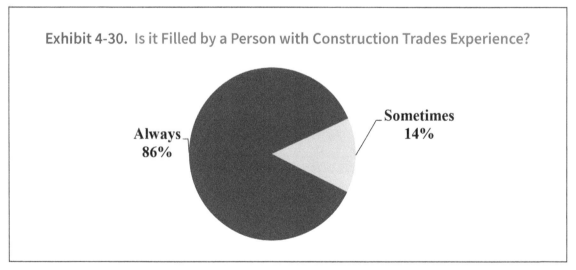

Exhibit 4-30. Is it Filled by a Person with Construction Trades Experience?

Always
86%

Sometimes
14%

Among firms that have the position, 10% report that their Head/Director of Production has an annual salary below $50,000, 52% between $50,000 and $99,999, and 39% report it at $100,000 or more. The average annual salary is $92,406, and the average bonus among all those reporting a salary is $27,824 (averaging in zero bonuses), for an average total compensation of $120,230 (Exhibit 4-31). Eighty-four percent of companies reporting a salary for this position also pay a bonus/commission. The average bonus among only those who reported a bonus (not averaging in zeroes) is $33,175 (Appendix B).

The chance that a builder has a full-time Head/Director of Production on staff increases with the size of the company. While only 2% and 8% of builders, respectively, with 1 to 10 starts or 11 to 25 starts have this position, the share rises to 25% of those with 26 to 99 starts and to 40% of those that start 100 or more units (Exhibit 4-32). Because of insufficient responses, average total compensation cannot be reported for this position for builders with fewer than 100 starts. At companies that start 100+ units, the job's annual compensation averages $133,167 (Appendix D).

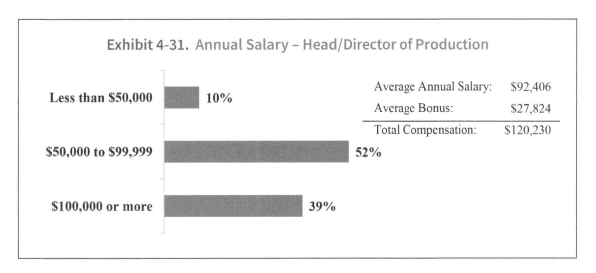

Exhibit 4-31. Annual Salary – Head/Director of Production

Less than $50,000		10%
$50,000 to $99,999		52%
$100,000 or more		39%

Average Annual Salary:	$92,406
Average Bonus:	$27,824
Total Compensation:	$120,230

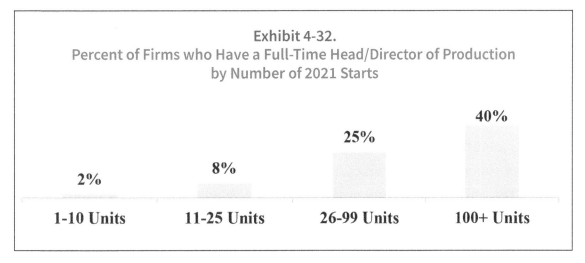

Exhibit 4-32.
Percent of Firms who Have a Full-Time Head/Director of Production
by Number of 2021 Starts

1-10 Units	11-25 Units	26-99 Units	100+ Units
2%	8%	25%	40%

All builders in the study who have the Head/Director of Production position on staff offer paid vacation leave. More than half also offer the following benefits: a 401K plan (90%), paid sick leave (84%), health insurance (84%), dental insurance (61%), a vision program (58%), training (52%), and a prescription program (52%). The remaining benefits are offered by a minority of firms: flex spending and life insurance (both by 39%), long term and short term disability (both by 29%), and tuition reimbursement (26%). Sixteen percent offer some other type of benefits, such as profit sharing and a company vehicle (Exhibit 4-33).

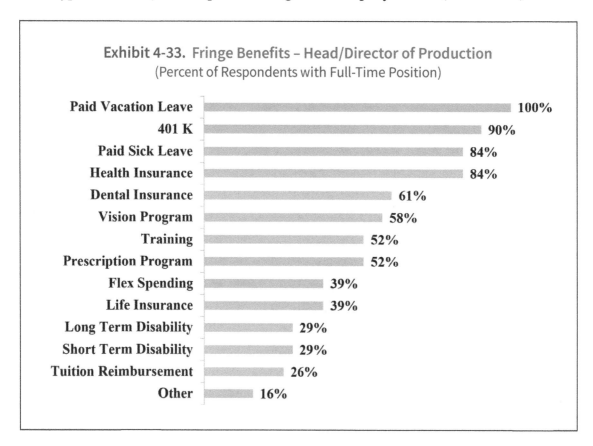

Exhibit 4-33. Fringe Benefits – Head/Director of Production
(Percent of Respondents with Full-Time Position)

Paid Vacation Leave	100%
401 K	90%
Paid Sick Leave	84%
Health Insurance	84%
Dental Insurance	61%
Vision Program	58%
Training	52%
Prescription Program	52%
Flex Spending	39%
Life Insurance	39%
Long Term Disability	29%
Short Term Disability	29%
Tuition Reimbursement	26%
Other	16%

Head/Director of Development and Training

Only 2% of builders report the position of Head/Director of Development & Training exists on a full-time basis at their firm (Exhibit 4-34). The salary, bonus, and benefits for this position cannot be reported due to its low incidence among builders responding to the survey.

Head/Director of Sales & Marketing

More than a quarter of builders report the position of Head/Director of Sales & Marketing exists in their firm, 21% in a full-time capacity and 5% as a part-time job (Exhibit 4-35). Almost half — 48% — of builders say the person in this job "always" has experience in the construction trades, 31% say "sometimes," and 20% "never/almost never" (Exhibit 4-36).

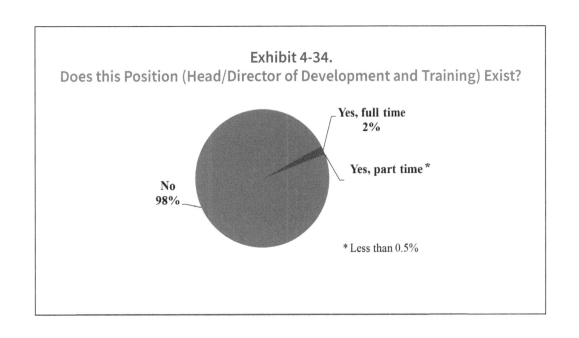

Exhibit 4-34.
Does this Position (Head/Director of Development and Training) Exist?

Yes, full time
2%

Yes, part time *

No
98%

* Less than 0.5%

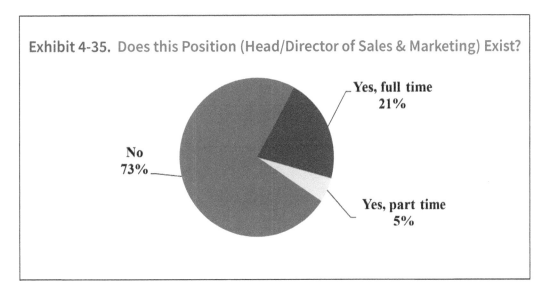

Exhibit 4-35. Does this Position (Head/Director of Sales & Marketing) Exist?

Yes, full time
21%

No
73%

Yes, part time
5%

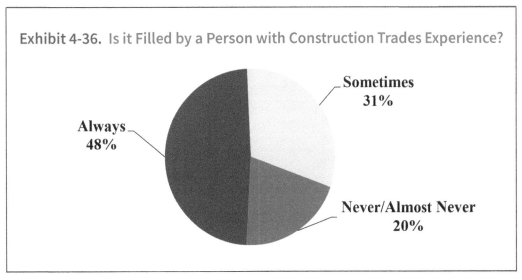

Exhibit 4-36. Is it Filled by a Person with Construction Trades Experience?

Sometimes
31%

Always
48%

Never/Almost Never
20%

Among firms that have the position full-time, 5% report that the Head/Director of Sales & Marketing has an average salary of less than $50,000, 41% between $50,000 and $99,999, and 55% report it at $100,000 or more. The average annual salary is $101,913 and the average bonus among all those reporting a salary is $44,377 (averaging in zero bonuses), for an average total compensation of $146,290 (Exhibit 4-37). Eighty-four percent of companies reporting a salary for this position also pay a bonus/commission. The average bonus among only those who reported a bonus (not averaging in zeroes) is $52,773 (Appendix B).

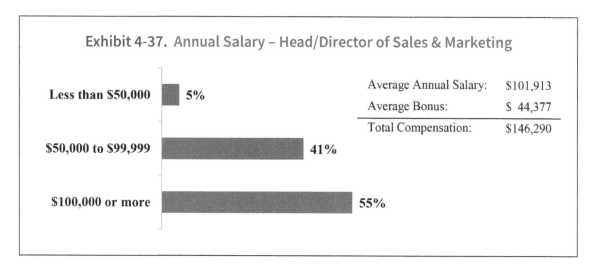

Exhibit 4-37. Annual Salary – Head/Director of Sales & Marketing

Less than $50,000	5%
$50,000 to $99,999	41%
$100,000 or more	55%

Average Annual Salary:	$101,913
Average Bonus:	$ 44,377
Total Compensation:	$146,290

The share of firms with a full-time Head/Director of Sales & Marketing increases steadily with the size of the company. Whereas only 6% of builders with 1 to 10 starts report the position exists in their companies, the share goes up to 17% at firms with 11 to 25 starts, 38% at those with 26 to 99 starts, and up to 73% of those with 100+ starts (Exhibit 4-38). Average total compensation for this job is $155,709 at builders with 26 to 99 starts and $163,953 at those with 100+ starts (Exhibit 4-39).

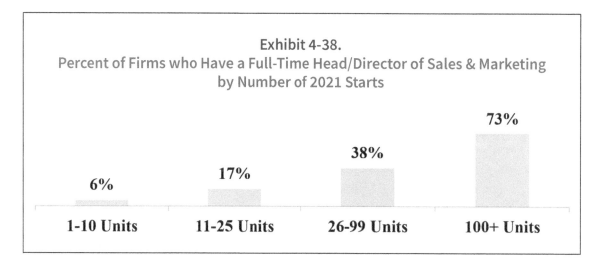

Exhibit 4-38.
Percent of Firms who Have a Full-Time Head/Director of Sales & Marketing by Number of 2021 Starts

1-10 Units	11-25 Units	26-99 Units	100+ Units
6%	17%	38%	73%

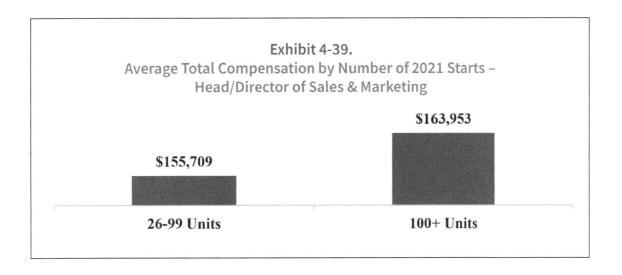

Exhibit 4-39.
Average Total Compensation by Number of 2021 Starts –
Head/Director of Sales & Marketing

$155,709

$163,953

26-99 Units

100+ Units

The most common benefit offered to the Head/Director of Sales & Marketing is paid vacation leave — 95% of firms who have this position offer it to them. More than half also offer health insurance (89%), paid sick leave (86%), a 401K plan (80%), dental insurance (77%), training (64%), life insurance (61%), a vision program (61%), and a prescription program (59%). Less than half offer the remaining benefits: short term disability (43%), flex spending (41%), long term disability (41%), and tuition reimbursement (32%). A quarter of builders offer some other type of benefits to the Head/Director of Sales & Marketing, such as a company vehicle and volunteer time off (Exhibit 4-40).

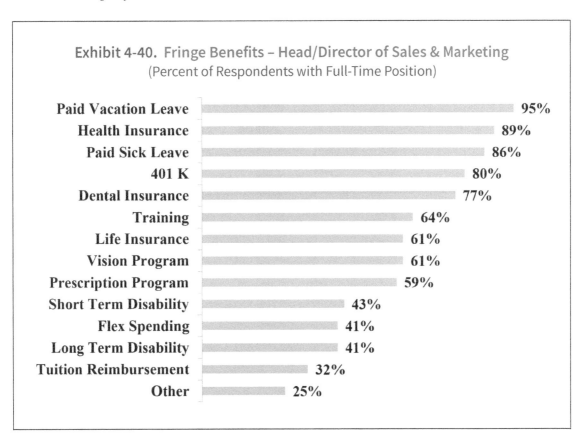

Exhibit 4-40. Fringe Benefits – Head/Director of Sales & Marketing
(Percent of Respondents with Full-Time Position)

Paid Vacation Leave	95%
Health Insurance	89%
Paid Sick Leave	86%
401 K	80%
Dental Insurance	77%
Training	64%
Life Insurance	61%
Vision Program	61%
Prescription Program	59%
Short Term Disability	43%
Flex Spending	41%
Long Term Disability	41%
Tuition Reimbursement	32%
Other	25%

Controller

A full-time Controller exists at 19% of the single-family building firms that took part in this study. Another 3% of builders have the job on a part-time basis (Exhibit 4-41). Among firms that have the position full-time, 72% report that the Controller has an annual average salary between $50,000 and $99,999 and 28% report it at $100,000 or more. The average annual salary is $92,182 and the average bonus among all those reporting a salary is $20,344 (averaging in zero bonuses), for an average total compensation of $112,526 (Exhibit 4-42). Eighty-six percent of companies reporting a salary for this position also pay a bonus/commission. The average bonus among only those who reported a bonus (not averaging in zeroes) is $23,643 (Appendix B).

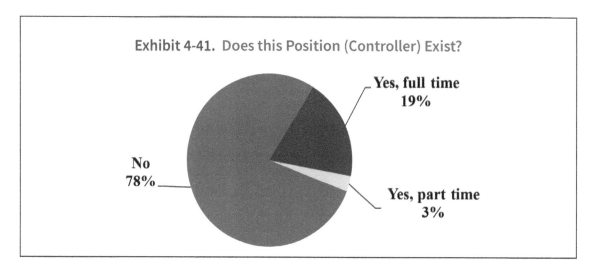

Exhibit 4-41. Does this Position (Controller) Exist?

Yes, full time
19%

No
78%

Yes, part time
3%

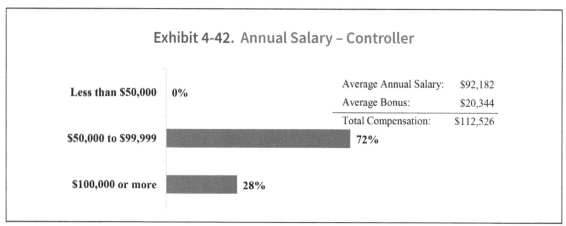

Exhibit 4-42. Annual Salary – Controller

Less than $50,000	0%
$50,000 to $99,999	72%
$100,000 or more	28%

Average Annual Salary:	$92,182
Average Bonus:	$20,344
Total Compensation:	$112,526

Except at large, production builders, a full-time Controller is not a common position at homebuilding companies. The share of builders who have this job is only 2% at firms with 1 to 10 starts, but it grows slightly to 22% among those with 11 to 99 starts, and then jumps among firms with 100 or more starts to 73% (Exhibit 4-43). Because of insufficient responses, average total compensation cannot be reported for this position for builders with fewer than 100 starts. At companies that start 100+ units, the job's annual compensation averages $124,908 (Appendix D).

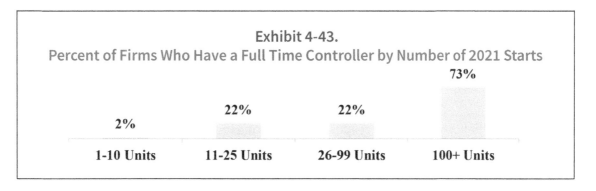

Exhibit 4-43.
Percent of Firms Who Have a Full Time Controller by Number of 2021 Starts

1-10 Units	11-25 Units	26-99 Units	100+ Units
2%	22%	22%	73%

Almost all builders — 98% — offer paid vacation leave to full-time Controllers. Other benefits offered to this position by a majority of companies where it exists include health insurance (90%), a 401K plan (88%), paid sick leave (83%), dental insurance (76%), a prescription program (60%), life insurance (57%), and a vision program (57%). Less than half offer the following benefits: short term disability (45%), training (43%), long term disability (43%), flex spending (36%), and tuition reimbursement (29%). Ten percent of builders offer the Controller other benefits, such as paid parental leave and profit sharing (Exhibit 4-44).

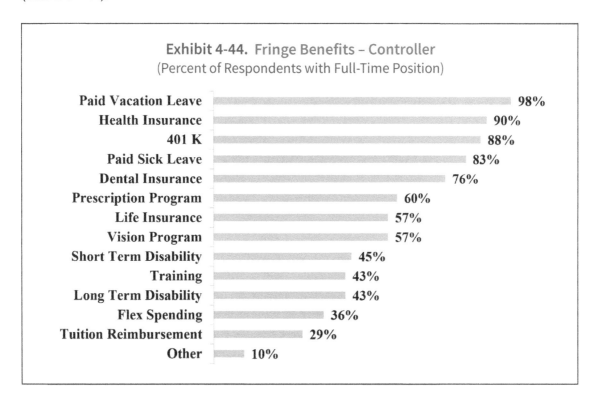

Exhibit 4-44. Fringe Benefits – Controller
(Percent of Respondents with Full-Time Position)

Paid Vacation Leave	98%
Health Insurance	90%
401 K	88%
Paid Sick Leave	83%
Dental Insurance	76%
Prescription Program	60%
Life Insurance	57%
Vision Program	57%
Short Term Disability	45%
Training	43%
Long Term Disability	43%
Flex Spending	36%
Tuition Reimbursement	29%
Other	10%

Payroll Manager

Only 7% of builders have a full time Payroll Manager position, while another 5% have it on a part-time basis (Exhibit 4-45). Among firms that have the position full-time, 21% report that the Payroll Manager has an annual salary of less than $50,000, 71% between $50,000 and $99,999, and 7% at $100,000 or more. The average annual salary is $64,763, and the average bonus among all those reporting a salary is $6,339 (averaging in zero bonuses), for an average total compensation of $71,102 (Exhibit 4-46). Fifty percent of companies reporting a salary for this position also pay a bonus/commission. The average bonus among those who reported a bonus (not averaging in zeroes) cannot be reported due to an insufficient number of responses to this question (Appendix B).

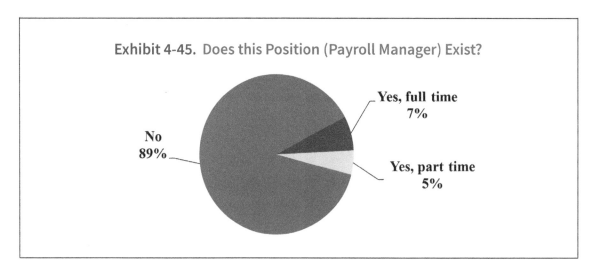

Exhibit 4-45. Does this Position (Payroll Manager) Exist?

Yes, full time
7%

No
89%

Yes, part time
5%

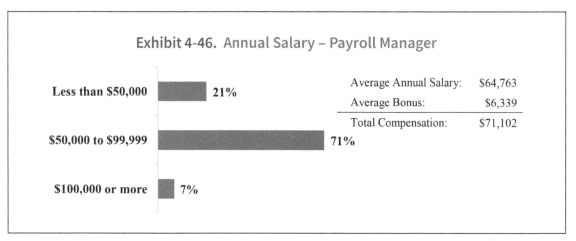

Exhibit 4-46. Annual Salary – Payroll Manager

Less than $50,000	21%	
$50,000 to $99,999	71%	
$100,000 or more	7%	

Average Annual Salary:	$64,763
Average Bonus:	$6,339
Total Compensation:	$71,102

Most single-family home building companies do not have a full-time Payroll Manager on staff, regardless of company size. In fact, fewer than 10% of builders that start less than 100 units a year report having this position. Among those with 100+ starts, the share is only 23% (Exhibit 4-47). Due to an insufficient number of responses to produce reliable estimates, average total compensation for Payroll Managers cannot be reported by company size.

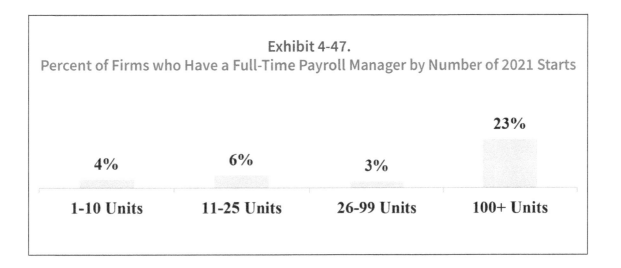

Exhibit 4-47.
Percent of Firms who Have a Full-Time Payroll Manager by Number of 2021 Starts

| 1-10 Units | 11-25 Units | 26-99 Units | 100+ Units |
| 4% | 6% | 3% | 23% |

At least half the builders with a full-time Payroll Manager on staff offer the following benefits: paid vacation leave (100%), a 401K plan (86%), health insurance (86%), paid sick leave (79%), a prescription program (64%), dental insurance (64%), a vision program (57%), and training (50%). A minority of builders offer life insurance (43%), flex spending (36%), long and short term disability (both 29%), and tuition reimbursement (14%). Fourteen percent offer some other type of benefit to the Payroll Manager, such as a fuel reimbursement and vehicle maintenance (Exhibit 4-48).

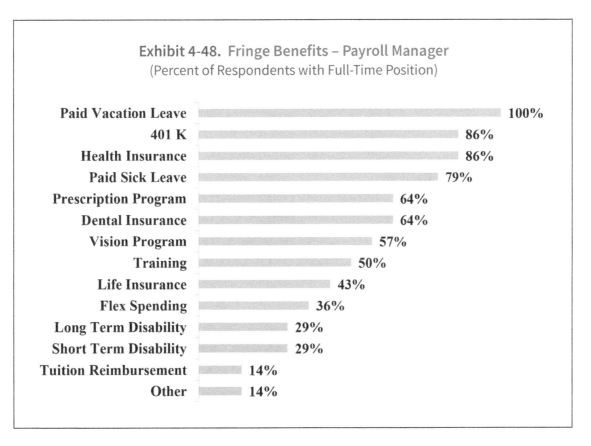

Exhibit 4-48. Fringe Benefits – Payroll Manager
(Percent of Respondents with Full-Time Position)

Benefit	Percent
Paid Vacation Leave	100%
401 K	86%
Health Insurance	86%
Paid Sick Leave	79%
Prescription Program	64%
Dental Insurance	64%
Vision Program	57%
Training	50%
Life Insurance	43%
Flex Spending	36%
Long Term Disability	29%
Short Term Disability	29%
Tuition Reimbursement	14%
Other	14%

Staff Accountant

Thirteen percent of builders in this study have a full-time Staff Accountant on staff. Another 3% have the position on a part-time basis (Exhibit 4-49). Among firms that have the position full-time, 10% pay it an annual salary of less than $50,000, 83% between $50,000 and $99,999, and 7% pay it $100,000 or more. The average annual salary is $67,488, and the average bonus among all those reporting a salary is $9,233 (averaging in zero bonuses), for an average total compensation of $76,721 (Exhibit 4-50). Seventy-three percent of companies reporting a salary for this position also pay a bonus/commission. The average bonus among only those who reported a bonus (not averaging in zeroes) is $12,590 (Appendix B).

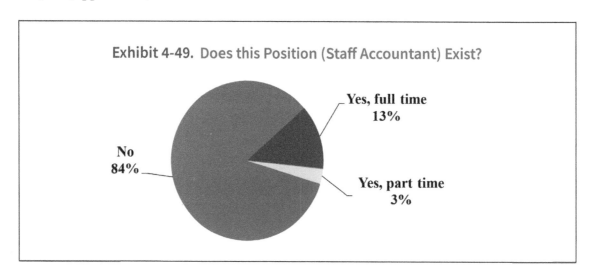

Exhibit 4-49. Does this Position (Staff Accountant) Exist?

Yes, full time
13%

No
84%

Yes, part time
3%

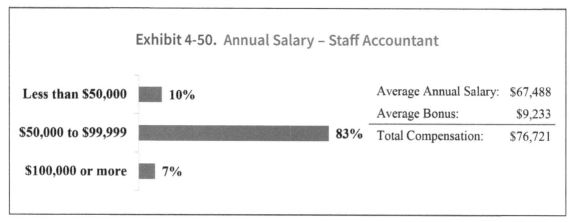

Exhibit 4-50. Annual Salary – Staff Accountant

Less than $50,000	10%
$50,000 to $99,999	83%
$100,000 or more	7%

Average Annual Salary:	$67,488
Average Bonus:	$9,233
Total Compensation:	$76,721

Exactly half of the largest builders (100 or more units) employ a full-time Staff Accountant. But the share is significantly lower among smaller builders: 4% among those with 1 to 10 starts, 14% among those with 11 to 25 starts, and 22% among those with 26 to 99 starts (Exhibit 4-51). Annual compensation for full-time Staff Accountants averages $77,071 at firms with 100 or more starts (Appendix D).

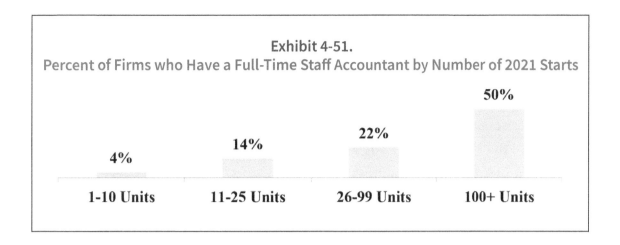

Exhibit 4-51.
Percent of Firms who Have a Full-Time Staff Accountant by Number of 2021 Starts

			50%
4%	14%	22%	
1-10 Units	11-25 Units	26-99 Units	100+ Units

One hundred percent of builders with a full-time Staff Accountant on staff offer paid vacation leave. Eighty-six percent offer this position both paid sick leave and health insurance. Most also offer dental insurance (83%), a 401K plan (79%), a vision program (66%), life insurance (62%), training (59%), and a prescription program (52%). A minority also offer long term disability (48%), short term disability (45%), flex spending (41%), and tuition reimbursement (38%). Ten percent offer some other type of benefit to the Staff Accountant, such as paid parental leave (Exhibit 4-52).

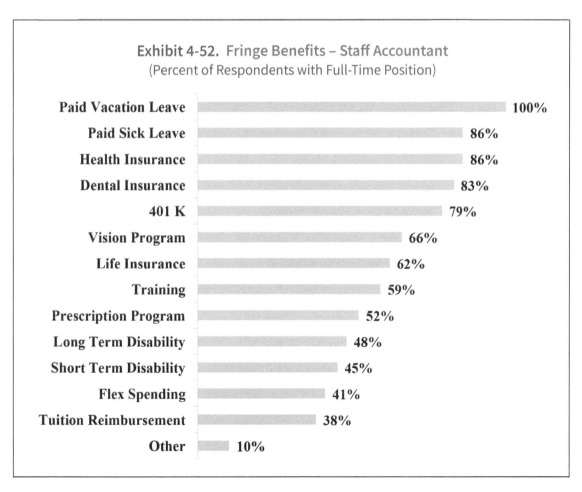

Exhibit 4-52. Fringe Benefits – Staff Accountant
(Percent of Respondents with Full-Time Position)

Paid Vacation Leave	100%
Paid Sick Leave	86%
Health Insurance	86%
Dental Insurance	83%
401 K	79%
Vision Program	66%
Life Insurance	62%
Training	59%
Prescription Program	52%
Long Term Disability	48%
Short Term Disability	45%
Flex Spending	41%
Tuition Reimbursement	38%
Other	10%

Bookkeeper

Twenty-nine percent of builders report the position of Bookkeeper exists as a full-time job in their firm, while 16% report it exists on a part-time basis (Exhibit 4-53). Among firms that have the position full time, half pay it an average annual salary of less than $50,000 and the other half between $50,000 and $99,999. The average annual salary is $49,693, and the average bonus among all those reporting a salary is $5,858 (averaging in zero bonuses), for an average total compensation of $55,551 (Exhibit 4-54). Sixty-one percent of companies reporting a salary for this position also pay a bonus/commission. The average bonus among only those who reported a bonus (not averaging in zeroes) is $9,665 (Appendix B).

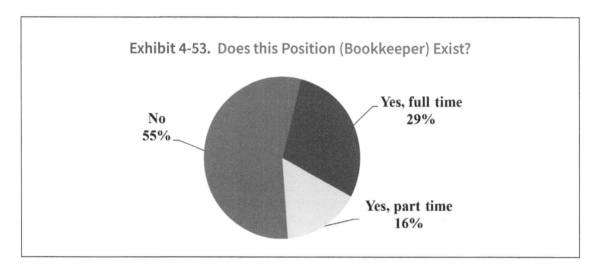

Exhibit 4-53. Does this Position (Bookkeeper) Exist?

No 55%

Yes, full time 29%

Yes, part time 16%

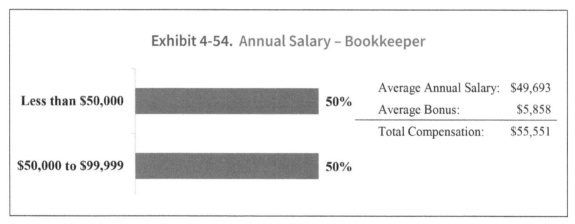

Exhibit 4-54. Annual Salary – Bookkeeper

Less than $50,000	50%
$50,000 to $99,999	50%

Average Annual Salary:	$49,693
Average Bonus:	$5,858
Total Compensation:	$55,551

Full-time Bookkeepers become more commonplace as single-family building companies get larger. Whereas only 16% of builders with 1 to 10 starts have the position, the share doubles to 33% among those with 11 to 25 starts, goes to 38% of those with 26 to 99 starts, and reaches 60% of builders with 100 or more starts (Exhibit 4-55). Total compensation for this position averages $50,984 among builders with 1 to 10 starts, $65,982 among those with 11 to 25 starts, and slightly above $55,000 among builders with 26 or more starts (Exhibit 4-56).

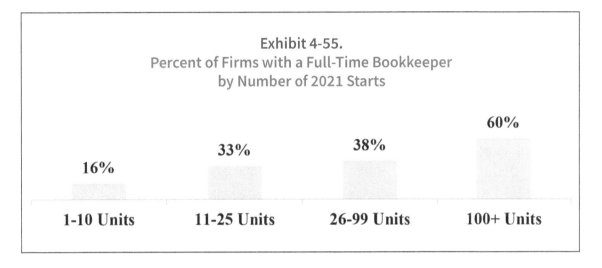

Exhibit 4-55.
Percent of Firms with a Full-Time Bookkeeper
by Number of 2021 Starts

16%	33%	38%	60%
1-10 Units	11-25 Units	26-99 Units	100+ Units

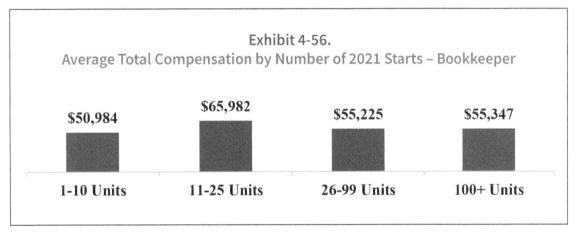

Exhibit 4-56.
Average Total Compensation by Number of 2021 Starts – Bookkeeper

$50,984	$65,982	$55,225	$55,347
1-10 Units	11-25 Units	26-99 Units	100+ Units

The most common benefit offered to the Bookkeeper is paid vacation leave — 95% of firms with this position offer it to them. Three additional benefits are offered by most builders: paid sick leave (77%), a 401K plan (73%), and health insurance (73%). The remaining nine benefits, on the other hand, are offered to the Bookkeeper by less than half the companies where the position exists: dental insurance (47%), training (45%), a vision program (39%), life insurance (37%), a prescription program (34%), long term disability (23%), short term disability (21%), tuition reimbursement (19%), and flex spending (16%). Three percent of the responding firms offer some other type of benefit to the Bookkeeper, such as paid holidays (Exhibit 4-57).

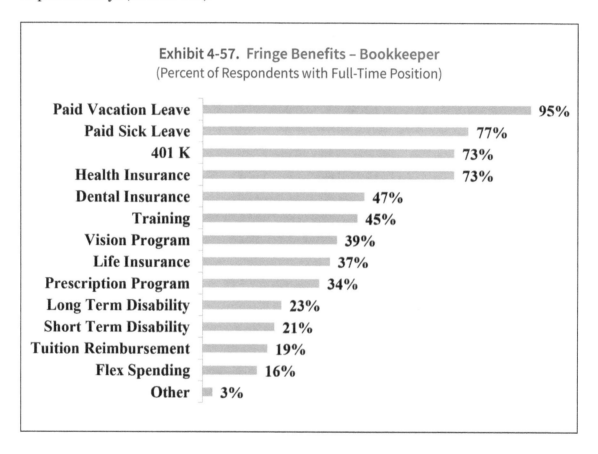

Exhibit 4-57. Fringe Benefits – Bookkeeper
(Percent of Respondents with Full-Time Position)

Benefit	Percent
Paid Vacation Leave	95%
Paid Sick Leave	77%
401 K	73%
Health Insurance	73%
Dental Insurance	47%
Training	45%
Vision Program	39%
Life Insurance	37%
Prescription Program	34%
Long Term Disability	23%
Short Term Disability	21%
Tuition Reimbursement	19%
Flex Spending	16%
Other	3%

Director of Human Resources

Most single-family home building companies do not employ a Director of Human Resources. In fact, only a small minority of 7% do: 5% full-time and 2% part-time (Exhibit 4-58). Among firms that have the position full-time, 75% pay it an annual average salary between $50,000 and $99,999 and 25% pay it $100,000 or more. The average annual salary is $89,567 and the average bonus among all those reporting a salary is $17,008 (averaging in zero bonuses), for an average total compensation of $106,575 (Exhibit 4-59). Seventy-five percent of companies reporting a salary for this position also pay a bonus/commission. The average bonus among those who reported a bonus (not averaging in zeroes) cannot be reported due to an insufficient number of responses to this question (Appendix B).

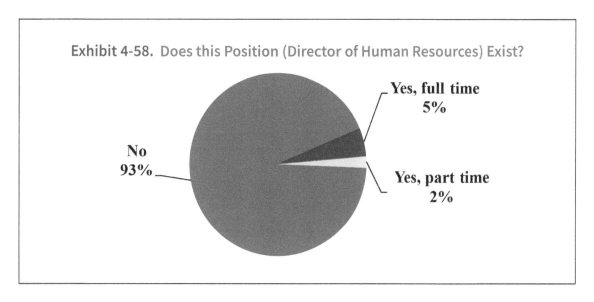

Exhibit 4-58. Does this Position (Director of Human Resources) Exist?

Yes, full time
5%

No
93%

Yes, part time
2%

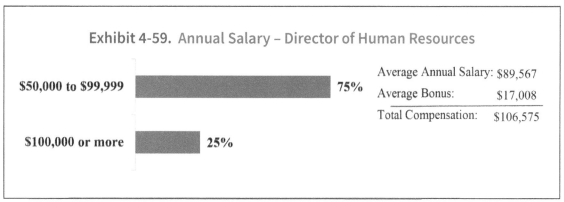

Exhibit 4-59. Annual Salary – Director of Human Resources

$50,000 to $99,999	75%
$100,000 or more	25%

Average Annual Salary: $89,567
Average Bonus: $17,008
Total Compensation: $106,575

Most single-family home building companies do not have a full-time Director of Human Resources on staff, regardless of company size. In fact, fewer than 10% of builders that start less than 100 units a year report this position. Among those with 100+ starts, the share is 30% (Exhibit 4-60). Due to an insufficient number of responses to produce reliable estimates, average total compensation for Director of Human Resources cannot be reported by company size.

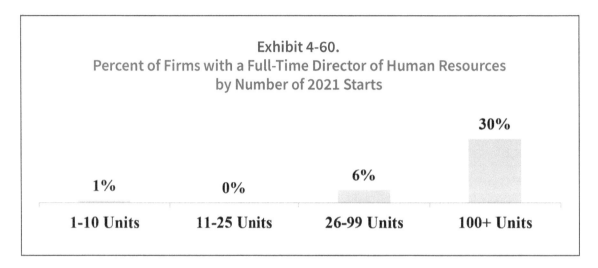

Exhibit 4-60.
Percent of Firms with a Full-Time Director of Human Resources
by Number of 2021 Starts

| 1% | 0% | 6% | 30% |
| 1-10 Units | 11-25 Units | 26-99 Units | 100+ Units |

Although only a small minority of builders employ a full-time Director of Human Resources, those that do are likely to offer him/her most fringe benefits. For example, 100% of companies that report this job offer paid vacation leave and health insurance, nearly all (92%) also offer paid sick leave and a 401K plan, and 83% offer both life insurance and dental insurance. Except for tuition reimbursement (42%), most builders offer all the remaining benefits: a prescription program (75%), long term disability (67%), training (58%), a vision program (58%), flex spending (50%), and short term disability (50%). Eight percent offer some other type of benefit to the Director of Human Resources, such as a week off for volunteer work. (Exhibit 4-61).

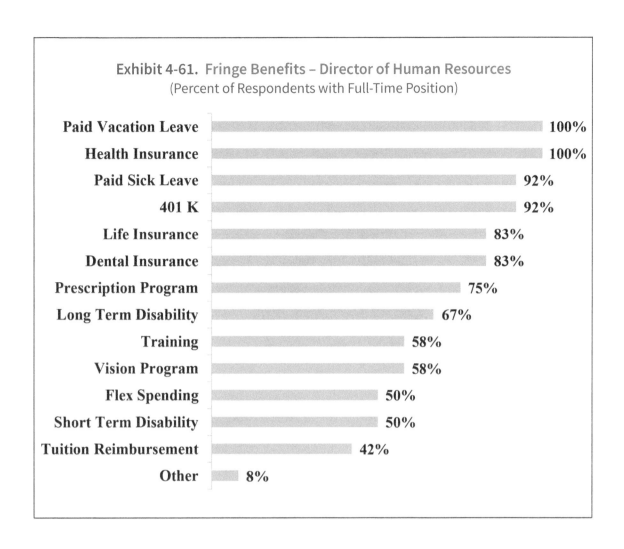

Exhibit 4-61. Fringe Benefits – Director of Human Resources
(Percent of Respondents with Full-Time Position)

Paid Vacation Leave	100%
Health Insurance	100%
Paid Sick Leave	92%
401 K	92%
Life Insurance	83%
Dental Insurance	83%
Prescription Program	75%
Long Term Disability	67%
Training	58%
Vision Program	58%
Flex Spending	50%
Short Term Disability	50%
Tuition Reimbursement	42%
Other	8%

Recruiter

Ninety-nine percent of builders in this study do not have a Recruiter on staff. One percent have the position part-time (Exhibit 4-62). Due to this job's low incidence, its average salary, bonus, and benefits cannot be reliably reported.

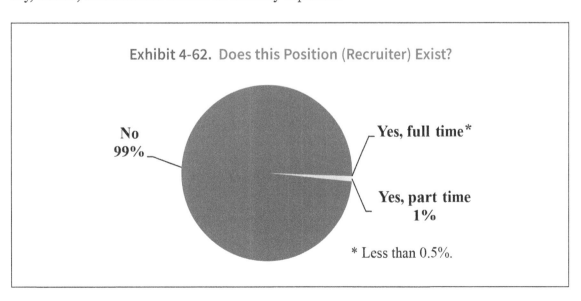

Exhibit 4-62. Does this Position (Recruiter) Exist?

No
99%

Yes, full time*

Yes, part time
1%

* Less than 0.5%.

In-House Legal Counsel

Ninety-eight percent of builders in the study do not have an In-House Legal Counsel position. Two percent have the position full-time (Exhibit 4-63). Due to this job's low incidence, its average salary, bonus, and benefits cannot be reliably reported.

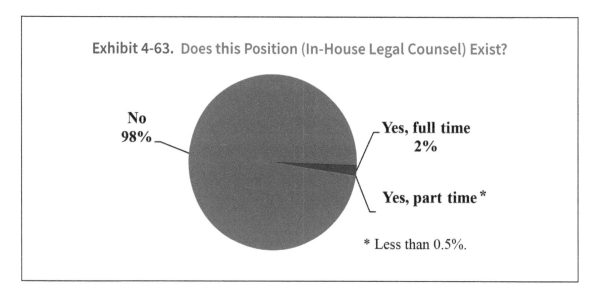

Exhibit 4-63. Does this Position (In-House Legal Counsel) Exist?

No
98%

Yes, full time
2%

Yes, part time*

* Less than 0.5%.

IT JOBS

Director of IT

Ninety-five percent of builders in the study do not have a Director of IT on staff. Three percent have the position full-time and 1% part-time (Exhibit 4-64). The job is uncommon on a full-time basis even at large builders with 100+ starts, as only 13% of that group report having this position. (Appendix A-58). Due to this job's low incidence, its average salary, bonus, and benefits cannot be reliably reported.

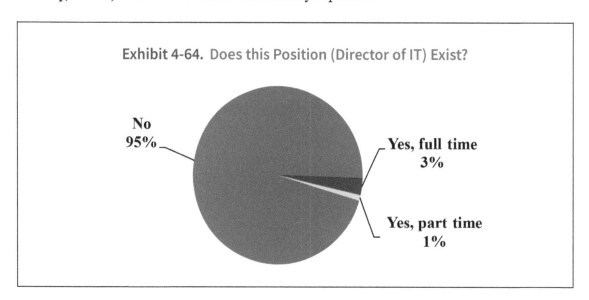

Exhibit 4-64. Does this Position (Director of IT) Exist?

No
95%

Yes, full time
3%

Yes, part time
1%

Network Engineer

Ninety-nine percent of builders in the study do not have a Network Engineer position (Exhibit 4-65). Due to this job's low incidence, its average salary, bonus, and benefits cannot be reliably reported.

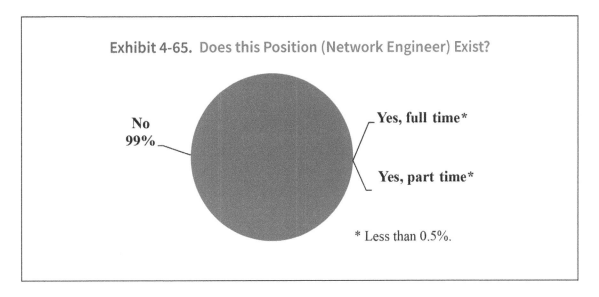

Exhibit 4-65. Does this Position (Network Engineer) Exist?

No
99%

Yes, full time*

Yes, part time*

* Less than 0.5%.

Web Design Specialist

Ninety-five percent of builders in the study do not have a Web Design Specialist position. One percent have the position full-time and 4% part-time (Exhibit 4-66). The job is uncommon on a full-time basis even at large builders with 100+ starts, as only 10% of that group report it (Appendix A-58). Due to this job's low incidence, its average salary, bonus, and benefits cannot be reliably reported.

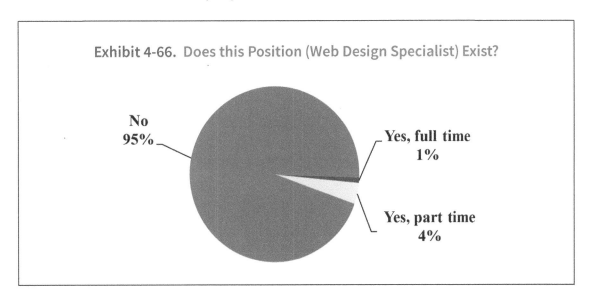

Exhibit 4-66. Does this Position (Web Design Specialist) Exist?

No
95%

Yes, full time
1%

Yes, part time
4%

Executive Assistant

The Executive Assistant position exists as a full-time job at 11% of the companies in the study, and as a part-time job at another 1%. (Exhibit 4-67). Among firms that have the position full-time, 42% pay an annual salary of less than $50,000 and 58% pay between $50,000 and $99,999. The average annual salary is $49,394, and the average bonus among all those reporting a salary is $4,227 (averaging in zero bonuses), for an average total compensation of $53,621 (Exhibit 4-68). Fifty percent of companies reporting a salary for this position also pay a bonus/commission. The average bonus among only those who reported a bonus (not averaging in zeroes) is $8,454 (Appendix B).

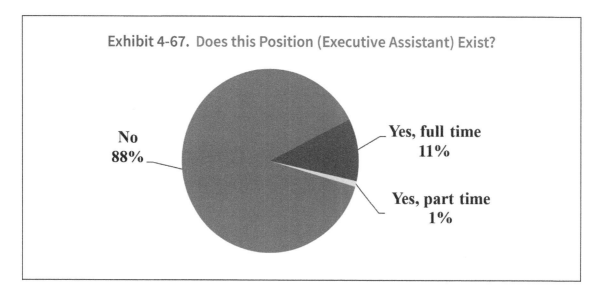

Exhibit 4-67. Does this Position (Executive Assistant) Exist?

No 88%

Yes, full time 11%

Yes, part time 1%

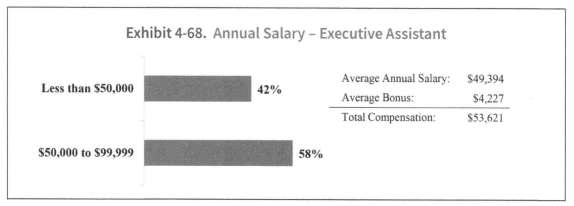

Exhibit 4-68. Annual Salary – Executive Assistant

Less than $50,000 — 42%

$50,000 to $99,999 — 58%

Average Annual Salary:	$49,394
Average Bonus:	$4,227
Total Compensation:	$53,621

The likelihood that a builder employs a full-time Executive Assistant is positively correlated to the size of the company. While only 6% of those with 1 to 10 starts have this position, the share is 11% among those with 11 to 25 starts, 16% among those with 26 to 99 starts, and 20% among those with starts of 100+ untis. (Exhibit 4-69). Due to an insufficient number of responses to produce reliable estimates, average total compensation for Executive Assistants cannot be reported by company size.

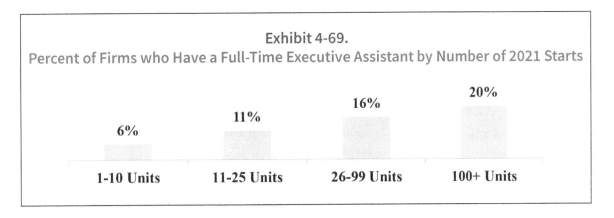

Exhibit 4-69.
Percent of Firms who Have a Full-Time Executive Assistant by Number of 2021 Starts

| 6% | 11% | 16% | 20% |
| 1-10 Units | 11-25 Units | 26-99 Units | 100+ Units |

The most common benefit extended to full-time Executive Assistants is paid vacation leave, offered by 96% of builders with the position on staff. At least half also offer health insurance (79%), paid sick leave (75%), a 401K plan (75%), training (67%), dental insurance (54%), and a vision program (50%). Less common benefits to Executive Assistants include life insurance (46%), flex spending (42%), long term disability (42%), tuition reimbursement (38%), short term disability (38%), and a prescription program (33%). Seventeen percent offered some other type of benefit, such as an IRA (Exhibit 4-70).

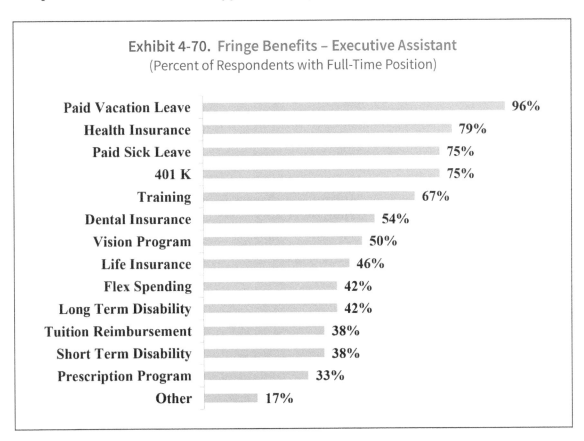

Exhibit 4-70. Fringe Benefits – Executive Assistant
(Percent of Respondents with Full-Time Position)

Benefit	Percent
Paid Vacation Leave	96%
Health Insurance	79%
Paid Sick Leave	75%
401 K	75%
Training	67%
Dental Insurance	54%
Vision Program	50%
Life Insurance	46%
Flex Spending	42%
Long Term Disability	42%
Tuition Reimbursement	38%
Short Term Disability	38%
Prescription Program	33%
Other	17%

Office Manager

The position of Office Manager exists on a full-time basis at 14% of the companies in the study. Another 4% have it on a part-time basis (Exhibit 4-71). Among firms that have the position full-time, 30% report an annual salary of less than $50,000, 67% between $50,000 and $99,999, and 3% $100,000 or more. The average annual salary is $58,348, and the average bonus among all those reporting a salary is $6,220 (averaging in zero bonuses), for an average total compensation of $64,568 (Exhibit 4-72). Sixty-four percent of companies reporting a salary for this position also pay a bonus/commission. The average bonus among those who reported a bonus (not averaging in zeroes) is $9,774 (Appendix B).

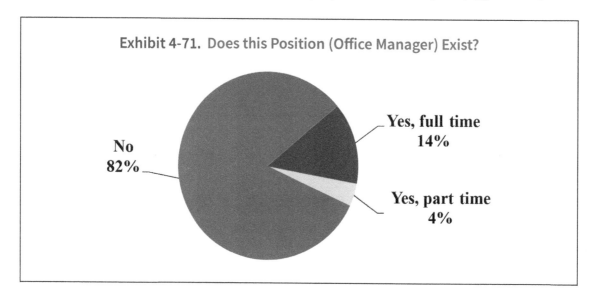

Exhibit 4-71. Does this Position (Office Manager) Exist?

No 82%

Yes, full time 14%

Yes, part time 4%

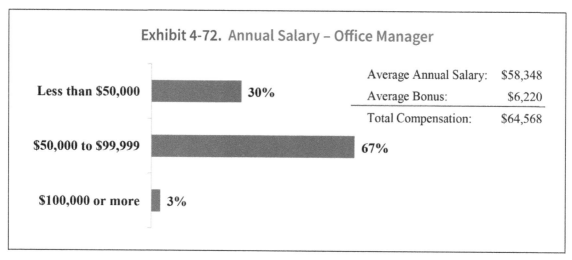

Exhibit 4-72. Annual Salary – Office Manager

Less than $50,000 — 30%

$50,000 to $99,999 — 67%

$100,000 or more — 3%

Average Annual Salary:	$58,348
Average Bonus:	$6,220
Total Compensation:	$64,568

Employing a full-time Office Manager is rare at companies with fewer than 26 housing starts (8% to 10%). The job is somewhat more common among those with 26 to 99 starts (25%) and those with 100+ starts (33%) (Exhibit 4-73). Total compensation for a full-time Office Managers averages $73,850 at builders with 100+ starts (Appendix D).

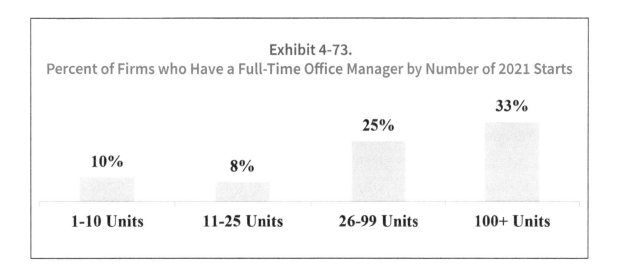

Exhibit 4-73.
Percent of Firms who Have a Full-Time Office Manager by Number of 2021 Starts

1-10 Units	11-25 Units	26-99 Units	100+ Units
10%	8%	25%	33%

Ninety-four percent of builders who have a full-time Office Manager offer this person paid vacation leave. At least half also offer health insurance (75%), paid sick leave (72%), a 401K plan (72%), dental insurance (56%), and a vision program (50%). The remaining benefits are offered by a minority of builders: a prescription program (47%), training (44%), life insurance (44%), long term disability (38%), flex spending (28%), short term disability (28%), and tuition reimbursement (16%). Six percent of respondents offered some other type of benefit, such as a Health Savings Account (Exhibit 4-74).

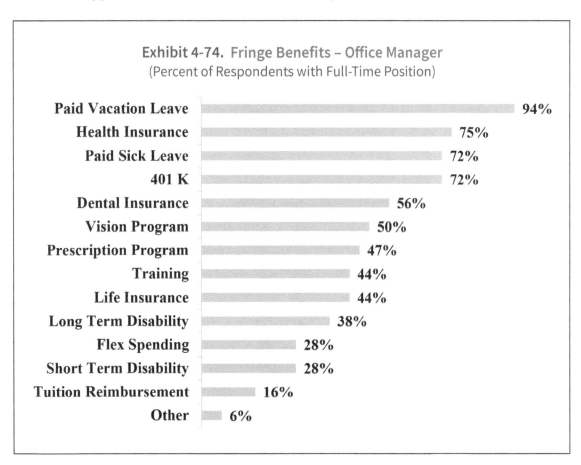

Exhibit 4-74. Fringe Benefits – Office Manager
(Percent of Respondents with Full-Time Position)

Paid Vacation Leave	94%
Health Insurance	75%
Paid Sick Leave	72%
401 K	72%
Dental Insurance	56%
Vision Program	50%
Prescription Program	47%
Training	44%
Life Insurance	44%
Long Term Disability	38%
Flex Spending	28%
Short Term Disability	28%
Tuition Reimbursement	16%
Other	6%

Administrative Assistant

Ten percent of builders have a full-time Administrative Assistant on staff and another 6% have it on a part-time basis (Exhibit 4-75). Among firms that have the position full-time, 75% report paying an annual salary of less than $50,000 and 25% between $50,000 and $99,999. The average annual salary is $44,956, and the average bonus among all those reporting a salary is $2,708 (averaging in zero bonuses), for an average total compensation of $47,664 (Exhibit 4-76). Fifty-eight percent of companies reporting a salary for this position also pay a bonus/commission. The average bonus among only those who reported a bonus (not averaging in zeroes) is $4,642 (Appendix B).

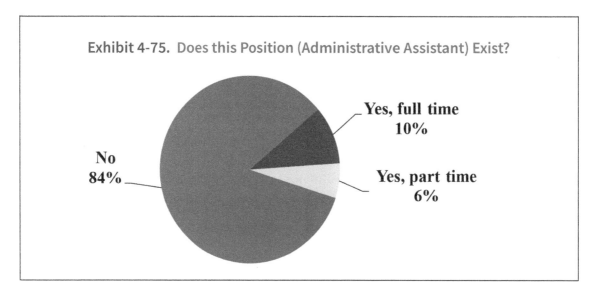

Exhibit 4-75. Does this Position (Administrative Assistant) Exist?

Yes, full time
10%

Yes, part time
6%

No
84%

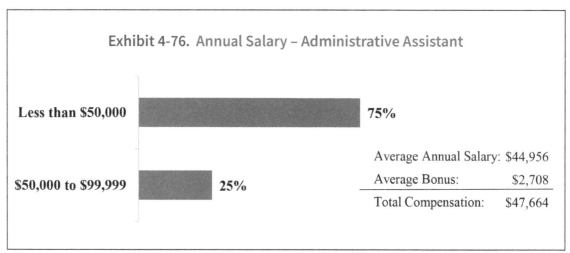

Exhibit 4-76. Annual Salary – Administrative Assistant

Less than $50,000   75%

$50,000 to $99,999   25%

Average Annual Salary:	$44,956
Average Bonus:	$2,708
Total Compensation:	$47,664

The job of full-time administrative assistant only exists in a minority of companies, regardless of size. In fact, less than 15% of builders with fewer than 100 starts report this position. The share barely reaches 23% among those with 100+ starts (Exhibit 4-77). Due to an insufficient number of responses to produce reliable estimates, average total compensation for Administrative Assistants cannot be reported by company size.

Exhibit 4-77.
Percent of Firms with a Full-Time Administrative Assistant
by Number of 2021 Starts

5%	11%	9%	23%
1-10 Units	11-25 Units	26-99 Units	100+ Units

All builders with a full-time Administrative Assistant on staff offer this person paid vacation leave. Three other benefits are offered by most builders: paid sick leave (87%), health insurance (74%), and a 401K plan (70%). The majority of benefits, however, are offered by only a minority of companies: a vision program (48%), dental insurance (48%), a prescription program (35%), training (30%), long term disability (30%), short term disability (26%), life insurance (26%), tuition reimbursement (22%), and flex spending (17%). Less than half of one percent offer some other type of benefit to their Administrative Assistant (Exhibit 4-78).

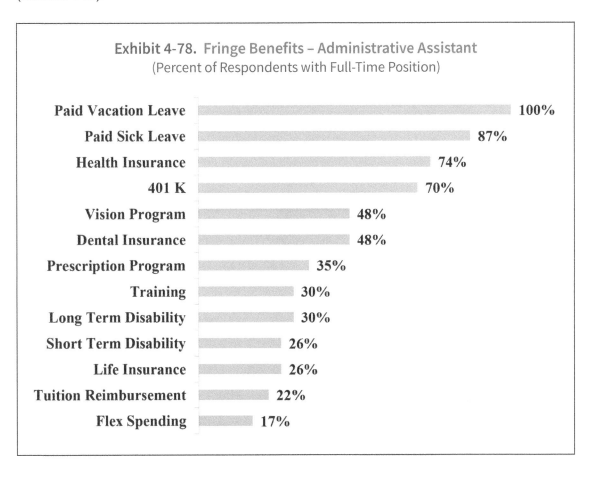

Exhibit 4-78. Fringe Benefits – Administrative Assistant
(Percent of Respondents with Full-Time Position)

Paid Vacation Leave	100%
Paid Sick Leave	87%
Health Insurance	74%
401 K	70%
Vision Program	48%
Dental Insurance	48%
Prescription Program	35%
Training	30%
Long Term Disability	30%
Short Term Disability	26%
Life Insurance	26%
Tuition Reimbursement	22%
Flex Spending	17%

Receptionist

Ten percent of builders in the study employ a Receptionist full-time, while 4% do it part-time (Exhibit 4-79). All companies where the position exists full-time report paying an annual salary of less than $50,000. The average annual salary is $35,971, and the average bonus among all those reporting a salary is $3,791 (averaging in zero bonuses), for an average total compensation of $39,762 (Exhibit 4-80).

Seventy-two percent of companies reporting a salary for this position also pay a bonus/commission. The average bonus among only those who reported a bonus (not averaging in zeroes) is $5,249 (Appendix B).

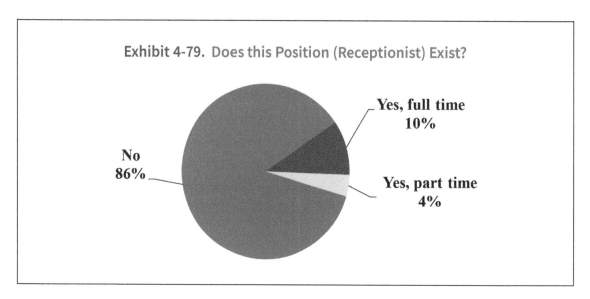

Exhibit 4-79. Does this Position (Receptionist) Exist?

Yes, full time
10%

No
86%

Yes, part time
4%

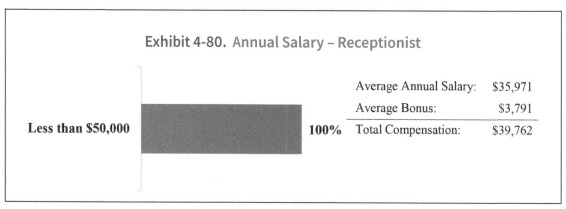

Exhibit 4-80. Annual Salary – Receptionist

Less than $50,000		100%

Average Annual Salary:	$35,971
Average Bonus:	$3,791
Total Compensation:	$39,762

Full-time Receptionists are rare at companies starting fewer than 100 units a year, with an incidence below 10%. The job is significantly more common among large building companies with 100+ annual starts, 43% of whom report having the position on staff (Exhibit 4-81). Total compensation for full-time Receptionists averages $41,940 at builders with 100+ starts (Appendix D).

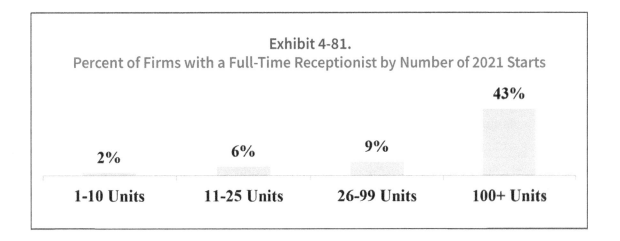

Exhibit 4-81.
Percent of Firms with a Full-Time Receptionist by Number of 2021 Starts

1-10 Units	11-25 Units	26-99 Units	100+ Units
2%	6%	9%	43%

All builders with a full-time Receptionist offer that person paid vacation leave. Most companies also offer them paid sick leave (94%), a 401k plan (88%), dental insurance (88%), health insurance (82%), a vision program (65%), a prescription program (59%), and life insurance (53%). A handful of benefits are afforded to this position by only a minority of builders: short term disability (47%), long term disability (41%), tuition reimbursement (29%), and flex spending (24%). Six percent of respondents offered some other type of benefit, such as a vehicle allowance (Exhibit 4-82).

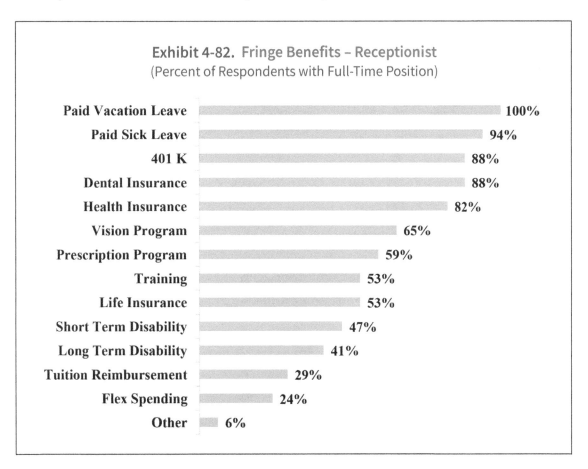

Exhibit 4-82. Fringe Benefits – Receptionist
(Percent of Respondents with Full-Time Position)

Benefit	Percent
Paid Vacation Leave	100%
Paid Sick Leave	94%
401 K	88%
Dental Insurance	88%
Health Insurance	82%
Vision Program	65%
Prescription Program	59%
Training	53%
Life Insurance	53%
Short Term Disability	47%
Long Term Disability	41%
Tuition Reimbursement	29%
Flex Spending	24%
Other	6%

Settlement Coordinator

A Settlement Coordinator exists as a full-time position at 8% of builders responding to the survey (Exhibit 4-83). The majority of those builders — 78% — pay this person an annual salary between $50,000 and $99,999, while the other 22% pay less than $50,000. The average annual salary is $56,838, and the average bonus among all those reporting a salary is $8,915 (averaging in zero bonuses), for an average total compensation of $65,753 (Exhibit 4-84). Seventy-eight percent of companies reporting a salary for this position also pay a bonus/commission. The average bonus among only those who reported a bonus (not averaging in zeroes) is $11,463 (Appendix B).

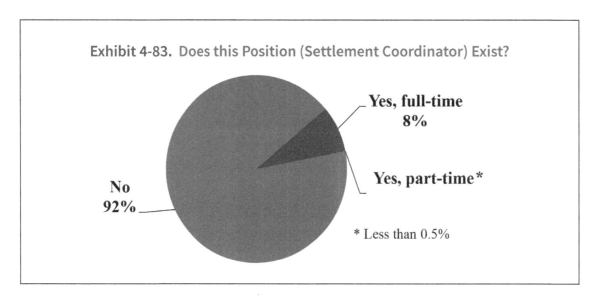

Exhibit 4-83. Does this Position (Settlement Coordinator) Exist?

Yes, full-time
8%

Yes, part-time*

No
92%

* Less than 0.5%

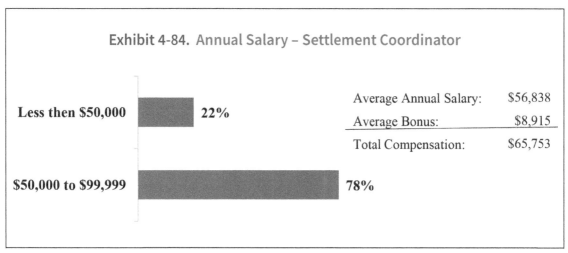

Exhibit 4-84. Annual Salary – Settlement Coordinator

Less then $50,000   22%

$50,000 to $99,999   78%

Average Annual Salary:	$56,838
Average Bonus:	$8,915
Total Compensation:	$65,753

Less than 10% of builders who start under 100 units a year have a full-time Settlement Coordinator. In contrast, one-third of those who start 100 or more units a year have this position on staff (Exhibit 4-85). Total compensation for Settlement Coordinators averages $60,784 at builders with 100+ starts (Appendix D).

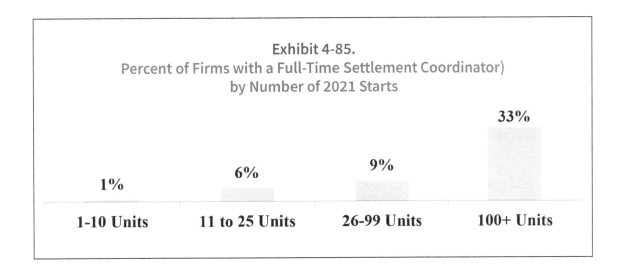

Exhibit 4-85.
Percent of Firms with a Full-Time Settlement Coordinator)
by Number of 2021 Starts

1%	6%	9%	33%
1-10 Units	11 to 25 Units	26-99 Units	100+ Units

All builders with a full-time Settlement Coordinator offer that person paid vacation leave. Most companies also offer them paid sick leave, a 401K plan, and health insurance (each by 82%) as well as training and dental insurance (each by 65%), life insurance (59%), and short term disability and a prescription program (53%). Fewer than half offer long term insurance and a vision program (each by 47%), tuition reimbursement (41%), and flex spending (35%). Twelve percent offer some other type of benefit to the Settlement Coordinator, such as paid holidays (Exhibit 4-86).

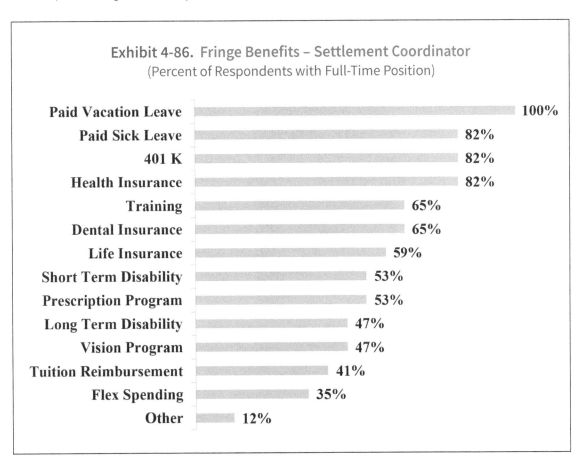

Exhibit 4-86. Fringe Benefits – Settlement Coordinator
(Percent of Respondents with Full-Time Position)

Benefit	Percent
Paid Vacation Leave	100%
Paid Sick Leave	82%
401 K	82%
Health Insurance	82%
Training	65%
Dental Insurance	65%
Life Insurance	59%
Short Term Disability	53%
Prescription Program	53%
Long Term Disability	47%
Vision Program	47%
Tuition Reimbursement	41%
Flex Spending	35%
Other	12%

Production Manager

About a quarter (24%) of builders who took part in the study report having a full-time Production Manager on staff (Exhibit 4-87). An overwhelming majority (90%) of those that have the position say it is "always" filled by someone with experience in the construction trades, while the other 10% say only 'sometimes" (Exhibit 4-88).

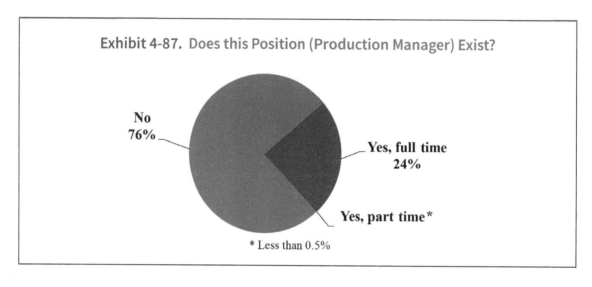

Exhibit 4-87. Does this Position (Production Manager) Exist?

No
76%

Yes, full time
24%

Yes, part time*

* Less than 0.5%

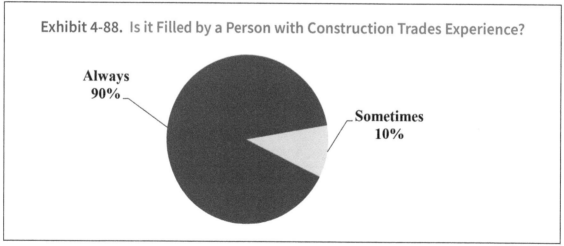

Exhibit 4-88. Is it Filled by a Person with Construction Trades Experience?

Always
90%

Sometimes
10%

For those firms that have a full-time Production Manager, 4% report paying an annual salary of less than $50,000, 70% between $50,000 and $99,999, and 26% pay this position $100,000 or more. The average annual salary is $80,842, and the average bonus among all those reporting a salary is $18,050 (averaging in zero bonuses), for an average total compensation of $98,892 (Exhibit 4-89). The majority of companies reporting a salary for this position — 80% — also pay a bonus/commission. The average bonus among only those who reported a bonus (not averaging in zeroes) is $22,668 (Appendix B).

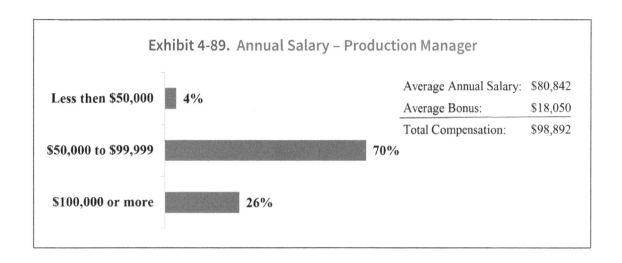

Exhibit 4-89. Annual Salary – Production Manager

Less then $50,000   4%

$50,000 to $99,999   70%

$100,000 or more   26%

Average Annual Salary:	$80,842
Average Bonus:	$18,050
Total Compensation:	$98,892

The more single-family units a firm starts, the more likely it is to have a full-time Production Manager on staff. As Exhibit 4-90 shows, 15% of those starting 1 to 10 units report having this job, compared to 31% of builders with 11 to 99 starts, and 50% of those with 100+ starts. Average total compensation also increases with company size, from $83,417 at builders with 1-10 starts, to $108,455 at those with 11-25 starts, and $112,789 at builders with 100+ starts (Exhibit 4-91).

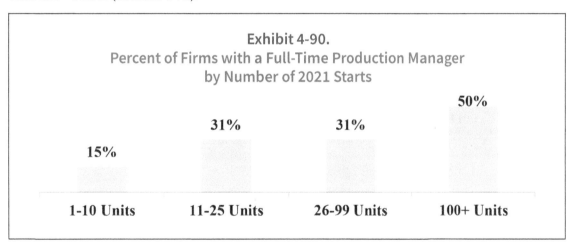

Exhibit 4-90.
Percent of Firms with a Full-Time Production Manager
by Number of 2021 Starts

15%	31%	31%	50%
1-10 Units	11-25 Units	26-99 Units	100+ Units

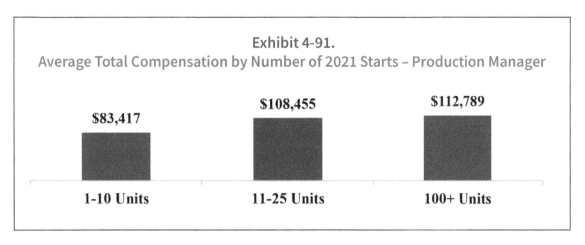

Exhibit 4-91.
Average Total Compensation by Number of 2021 Starts – Production Manager

$83,417	$108,455	$112,789
1-10 Units	11-25 Units	100+ Units

Most companies with a Production Manager on staff offer that person the following fringe benefits: paid vacation leave (92%), health insurance (81%), paid sick leave (75%), a 401K plan (69%), and training (52%). The other eight benefits are offered by a minority of builders: dental insurance (48%), a vision program (42%), a prescription program (40%), long term disability (33%), short term disability (31%), life insurance (29%), flex spending (27%), and tuition reimbursement (19%). Ten percent of the responding firms offer the Production Manager some other type of benefit, such as paid parental leave (Exhibit 4-92).

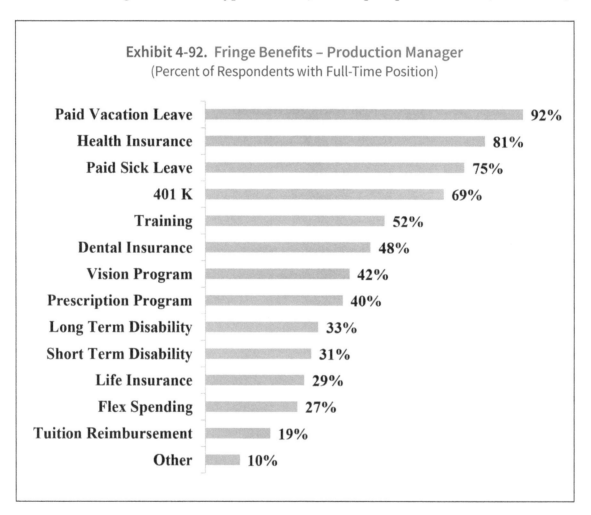

Exhibit 4-92. Fringe Benefits – Production Manager
(Percent of Respondents with Full-Time Position)

Paid Vacation Leave	92%
Health Insurance	81%
Paid Sick Leave	75%
401 K	69%
Training	52%
Dental Insurance	48%
Vision Program	42%
Prescription Program	40%
Long Term Disability	33%
Short Term Disability	31%
Life Insurance	29%
Flex Spending	27%
Tuition Reimbursement	19%
Other	10%

Land Manager

Ninety-five percent of builders do not have a Land Manager on staff, while 4% have it as a full-time position (Exhibit 4-93). The job is uncommon on a full-time basis even at large builders with 100+ starts, as only 20% of that group report it (Appendix A-82). Due to this job's low incidence, its average salary, bonus, and benefits cannot be reliably reported.

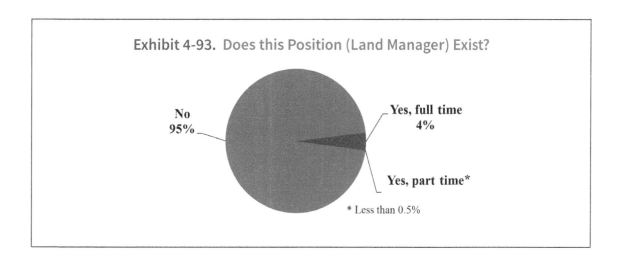

Exhibit 4-93. Does this Position (Land Manager) Exist?

No
95%

Yes, full time
4%

Yes, part time*

* Less than 0.5%

Purchasing Manager

The position of Purchasing Manager exists on a full-time basis at 9% of the builders in this survey, while none have it as a part-time job (Exhibit 4-94). Among builders that do have the position, 76% say that it is "always" filled by someone with experience in the construction trades, 12% say "sometimes," and 12% say "never/almost never" (Exhibit 4-95).

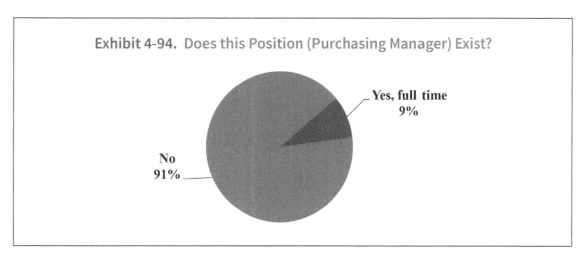

Exhibit 4-94. Does this Position (Purchasing Manager) Exist?

Yes, full time
9%

No
91%

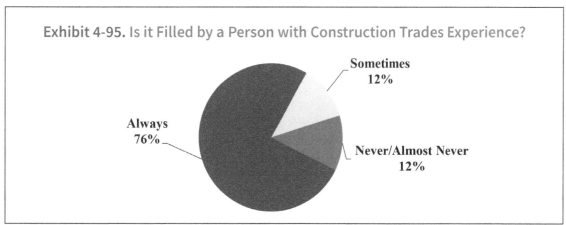

Exhibit 4-95. Is it Filled by a Person with Construction Trades Experience?

Sometimes
12%

Always
76%

Never/Almost Never
12%

Among builders that have a full-time Purchasing Manager position, 5% report paying an annual salary of less than $50,000, 86% between $50,000 and $99,999, and 10% pay $100,000 or more. The average annual salary is $69,567, and the average bonus among all those reporting a salary is $7,476 (averaging in zero bonuses), for an average total compensation of $77,043 (Exhibit 4-96). Sixty-two percent of companies reporting a salary for this position also pay a bonus/commission. The average bonus among only those who reported a bonus (not averaging in zeroes) is $12,077 (Appendix B).

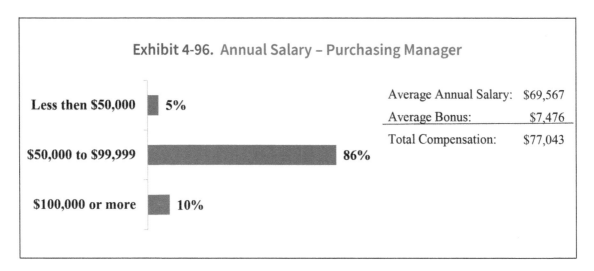

Exhibit 4-96. Annual Salary – Purchasing Manager

Less then $50,000	5%
$50,000 to $99,999	86%
$100,000 or more	10%

Average Annual Salary: $69,567
Average Bonus: $7,476
Total Compensation: $77,043

Less than 15% of builders who start under 100 units a year have a full-time Purchasing Manager. The position is somewhat more common among large builders with 100+ starts a year, as 33% of them report having the job on payroll (Exhibit 4-97). Total compensation for Purchasing Managers averages $74,840 at builders with 100+ starts (Appendix D).

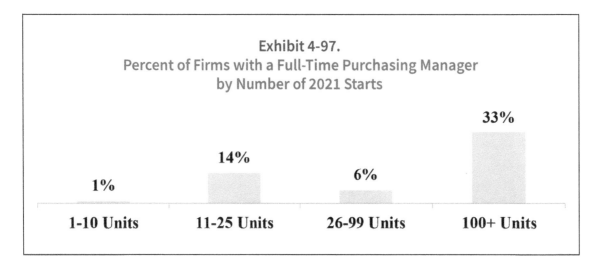

Exhibit 4-97.
Percent of Firms with a Full-Time Purchasing Manager
by Number of 2021 Starts

1-10 Units	11-25 Units	26-99 Units	100+ Units
1%	14%	6%	33%

All builders who employ a Purchasing Manager offer that person paid vacation leave. More than half also offer paid sick leave, a 401k plan, a vision program, and health insurance (each by 84%), dental insurance (79%), a prescription program (68%), and training (53%). A minority offer long and short term disability (each by 47%), life insurance (42%), flex spending (37%), and tuition reimbursement (21%). Eleven percent of respondents offer some other type of benefit, such as auto reimbursement (Exhibit 4-98).

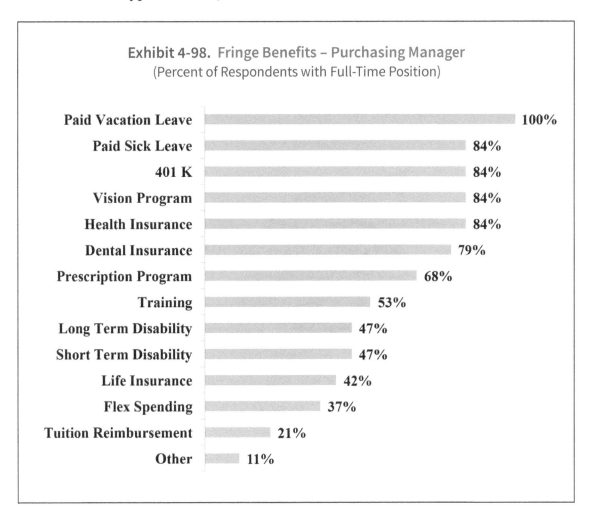

Exhibit 4-98. Fringe Benefits – Purchasing Manager
(Percent of Respondents with Full-Time Position)

Benefit	Percent
Paid Vacation Leave	100%
Paid Sick Leave	84%
401 K	84%
Vision Program	84%
Health Insurance	84%
Dental Insurance	79%
Prescription Program	68%
Training	53%
Long Term Disability	47%
Short Term Disability	47%
Life Insurance	42%
Flex Spending	37%
Tuition Reimbursement	21%
Other	11%

Home Services/Warranty Manager

Twenty percent of builders have a Home Services/Warranty Manager on staff on a full-time basis and 3% on a part-time basis (Exhibit 4-99). Among firms that have a full-time Home Services/Warranty Manager, 21% pay an annual salary of less than $50,000, 72% between $50,000 and $99,999, and 6% $100,000 or more. The average annual salary is $64,239, and the average bonus among all those reporting a salary is $8,818 (averaging in zero bonuses), for an average total compensation of $73,057 (Exhibit 4-100). Seventy-four percent of companies reporting a salary for this position also pay a bonus/commission. The average bonus among only those who reported a bonus (not averaging in zeroes) is $11,841 (Appendix B).

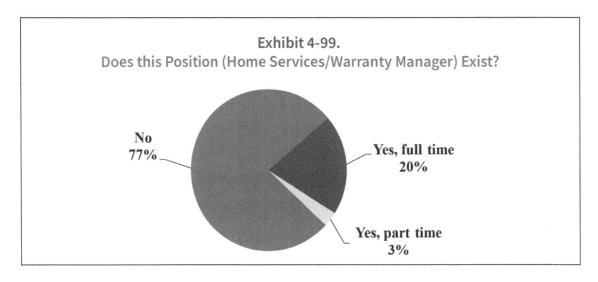

Exhibit 4-99.
Does this Position (Home Services/Warranty Manager) Exist?

No 77%

Yes, full time 20%

Yes, part time 3%

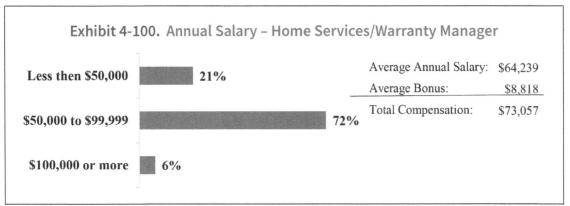

Exhibit 4-100. Annual Salary – Home Services/Warranty Manager

Less then $50,000	21%	
$50,000 to $99,999	72%	
$100,000 or more	6%	

Average Annual Salary: $64,239
Average Bonus: $8,818
Total Compensation: $73,057

The likelihood that a builder employs a full-time Home Services/Warranty Manager increases significantly with company size. Whereas none of the builders with 1 to 10 starts and only 3% of those with 11 to 25 starts have the position, the share rises to 28% among those starting 11 to 99 units and to 83% of those with 100+ starts (Exhibit 4-101). Total compensation for Purchasing Managers averages $79,424 at builders with 100+ starts (Appendix D).

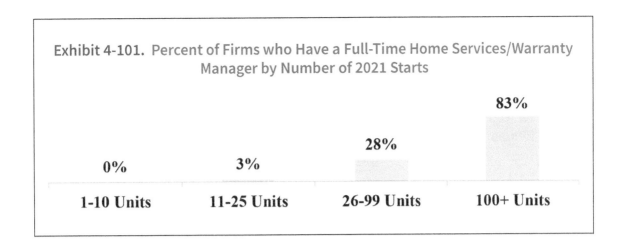

Exhibit 4-101. Percent of Firms who Have a Full-Time Home Services/Warranty Manager by Number of 2021 Starts

1-10 Units	11-25 Units	26-99 Units	100+ Units
0%	3%	28%	83%

All builders who employ a full-time Home Services/Warranty Manager offer that person paid vacation leave. More than half also offer health insurance (89%), a 401 K plan (87%), paid sick leave (85%), dental insurance (64%), a prescription program (55%), a vision program (55%), and life insurance (53%). A minority of builders offer training (47%), long term disability (40%), and tuition reimbursement, flex spending, and short term disability (each by 34%). Thirteen percent of builders offer some other type of benefit, such as a health savings account (Exhibit 4-102).

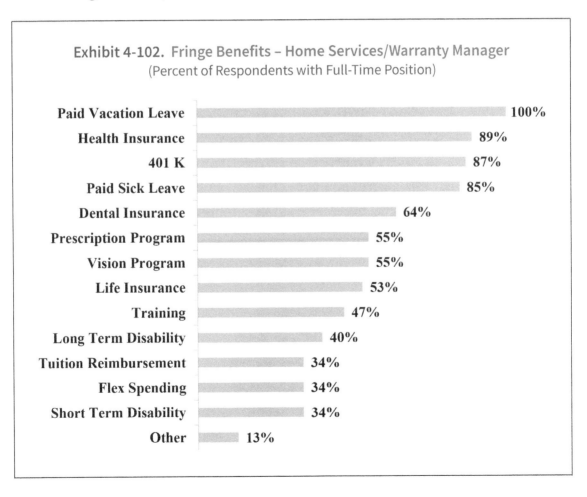

Exhibit 4-102. Fringe Benefits – Home Services/Warranty Manager
(Percent of Respondents with Full-Time Position)

Benefit	Percent
Paid Vacation Leave	100%
Health Insurance	89%
401 K	87%
Paid Sick Leave	85%
Dental Insurance	64%
Prescription Program	55%
Vision Program	55%
Life Insurance	53%
Training	47%
Long Term Disability	40%
Tuition Reimbursement	34%
Flex Spending	34%
Short Term Disability	34%
Other	13%

Contract Manager

While the vast majority of builders do not employ a Contract Manager (96%), 4% do on a full-time basis (Exhibit 4-103). The job is uncommon on a full-time basis even at large builders with 100+ starts, as only 17% of that group report it (Appendix A-90). Due to this job's low incidence, its average salary, bonus, and benefits cannot be reliably reported.

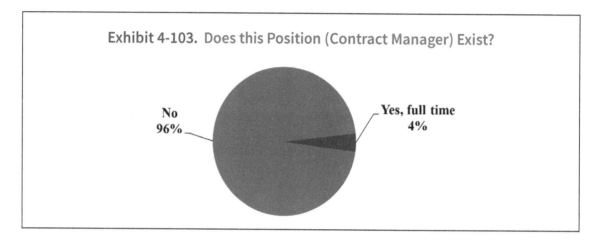

Exhibit 4-103. Does this Position (Contract Manager) Exist?

No
96%

Yes, full time
4%

Project Manager

About one-third of builders (34%) report that the position of Project Manager exists in their firm on a full-time basis. Another 1% report it exists as a part-time job (Exhibit 4-104). Among firms that have the position, 12% report that their Project Manager has an annual salary of less than $50,000, 69% between $50,000 and $99,999, and 19% report it at $100,000 or more. The average annual salary is $78,294 and the average bonus among all those reporting a salary is $13,724 (averaging in zero bonuses), for an average total compensation of $92,018 (Exhibit 4-105). Seventy-seven percent of companies reporting a salary for this position also pay a bonus/commission. The average bonus among only those who reported a bonus (not averaging in zeroes) is $17,842 (Appendix B).

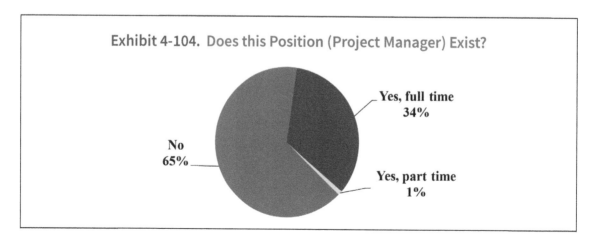

Exhibit 4-104. Does this Position (Project Manager) Exist?

Yes, full time
34%

No
65%

Yes, part time
1%

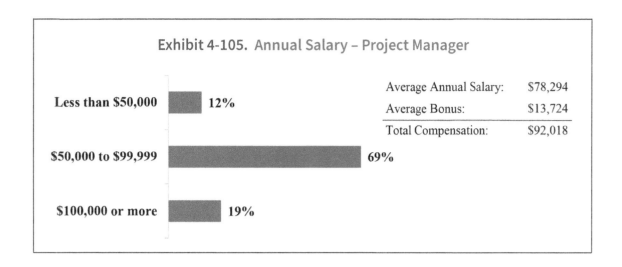

Exhibit 4-105. Annual Salary – Project Manager

Average Annual Salary:	$78,294
Average Bonus:	$13,724
Total Compensation:	$92,018

Less than $50,000 12%

$50,000 to $99,999 69%

$100,000 or more 19%

The share of builders with a full-time Project Manager on staff is 29% at companies with 1 to 10 starts a year and above 40% among companies of larger size (Exhibit 4-106). Total annual compensation for Project Managers averages $100,062 at builders with 1-10 starts and $102,185 at those with 100+ starts. In between, it averages $73,331 at builders with 11-25 starts and $84,306 at those with 26-99 starts (Exhibit 4-107).

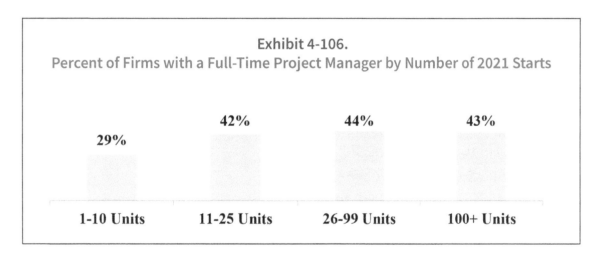

Exhibit 4-106.
Percent of Firms with a Full-Time Project Manager by Number of 2021 Starts

1-10 Units	11-25 Units	26-99 Units	100+ Units
29%	42%	44%	43%

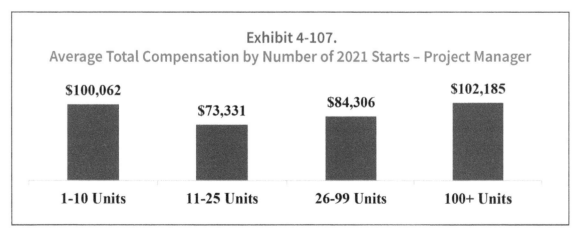

Exhibit 4-107.
Average Total Compensation by Number of 2021 Starts – Project Manager

1-10 Units	11-25 Units	26-99 Units	100+ Units
$100,062	$73,331	$84,306	$102,185

At least half the builders with a full-time Project Manager on staff offer that person six benefits: paid vacation leave (96%), paid sick leave (79%), health insurance (76%), a 401K plan (69%), training (61%), and dental insurance (50%). The other seven benefits listed in the survey are offered to this position by a minority of companies: vision program (43%), prescription program (36%), life insurance (35%), short term disability (25%), tuition reimbursement (22%), long term disability (22%), and flex spending (18%). Thirteen percent offer some other type of benefit, such as profit sharing (Exhibit 4-108).

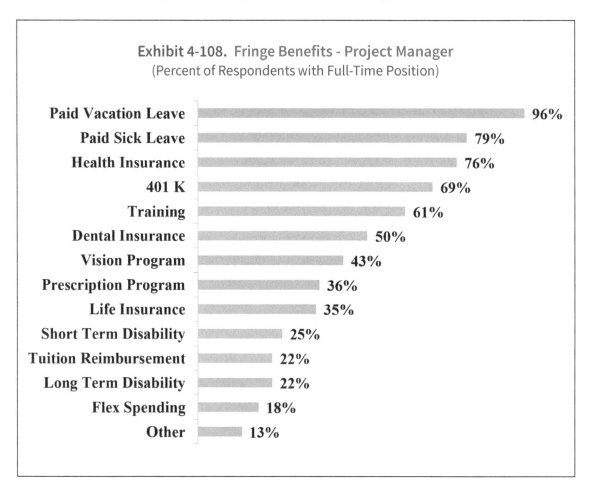

Exhibit 4-108. Fringe Benefits - Project Manager
(Percent of Respondents with Full-Time Position)

Paid Vacation Leave	96%
Paid Sick Leave	79%
Health Insurance	76%
401 K	69%
Training	61%
Dental Insurance	50%
Vision Program	43%
Prescription Program	36%
Life Insurance	35%
Short Term Disability	25%
Tuition Reimbursement	22%
Long Term Disability	22%
Flex Spending	18%
Other	13%

Architect

Eight percent of builders have a full-time architect on staff. Two percent have the position on a part-time basis (Exhibit 4-109). Among firms that have the position full-time, 15% report paying it an annual salary of less than $50,000, 55% between $50,000 and $99,999, and 30% $100,000 or more. The average annual salary is $81,618 and the average bonus among all those reporting a salary is $14,835 (averaging in zero bonuses), for an average total compensation of $96,453 (Exhibit 4-110). Seventy-five percent of companies reporting a salary for this position also pay a bonus/commission. The average bonus among only those who reported a bonus (not averaging in zeroes) is $19,779 (Appendix B).

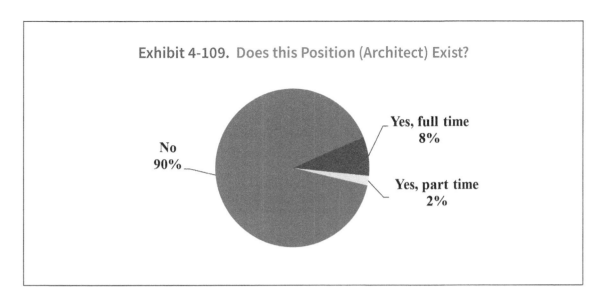

Exhibit 4-109. Does this Position (Architect) Exist?

Yes, full time
8%

No
90%

Yes, part time
2%

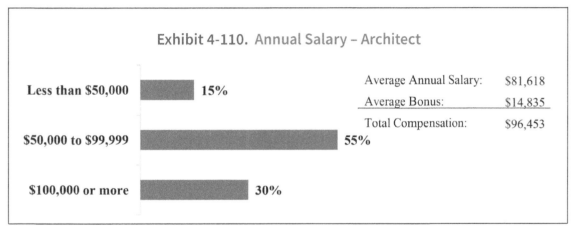

Exhibit 4-110. Annual Salary – Architect

Less than $50,000   15%

$50,000 to $99,999   55%

$100,000 or more   30%

Average Annual Salary:	$81,618
Average Bonus:	$14,835
Total Compensation:	$96,453

Builders do not commonly employ a full-time Architect. The share is in the single digits among companies with 1 to 25 starts a year, and barely reaches 16% and 23% at those with 26 to 99 starts and 100+starts, respectively (Exhibit 4-111). Due to an insufficient number of responses to produce reliable estimates, average total compensation for Architects cannot be reported by company size.

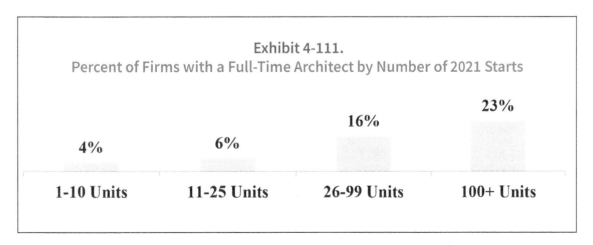

Exhibit 4-111.
Percent of Firms with a Full-Time Architect by Number of 2021 Starts

4%	6%	16%	23%
1-10 Units	11-25 Units	26-99 Units	100+ Units

The two most common benefits firms offer to their full-time Architects are paid vacation leave (94%) and paid sick leave (83%). At least half also offer them a 401K plan and health insurance (78% each), training (67%), dental insurance (61%), life insurance and a vision program (50% each). Less than half offer them short term disability (44%), long term disability and a prescription program (39% each), tuition reimbursement (22%), and flex spending (17%). Twenty-eight percent offer some other type of benefit, such as an IRA, profit sharing, and a vehicle allowance (Exhibit 4-112).

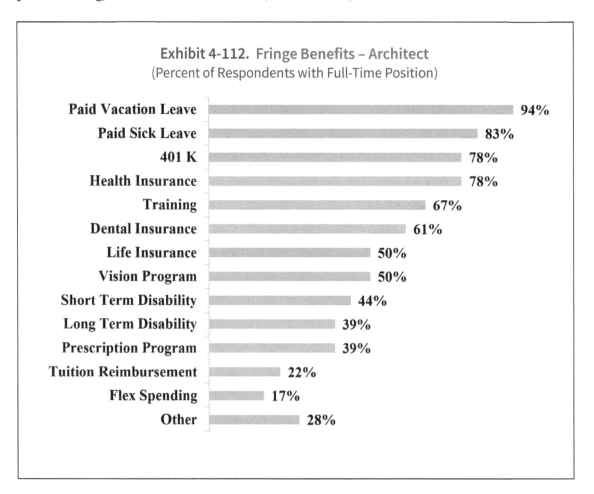

Exhibit 4-112. Fringe Benefits – Architect
(Percent of Respondents with Full-Time Position)

Paid Vacation Leave	94%
Paid Sick Leave	83%
401 K	78%
Health Insurance	78%
Training	67%
Dental Insurance	61%
Life Insurance	50%
Vision Program	50%
Short Term Disability	44%
Long Term Disability	39%
Prescription Program	39%
Tuition Reimbursement	22%
Flex Spending	17%
Other	28%

Estimator

Estimators exist in a full-time capacity at 15% of the building companies in this study and as part-time at another 1% (Exhibit 4-113). Among firms that have the position full-time, 14% report paying an annual salary of less than $50,000, 83% between $50,000 and $99,999, and 3% pay $100,000 or more. The average annual salary is $62,155 and the average bonus among all those reporting a salary is $9,295 (averaging in zero bonuses), for an average total compensation of $71,450 (Exhibit 4-114). Seventy-one percent of companies reporting a salary for this position also pay a bonus/commission. The average bonus among only those who reported a bonus (not averaging in zeroes) is $13,014 (Appendix B).

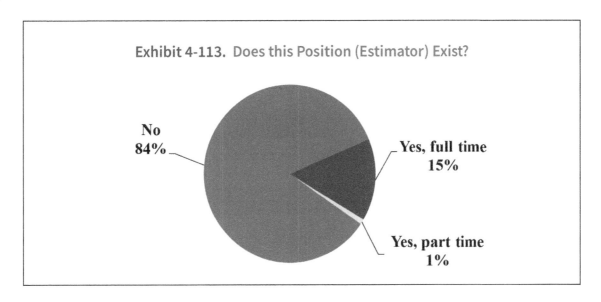

Exhibit 4-113. Does this Position (Estimator) Exist?

No
84%

Yes, full time
15%

Yes, part time
1%

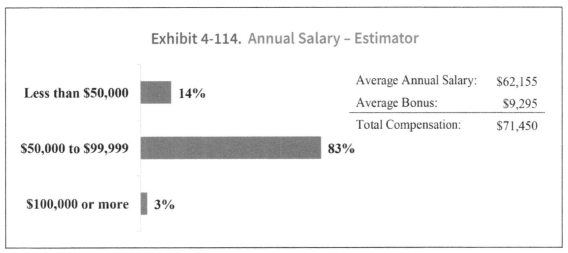

Exhibit 4-114. Annual Salary – Estimator

Less than $50,000　14%

$50,000 to $99,999　83%

$100,000 or more　3%

Average Annual Salary:	$62,155
Average Bonus:	$9,295
Total Compensation:	$71,450

The likelihood of having a full-time Estimator is significantly higher for companies starting 100+ units a year than for their smaller counterparts: whereas only 11% to 13% of builders starting 99 or fewer units have this position on staff, the share is 47% among builders starting 100+ units (Exhibit 4-115). Total compensation for Estimators averages $74,632 at builders with 100+ starts (Appendix D).

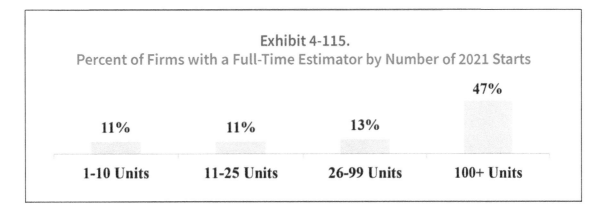

Exhibit 4-115.
Percent of Firms with a Full-Time Estimator by Number of 2021 Starts

1-10 Units	11-25 Units	26-99 Units	100+ Units
11%	11%	13%	47%

All builders with a full-time Estimator offer this person paid vacation leave. At least half also offer a 401K plan and health insurance (each by 88%), paid sick leave (79%), dental insurance (68%), training (56%), a vision program (53%), and life insurance (50%). The other five benefits are offered by a minority of builders: a prescription program (47%), tuition reimbursement and short term disability (each by 35%), long term disability (26%), and flex spending (24%). Fifteen percent offer some other type of benefit, such as an IRA (Exhibit 4-116).

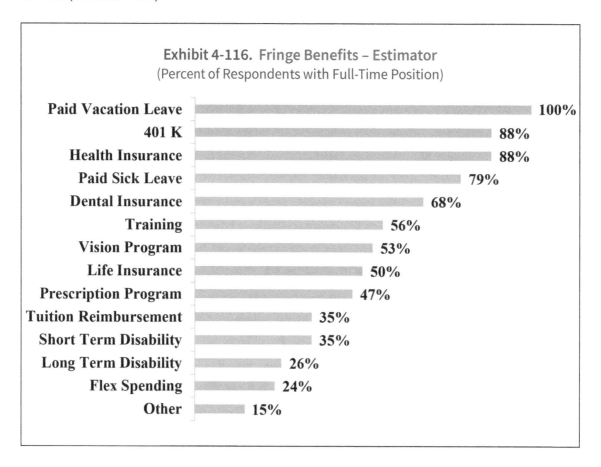

Exhibit 4-116. Fringe Benefits – Estimator
(Percent of Respondents with Full-Time Position)

Benefit	Percent
Paid Vacation Leave	100%
401 K	88%
Health Insurance	88%
Paid Sick Leave	79%
Dental Insurance	68%
Training	56%
Vision Program	53%
Life Insurance	50%
Prescription Program	47%
Tuition Reimbursement	35%
Short Term Disability	35%
Long Term Disability	26%
Flex Spending	24%
Other	15%

Superintendent

Nearly half of all builders responding have a Superintendent on staff: 47% as a full-time job and 1% as a part-time job (Exhibit 4-117). Among firms that have the position full-time, 8% report an annual salary of less than $50,000, 86% between $50,000 and $99,999, and 5% of $100,000 or more. The average annual salary is $69,361 and the average bonus among all those reporting a salary is $11,045 (averaging in zero bonuses), for an average total compensation of $80,406 (Exhibit 4-118). Seventy-four percent of companies reporting a salary for this position also pay a bonus/commission. The average bonus among only those who reported a bonus (not averaging in zeroes) is $14,951 (Appendix B).

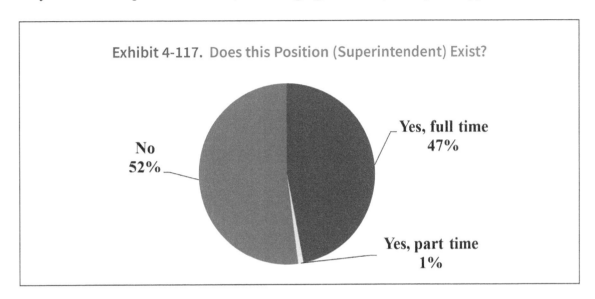

Exhibit 4-117. Does this Position (Superintendent) Exist?

No 52%
Yes, full time 47%
Yes, part time 1%

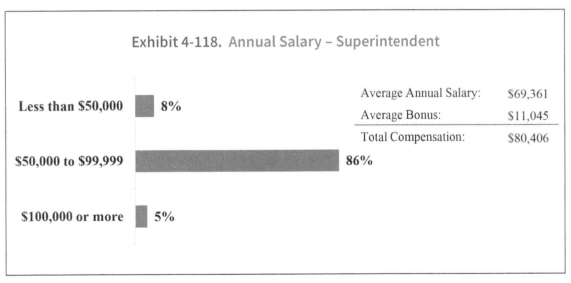

Exhibit 4-118. Annual Salary – Superintendent

Less than $50,000 8%
$50,000 to $99,999 86%
$100,000 or more 5%

Average Annual Salary:	$69,361
Average Bonus:	$11,045
Total Compensation:	$80,406

The likelihood of having a full-time Superintendent increases with company size. While 30% of builders with 1-10 annual starts have this position on staff, the share rises to 44% of those with 11-25 starts, and to 77% of those with 26 or more starts a year (Exhibit 4-119). The Superintendent's average total compensation is $73,520 at firms with 1-10 starts and $82,622 at those with 100+ starts (Exhibit 4-120).

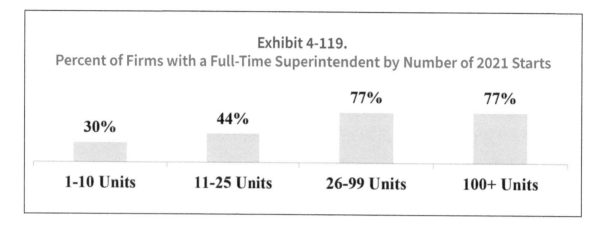

Exhibit 4-119.
Percent of Firms with a Full-Time Superintendent by Number of 2021 Starts

30%	44%	77%	77%
1-10 Units	11-25 Units	26-99 Units	100+ Units

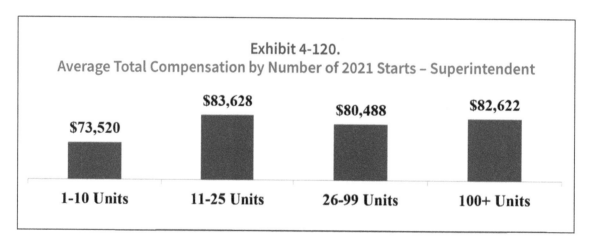

Exhibit 4-120.
Average Total Compensation by Number of 2021 Starts – Superintendent

$73,520	$83,628	$80,488	$82,622
1-10 Units	11-25 Units	26-99 Units	100+ Units

Nearly all (98%) builders who employ a full-time Superintendent offer that person paid vacation leave. Another four benefits are offered by most builders: paid sick leave (81%), health insurance (79%), a 401K plan (65%), and training (54%). The remaining eight benefits listed in the survey are only offered by a minority of builders: dental insurance (49%), a vision program (42%), a prescription program (38%), life insurance (37%), short term disability (30%), long term disability (27%), tuition reimbursement (26%), and flex spending (22%). Thirteen percent offer their Superintendent some other type of benefit, such as volunteer week off (Exhibit 4-121).

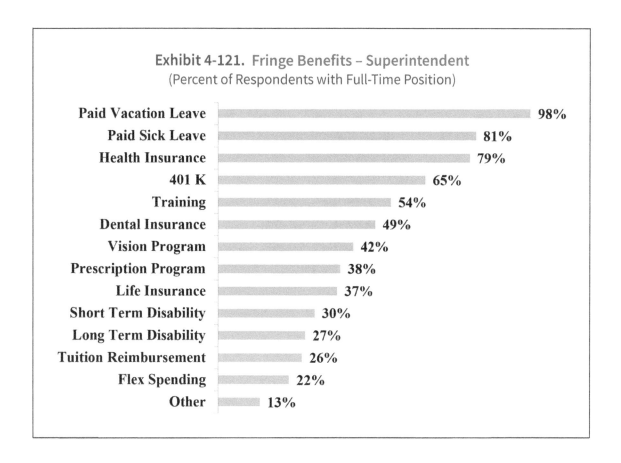

Exhibit 4-121. Fringe Benefits – Superintendent
(Percent of Respondents with Full-Time Position)

Benefit	Percent
Paid Vacation Leave	98%
Paid Sick Leave	81%
Health Insurance	79%
401 K	65%
Training	54%
Dental Insurance	49%
Vision Program	42%
Prescription Program	38%
Life Insurance	37%
Short Term Disability	30%
Long Term Disability	27%
Tuition Reimbursement	26%
Flex Spending	22%
Other	13%

SALES & MARKETING JOBS

Sales Manager

Fifteen percent of builders have a full-time Sales Manager on staff. Another 1% do on a part-time basis (Exhibit 4-122). Among builders that have the position, 47% say that it is "always" filled by someone with experience in the construction trades, 31% say "sometimes," and 22% say "never/almost never" (Exhibit 4-123).

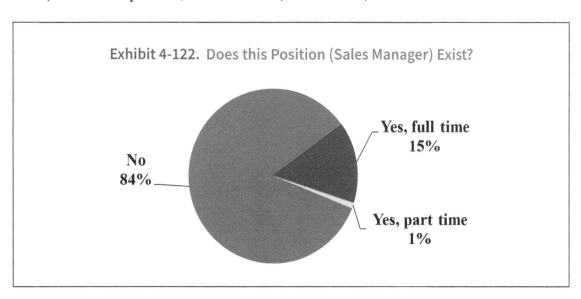

Exhibit 4-122. Does this Position (Sales Manager) Exist?

No 84%
Yes, full time 15%
Yes, part time 1%

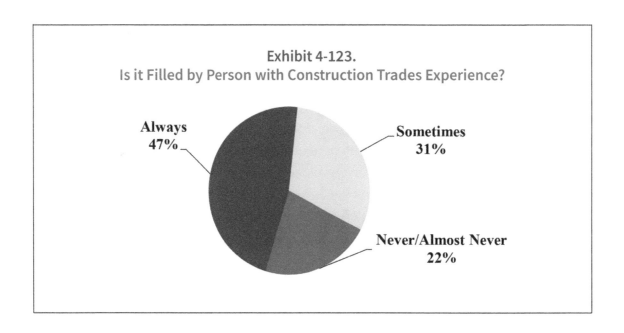

Exhibit 4-123.
Is it Filled by Person with Construction Trades Experience?

Always
47%

Sometimes
31%

Never/Almost Never
22%

Among firms that have the position full-time, one-third pay an annual salary of less than $50,000, 36% between $50,000 and $99,999, and 31% pay $100,000 or more. The average annual salary is $69,133 and the average bonus among all those reporting a salary is $46,847 (averaging in zero bonuses), for an average total compensation of $115,980 (Exhibit 4-124). Most companies reporting a salary for this position (86%) also pay a bonus/commission. The average bonus among only those who reported a bonus (not averaging in zeroes) is $54,403 (Appendix B).

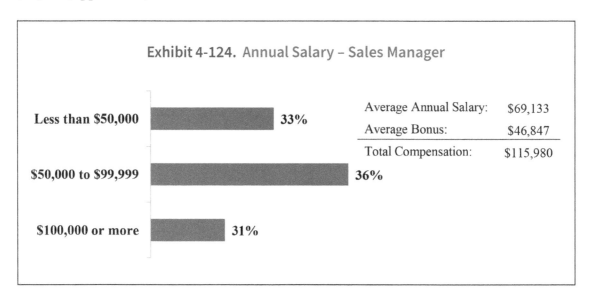

Exhibit 4-124. Annual Salary – Sales Manager

Less than $50,000	33%
$50,000 to $99,999	36%
$100,000 or more	31%

Average Annual Salary:	$69,133
Average Bonus:	$46,847
Total Compensation:	$115,980

Full-time Sales Managers are rather uncommon at small single-family home building companies. Results show only 2% of those with 1-10 starts and 11% of those with 11-25 starts a year have this job on payroll. Yet the share increases significantly at larger companies: 31% of those with 26-99 starts and 50% of builders who start 100+ units a year have a full-time Sales Manager (Exhibit 4-125). In terms of total compensation by company size, the average exceeds $130,000 across companies with more than 25 starts a year (Exhibit 4-126).

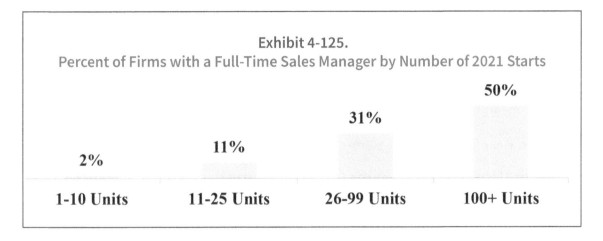

Exhibit 4-125.
Percent of Firms with a Full-Time Sales Manager by Number of 2021 Starts

| 2% | 11% | 31% | 50% |
| 1-10 Units | 11-25 Units | 26-99 Units | 100+ Units |

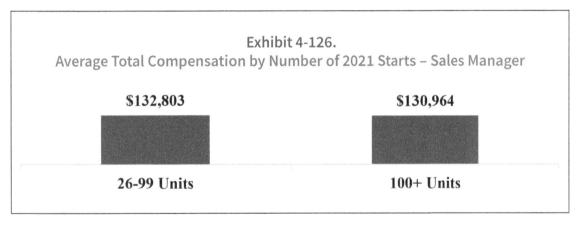

Exhibit 4-126.
Average Total Compensation by Number of 2021 Starts – Sales Manager

| $132,803 | $130,964 |
| 26-99 Units | 100+ Units |

All builders who employ a full-time Sales Manager offer that person paid vacation leave. A majority also offer health insurance (91%), paid sick leave (82%), a 401K plan (73%), dental insurance (73%), and a vision program (58%). A minority offer life insurance (48%), a prescription program (48%), training (36%), tuition reimbursement (30%), long term disability (30%), short term disability (30%), and flex spending (27%). Fifteen percent offer the Sales Manager some other type of benefit, such as vehicle allowance (Exhibit 4-127).

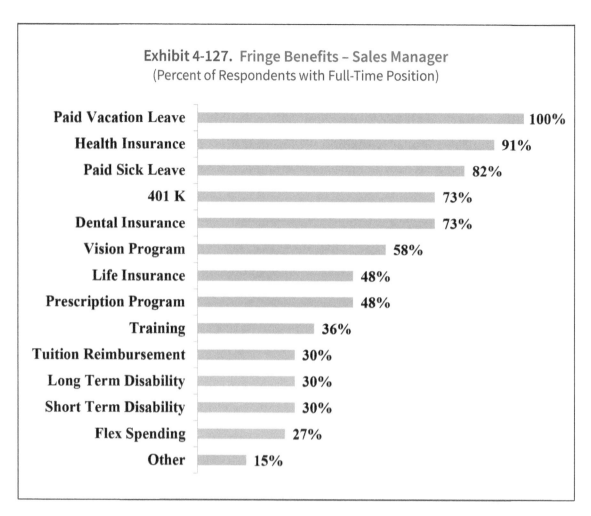

Exhibit 4-127. Fringe Benefits – Sales Manager
(Percent of Respondents with Full-Time Position)

Benefit	Percent
Paid Vacation Leave	100%
Health Insurance	91%
Paid Sick Leave	82%
401 K	73%
Dental Insurance	73%
Vision Program	58%
Life Insurance	48%
Prescription Program	48%
Training	36%
Tuition Reimbursement	30%
Long Term Disability	30%
Short Term Disability	30%
Flex Spending	27%
Other	15%

Model Home Host

Ninety-five percent of builders report the absence of a Model Home Host on staff, while 3% report the job on a full-time basis and 3% on a part-time basis (Exhibit 4-128). The job is uncommon on a full-time basis even at large builders with 100+ starts, as only 13% of that group have it (Appendix A-110). Due to this job's low incidence, its average salary, bonus, and benefits cannot be reliably reported.

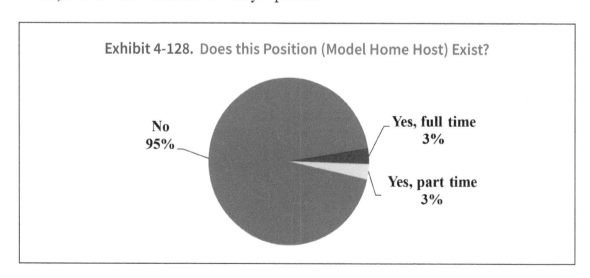

Exhibit 4-128. Does this Position (Model Home Host) Exist?

No 95%
Yes, full time 3%
Yes, part time 3%

Salesperson

Sixteen percent of builders have a full-time Salesperson on staff, while another 1% have a part-time Salesperson (Exhibit 4-129). Among firms that have the position, 70% pay an annual salary of less than $50,000, 19% between $50,000 and $99,999, and 11% pay $100,000 or more. The average annual salary is $36,199 and the average bonus among all those reporting a salary is $95,928 (averaging in zero bonuses), for an average total compensation of $132,127 (Exhibit 4-130). Seventy-eight percent of companies reporting a salary for this position also pay a bonus/commission. The average bonus among only those who reported a bonus (not averaging in zeroes) is $122,391 (Appendix B).

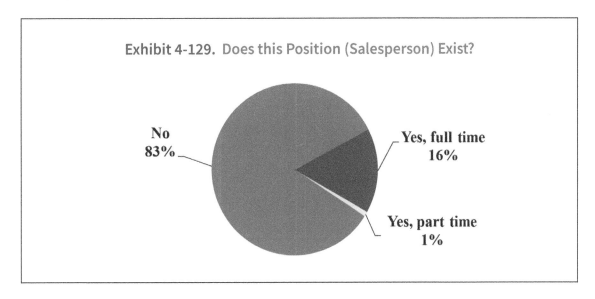

Exhibit 4-129. Does this Position (Salesperson) Exist?

No
83%

Yes, full time
16%

Yes, part time
1%

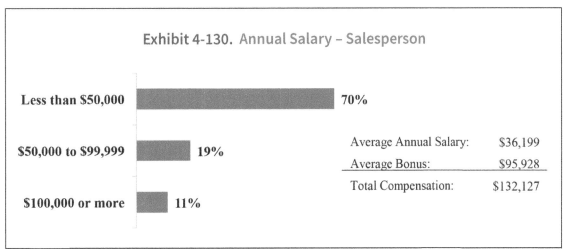

Exhibit 4-130. Annual Salary – Salesperson

Less than $50,000 — 70%

$50,000 to $99,999 — 19%

$100,000 or more — 11%

Average Annual Salary:	$36,199
Average Bonus:	$95,928
Total Compensation:	$132,127

Full-time Salespersons are rare at all but the largest home builders: 67% of those with 100+ starts have the position on staff, compared to less than 15% among smaller companies (Exhibit 4-131). Total compensation for a Salesperson averages $142,176 at companies with 100+ starts (Appendix D).

Exhibit 4-131. Percent of Firms with a Full-Time Salesperson by Number of 2021 Starts

1-10 Units	11-25 Units	26-99 Units	100+ Units
2%	14%	13%	67%

The three most common benefits offered by builders to the Salesperson are paid vacation leave (92%), health insurance (81%), and a 401K plan (78%). At least half also offer dental insurance (67%), paid sick leave (64%), life insurance (56%), a prescription program (56%), a vision program (56%), and training (50%). Less than half offer long and short term disability (each by 47%), flex spending (36%), and tuition reimbursement (22%). Eight percent offer some other type of benefit to the Salesperson, such as holiday pay (Exhibit 4-132).

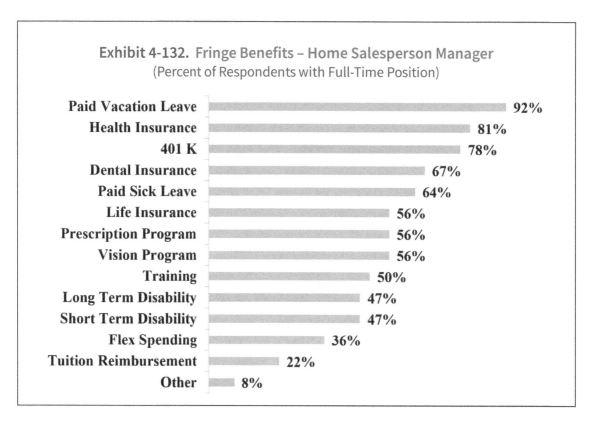

Exhibit 4-132. Fringe Benefits – Home Salesperson Manager
(Percent of Respondents with Full-Time Position)

Benefit	Percent
Paid Vacation Leave	92%
Health Insurance	81%
401 K	78%
Dental Insurance	67%
Paid Sick Leave	64%
Life Insurance	56%
Prescription Program	56%
Vision Program	56%
Training	50%
Long Term Disability	47%
Short Term Disability	47%
Flex Spending	36%
Tuition Reimbursement	22%
Other	8%

Design Center Manager

Only a small minority of builders (8%) employ a full-time Design Center Manager (Exhibit 4-133). All firms that have the position full-time pay it an annual salary between $50,000 and $99,999. The average annual salary is $65,819 and the average bonus among all those reporting a salary is $17,630 (averaging in zero bonuses), for an average total compensation of $83,449 (Exhibit 4-134). Sixty-nine percent of companies reporting a salary for this position also pay a bonus/commission. The average bonus among only those who reported a bonus (not averaging in zeroes) is $25,643 (Appendix B).

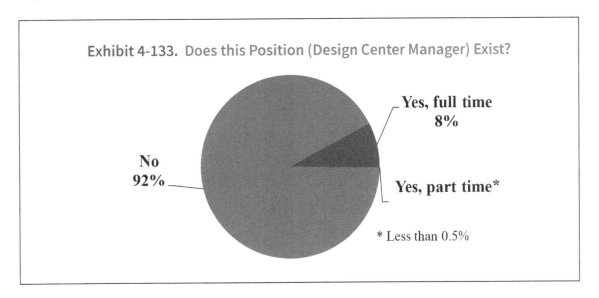

Exhibit 4-133. Does this Position (Design Center Manager) Exist?

Yes, full time
8%

No
92%

Yes, part time*

* Less than 0.5%

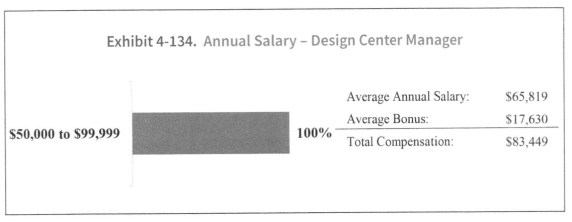

Exhibit 4-134. Annual Salary – Design Center Manager

$50,000 to $99,999   100%

Average Annual Salary:	$65,819
Average Bonus:	$17,630
Total Compensation:	$83,449

Much like Salespersons, full-time Design Center Managers are rare at all but the largest home builders: 40% of those with 100+ starts have this position on staff, compared to less than 10% among smaller companies (Exhibit 4-135). Total annual compensation for full-time Design Center Managers averages $84,767 at large companies (100+ starts), the only group for which it can be reliably estimated (Appendix D).

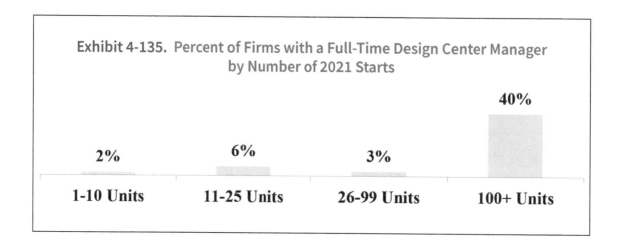

Exhibit 4-135. Percent of Firms with a Full-Time Design Center Manager by Number of 2021 Starts

Design Center Managers may not be a common position at single-family building companies, but they are likely to receive many benefits. In fact, a majority of builders that have the job offer every benefit: paid vacation leave, a 401k plan, and health insurance (each by 93%), dental insurance (87%), training and paid sick leave (each by 80%), life insurance, a prescription program, and a vision program (each by 67%), long and short term disability (each by 60%), and tuition reimbursement and flex spending (each by 53%). One-third offer the Design Center Manager some other type of benefit, such as automobile reimbursement (Exhibit 4-136).

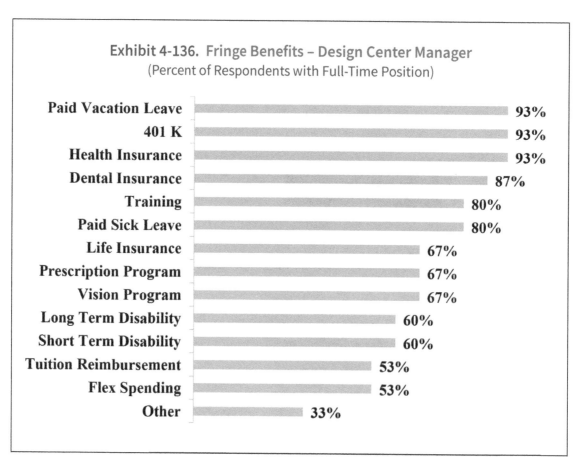

Exhibit 4-136. Fringe Benefits – Design Center Manager
(Percent of Respondents with Full-Time Position)

Selections Coordinator

In all, 15% of builders report having a Selections Coordinator on staff: 14% as a full-time job and 1% as part-time (Exhibit 4-137). Among firms that have the position full-time, 42% pay an annual salary of less than $50,000, 55% between $50,000 and $99,999, and 3% pay it $100,000 or more. The average annual salary is $53,930 and the average bonus among all those reporting a salary is $8,585 (averaging in zero bonuses), for an average total compensation of $62,515 (Exhibit 4-138). Seventy-three percent of companies reporting a salary for this position also pay a bonus/commission. The average bonus among only those who reported a bonus (not averaging in zeroes) is $11,804 (Appendix B).

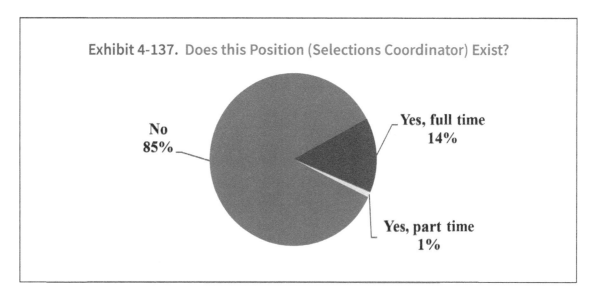

Exhibit 4-137. Does this Position (Selections Coordinator) Exist?

No 85%

Yes, full time 14%

Yes, part time 1%

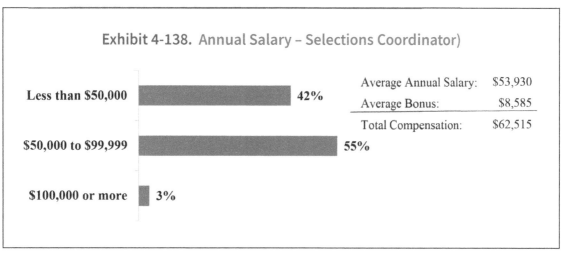

Exhibit 4-138. Annual Salary – Selections Coordinator)

Less than $50,000 — 42%

$50,000 to $99,999 — 55%

$100,000 or more — 3%

Average Annual Salary:	$53,930
Average Bonus:	$8,585
Total Compensation:	$62,515

The likelihood that builders have a full-time Selections Coordinator is low among builders who start fewer than 100 units a year (below 15%), but significantly higher among those who start 100+ units (47%) (Exhibit 4-139). Total compensation for a Selection Coordinator averages $64,175 at companies with 100+ starts (Appendix D).

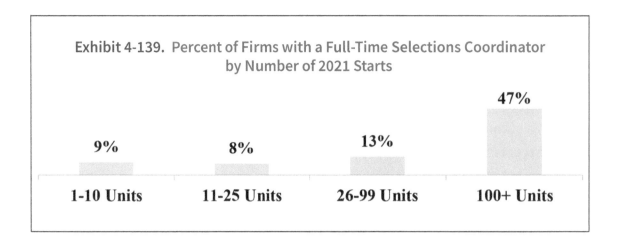

Exhibit 4-139. Percent of Firms with a Full-Time Selections Coordinator
by Number of 2021 Starts

1-10 Units	11-25 Units	26-99 Units	100+ Units
9%	8%	13%	47%

Ninety-four percent of builders that have a full-time Selections Coordinator offer this person paid vacation leave. More than half also offer health insurance (77%), a 401K plan (74%), paid sick leave (68%), dental insurance (65%), training (55%), and a vision program (52%). A minority of builders also offer life insurance (45%), a prescription program (39%), short term disability (32%), tuition reimbursement and long term disability (each by 26%), and flex spending (23%). Thirteen percent offer the Selections Coordinator some other type of benefit, such as profit sharing (Exhibit 4-140).

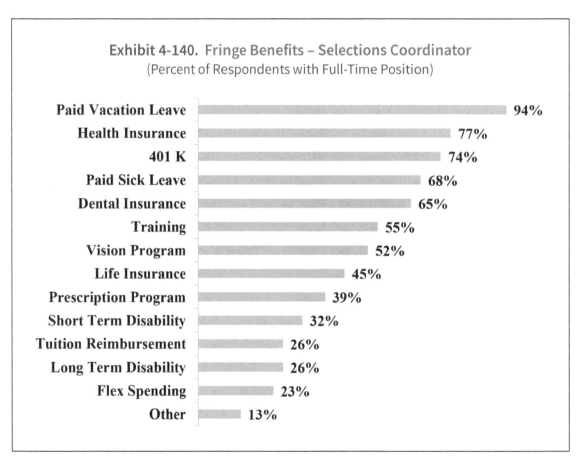

Exhibit 4-140. Fringe Benefits – Selections Coordinator
(Percent of Respondents with Full-Time Position)

Paid Vacation Leave	94%
Health Insurance	77%
401 K	74%
Paid Sick Leave	68%
Dental Insurance	65%
Training	55%
Vision Program	52%
Life Insurance	45%
Prescription Program	39%
Short Term Disability	32%
Tuition Reimbursement	26%
Long Term Disability	26%
Flex Spending	23%
Other	13%

Customer Service Manager

Most single-family building companies do not employ a Customer Service Manager. Among this study's respondents, only 5% have the position full-time and 1% part-time (Exhibit 4-141). Among firms that have the position full-time, 64% report an annual salary of less than $50,000 and 36% between $50,000 and $99,999. The average annual salary is $47,109 and the average bonus among all those reporting a salary is $5,309 (averaging in zero bonuses), for an average total compensation of $52,418 (Exhibit 4-142). Fifty-five percent of companies reporting a salary for this position also pay a bonus/commission, but not enough of them reported the actual bonus to reliably estimate an average.

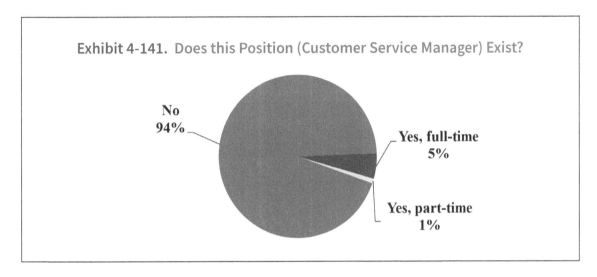

Exhibit 4-141. Does this Position (Customer Service Manager) Exist?

No
94%

Yes, full-time
5%

Yes, part-time
1%

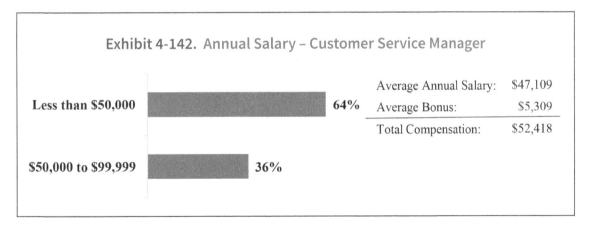

Exhibit 4-142. Annual Salary – Customer Service Manager

Less than $50,000 64%

$50,000 to $99,999 36%

Average Annual Salary:	$47,109
Average Bonus:	$5,309
Total Compensation:	$52,418

The likelihood that builders have a full-time Customer Service Manager is low across companies of every size. This is particularly true among those who start fewer than 100 units a year, as less than 10% of them report this job. The share does increase among large builders with 100+ starts, to 27%, but even that is relatively low (Exhibit 4-143). Due to an insufficient number of responses to produce reliable estimates, average total compensation for Customer Service Managers cannot be reported by company size (Appendix D).

Exhibit 4-143. Percent of Firms with a Full-Time Customer Service Manager by Number of 2021 Starts

1%	3%	6%	27%
1-10 Units	11-25 Units	26-99 Units	100+ Units

The four most typical benefits afforded to full-time Customer Service Managers are paid vacation leave, a vision program, dental insurance, and health insurance (each by 91% of builders where the job exists). Most builders also offer paid sick leave and a 401K program (each by 82%), a prescription program (64%), and training (55%). A minority also offer flex spending, long and short term disability, and life insurance (each by 36%), and tuition reimbursement (27%). Twenty-seven percent offer the Customer Service Manager some other type of benefit, such as a vehicle (Exhibit 4-144).

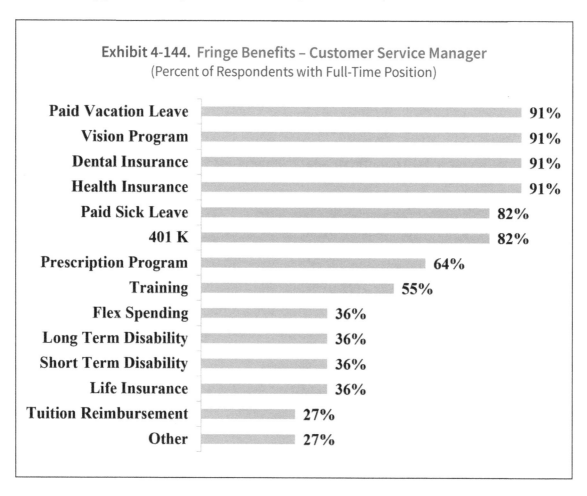

Exhibit 4-144. Fringe Benefits – Customer Service Manager
(Percent of Respondents with Full-Time Position)

Benefit	Percent
Paid Vacation Leave	91%
Vision Program	91%
Dental Insurance	91%
Health Insurance	91%
Paid Sick Leave	82%
401 K	82%
Prescription Program	64%
Training	55%
Flex Spending	36%
Long Term Disability	36%
Short Term Disability	36%
Life Insurance	36%
Tuition Reimbursement	27%
Other	27%

Detailed Tables

Appendix A.   Detailed Tables by Region, Dollar Volume, Starts & No. of Employees

Q1. What is your company's principal operation?
(Percent of Respondents)

| | Total | Region | | | | 2021 Dollar Volume | | | | |
		Northeast	Midwest	South	West	<$1M	$1M to $4.9M	$5M to $9.9M	$10M to $14.9M	$15M+
Single-Family Spec/Tract Builder	34	32	24	32	51	27	12	17	42	71
Single-Family Custom Builder	50	55	60	55	29	46	66	69	50	23
Single-Family General Contractor	15	14	17	13	20	27	22	14	8	6
Responses	338	22	72	169	75	26	103	65	38	95

Q2. How many single-family units does your company expect to start in 2021?
(Percent of Respondents)

| | Total | Region | | | | 2021 Dollar Volume | | | | |
		Northeast	Midwest	South	West	<$1M	$1M to $4.9M	$5M to $9.9M	$10M to $14.9M	$15M+
Zero Units	1			1	2	1				1
1 to 10	43	53	53	44	30	72	84	40	22	
11 to 25	20	13	18	21	20	17	14	42	33	4
26 to 99	19	20	15	20	22	11	1	16	41	36
100 to 499	14	13	13	11	20			2	4	46
500 Units or more	3	3	2	3	6					12
Mean	64	53	45	61	93	11	7	17	36	192
Median	15	9	10	15	24	3	5	15	22	133
Responses	249	15	55	125	54	18	79	55	27	69

Notes:
1) Results were suppressed in cells where the number of responses was below 10. This process eliminated most tabulations for several of the 39 jobs.
2) Throughout this and all appendices, the character "*" means less than 0.5%.

A-1

Q1. What is your company's principal operation?
(Percent of Respondents)

	2021 Single-Family Starts				Number of Employees			
	1 to 10	11 to 25	26 to 99	100+	0 to 2	3 to 4	5 to 9	10 or more
Single-Family Spec/Tract Builder	6	35	54	86	13	13	27	56
Single-Family Custom Builder	72	49	31	7	68	73	55	30
Single-Family General Contractor	21	16	15	7	20	15	18	14
Responses	108	49	48	42	40	48	93	96

Q2. How many single-family units does your company expect to start in 2021?
(Percent of Respondents)

	2021 Single-Family Starts				Number of Employees			
	1 to 10	11 to 25	26 to 99	100+	0 to 2	3 to 4	5 to 9	10 or more
Zero Units					3		1	
1 to 10	100				88	81	34	20
11 to 25		100			9	19	39	9
26 to 99			100				22	25
100 to 499				81			3	36
500 Units or more				19				11
Mean	5	17	46	294	4	7	22	161
Median	5	16	42	222	3	6	15	60
Responses	108	49	48	42	34	36	67	76

A–2

Q3. Approximately, what is the expected total volume of business in 2021?
(Percent of Respondents)

	Total	Region				2021 Dollar Volume				
		Northeast	Midwest	South	West	<$1M	$1M to $4.9M	$5M to $9.9M	$10M to $14.9M	$15M+
Under $500,000	2		6	1	3	31				
$500,000 - $999,999	5	5	9	4	5	69				
$1 million - $4,999,999	31	55	32	31	26		100			
$5 million - $9,999,999	20	9	17	24	16			100		
$10 million - $14,999,999	12	5	10	15	8				100	
$15 million or over	29	27	26	25	42					100
No business activity	*			1						
Median	$ 7,653,845	$ 4,333,332	$ 6,041,665	$ 7,820,511	$ 9,999,998	$ 638,888				
Responses	328	22	69	163	74	26	103	65	38	95

Q4. How many years has your company been in the home building business?
(Percent of Respondents)

	Total	Region				2021 Dollar Volume				
		Northeast	Midwest	South	West	<$1M	$1M to $4.9M	$5M to $9.9M	$10M to $14.9M	$15M+
Less then 5 years	4		3	5	2	4	6	7		12
5 to 10 years	13		7	16	15	13	11	14	21	11
11 to 15 years	14	6	11	16	14	25	8	22	14	16
16 to 20 years	14	24	13	15	8	17	13	14	7	7
More than 20 years	56	71	66	48	61	42	62	44	59	61
Mean (years)	25	34	29	23	23	25	25	23	24	28
Median (years)	23	35	27	20	24	19	24	18	24	25
Responses	278	17	61	141	59	24	90	59	29	75

A-3

Q3. Approximately, what is the expected total volume of business in 2021?
(Percent of Respondents)

	2021 Single-Family Starts				Number of Employees			
	1 to 10	11 to 25	26 to 99	100+	0 to 2	3 to 4	5 to 9	10 or more
Under $500,000	3	2	2		10	2	1	1
$500,000 - $999,999	9	4	2		13	10	5	5
$1 million - $4,999,999	61	22	2		65	52	34	8
$5 million - $9,999,999	20	47	19	2	5	29	28	18
$10 million - $14,999,999	6	18	23	2	5	6	15	10
$15 million or over	1	6	52	95			16	61
No business activity					3			
Median	$ 3,484,847	$ 7,282,607			$ 2,615,383	$ 3,879,998	$ 6,634,614	
Responses	108	49	48	42	40	48	93	96

Q4. How many years has your company been in the home building business?
(Percent of Respondents)

	2021 Single-Family Starts				Number of Employees			
	1 to 10	11 to 25	26 to 99	100+	0 to 2	3 to 4	5 to 9	10 or more
Less then 5 years	7	2	3	11	5	4	5	10
5 to 10 years	11	16	17	11	8	23	13	10
11 to 15 years	9	16	14	19	8	21	16	10
16 to 20 years	15	14	6	19	15	10	12	17
More than 20 years	57	51	60	59	65	42	53	61
Mean (years)	24	25	27	27	24	22	25	28
Median (years)	22	21	24	25	23	16	21	25
Responses	97	43	35	37	40	48	92	96

A-4

Q5. How many employees were on your payroll as of September 30, 2021? (Include Owner/President/CEO)
(Percent of Respondents)

	Total	Region				2021 Dollar Volume				
		Northeast	Midwest	South	West	<$1M	$1M to $4.9M	$5M to $9.9M	$10M to $14.9M	$15M+
Zero	2		5	2		9	3			
1 to 2	12		11	15	10	30	25	3	7	
3 to 4	17	22	13	19	15	26	27	24	10	
5 to 9	34	22	43	34	27	26	35	44	48	20
10 or more	35	56	28	29	47	9	9	29	34	80
Mean	18	17	12	20	22	5	5	9	10	50
Median	7	11	6	6	9	3	4	6	7	25
Responses	277	18	61	139	59	23	91	59	29	74
Did not report	*18*	*18*	*15*	*18*	*21*	*12*	*12*	*24*	*24*	*22*

Q6. What was your total payroll as of September 30, 2021? (Include Owner/President/CEO).
(Percent of Respondents)

	Total	Region				2021 Dollar Volume				
		Northeast	Midwest	South	West	<$1M	$1M to $4.9M	$5M to $9.9M	$10M to $14.9M	$15M+
Less then $100,000	9		11	10	5	36	17			7
$100,000 to $499,999	48	70	48	48	42	50	71	57	44	20
$500,000 to $999,999	22	20	16	25	21	14	11	35	38	39
$1,000,000 to $1,999,999	13	10	14	13	13		2	6	19	35
$2,000,000 to $4,999,999	9		11	5	18			2		
Mean	$727,314	$427,403	$801,070	$592,161	$1,080,059	$209,047	$248,494	$574,585	$593,083	$1,793,470
Median	$432,000	$400,000	$368,415	$443,407	$502,500	$144,500	$192,000	$470,000	$509,042	$1,337,500
Responses	193	10	44	101	38	14	65	22	16	46
Did not report	*43*	*55*	*39*	*40*	*49*	*46*	*37*	*58*	*52*	*52*

A-5

Q5. How many employees were on your payroll as of September 30, 2021? (Include Owner/President/CEO)
(Percent of Respondents)

	2021 Single-Family Starts				Number of Employees			
	1 to 10	11 to 25	26 to 99	100+	0 to 2	3 to 4	5 to 9	10 or more
Zero	4	2			15			
1 to 2	27	5			85			
3 to 4	30	16				100		
5 to 9	24	60	44	5			100	
10 or more	15	16	56	95				100
Mean	5	8	14	54	1	3	7	44
Median	4	6	11	42	2	4	7	23
Responses	97	43	34	37	40	48	93	96
Did not report	10	12	29	12				

Q6. What was your total payroll as of September 30, 2021? (Include Owner/President/CEO).
(Percent of Respondents)

	2021 Single-Family Starts				Number of Employees			
	1 to 10	11 to 25	26 to 99	100+	0 to 2	3 to 4	5 to 9	10 or more
Less then $100,000	18	4	4		52	3		5
$100,000 to $499,999	55	67	29		48	86	68	32
$500,000 to $999,999	22	22	29	6		11	27	39
$1,000,000 to $1,999,999	4	4	32	33			2	
$2,000,000 to $4,999,999	1	4	7	61			3	24
Mean	$386,914	$457,079	$951,353	$2,593,273	$108,594	$269,439	$470,621	$1,560,178
Median	$245,000	$361,535	$791,479	$2,557,151	$96,000	$240,000	$384,941	$1,200,000
Responses	74	27	28	18	29	35	66	62
Did not report	31	45	42	57	28	27	29	35

Q7. President/CEO
(Percent of Respondents)

	Total	Region				2021 Dollar Volume				
		Northeast	Midwest	South	West	<$1M	$1M to $4.9M	$5M to $9.9M	$10M to $14.9M	$15M+
Does Position Exist?										
Yes, full time	94	100	92	94	94	89	97	88	86	100
Yes, part time	3		2	3	6	5	3	8	4	
No	3		6	2		5		4	11	
Responses	240	15	49	122	54	19	77	52	28	63
Is it filled by a person(s) with experience in construction trades?										
Always	90	93	88	90	92	100	96	89	83	85
Sometimes	6	7	7	6	6		1	7	9	12
Never/Almost never	4		5	5	2		3	4	9	3
Responses	216	15	43	107	51	14	72	46	23	60
Salary										
Less then $50,000	6	21	12	5		25	13	2		
$50,000 to $99,999	27	21	26	29	26	33	49	23	13	7
$100,000 or more	67	57	62	66	74	42	38	75	88	93
Mean	$150,426	$134,643	$137,160	$141,689	$184,163	$98,667	$95,423	$132,229	$172,425	$239,006
Median	$120,000	$112,000	$110,000	$117,500	$127,500	$68,500	$90,000	$113,900	$150,000	$200,000
Responses	210	14	42	104	50	12	71	48	24	55
Bonus/Commissions										
Yes	55	43	64	49	62	58	51	63	46	56
No	45	57	36	51	38	42	49	38	54	44
Responses	210	14	42	104	50	12	71	48	24	55
Bonus (among all with salary)										
Zero	45	57	36	51	38	42	49	38	54	44
$1,000 to $4,999	1		7		6	8		2		2
$5,000 to $9,999	4	7	7	3	4	8	7		8	2
$10,000 or more	49	36	57	46	52	42	44	60	38	53
Mean	$68,432	$12,857	$68,914	$69,034	$82,338	$36,042	$20,154	$43,330	$59,063	$163,819
Median	$6,750	$0	$17,500	$0	$11,750	$3,750	$5,000	$14,662	$0	$20,000
Responses	210	14	42	104	50	12	71	48	24	55

A-7

EXECUTIVE JOBS
Q7. President/CEO
(Percent of Respondents)

	2021 Single-Family Starts				Number of Employees			
	1 to 10	11 to 25	26 to 99	100+	0 to 2	3 to 4	5 to 9	10 or more
Does Position Exist?								
Yes, full time	95	89	91	100	94	90	94	96
Yes, part time	2	6	6		3	7	1	4
No	2	6	3		3	2	5	
Responses	82	36	32	30	32	42	79	85
Is it filled by a person(s) with experience in construction trades?								
Always	95	94	93	83	96	89	92	88
Sometimes	1	6	4	13	3	3	6	10
Never/Almost never	4		4	3	4	8	3	2
Responses	74	33	28	30	24	38	72	81
Salary								
Less then $50,000	9	9				16	10	
$50,000 to $99,999	41	25	11	4	45	38	33	12
$100,000 or more	49	66	89	96	55	46	58	88
Mean	$110,515	$122,833	$205,856	$281,413	$94,955	$100,759	$132,405	$206,498
Median	$96,000	$110,300	$185,616	$225,000	$100,000	$90,000	$102,000	$192,116
Responses	75	32	28	28	22	37	73	78
Bonus/Commissions								
Yes	49	50	54	64	45	65	53	54
No	51	50	46	36	55	35	47	46
Responses	75	32	28	28	22	37	73	78
Bonus (among all with salary)								
Zero	51	50	46	36	55	35	47	46
$1,000 to $4,999	1	3	4	4	5			3
$5,000 to $9,999	3	3					11	1
$10,000 or more	45	44	50	61	41	65	42	50
Mean	$21,645	$51,813	$152,635	$155,736	$18,159	$40,781	$56,774	$106,640
Median	$0	$1,750	$8,000	$72,500	$0	$20,000	$5,000	$8,750
Responses	75	32	28	28	22	37	73	78

A-8

Q7. President/CEO - continued
(Percent of Respondents)

		Region				2021 Dollar Volume				
	Total	Northeast	Midwest	South	West	<$1M	$1M to $4.9M	$5M to $9.9M	$10M to $14.9M	$15M+
Bonus (among only those who actually got bonuses)										
$1,000 to $4,999	3				10			3		3
$5,000 to $9,999	8		11	6	6		14		18	3
$10,000 or more	90		89	94	84		86	97	82	94
Mean	$124,963		$107,200	$140,775	$132,803		$39,747	$69,327	$128,864	$290,647
Median	$43,500		$39,000	$47,500	$50,000		$25,000	$46,750	$30,000	$150,000
Responses	115		27	51	31		36	30	11	31
Benefits										
Health Insurance	74	64	66	72	87	62	59	73	78	91
Dental Insurance	42	21	39	40	52	31	17	44	57	63
Vision Program	33	21	29	33	39	38	14	33	43	47
Prescription Program	31	29	18	33	39	8	16	29	39	53
Life Insurance	44	50	37	43	48	15	34	36	61	60
Short Term Disability	20	21	26	18	17	8	11	13	26	35
Long Term Disability	22	14	13	20	35	8	13	18	22	39
Flex Spending	18	14	18	19	15	*	6	16	26	33
401 K	63	71	71	53	76	46	56	51	65	82
Paid Vacation Leave	90	93	87	90	89	77	78	98	100	95
Paid Sick Leave	72	71	63	75	74	46	56	84	87	81
Tuition Reimbursement	16	14	13	18	15	23	14	11	26	18
Training	44	29	45	47	41	46	34	47	61	46
Other	10	7	8	9	17	8	8	4	4	21
Responses	202	14	38	104	46	13	64	45	23	57

A-9

	2021 Single-Family Starts				Number of Employees			
	1 to 10	11 to 25	26 to 99	100+	0 to 2	3 to 4	5 to 9	10 or more
Bonus (among only those who actually got bonuses)								
$1,000 to $4,999	3	6		6	10			5
$5,000 to $9,999	5	6	7				21	2
$10,000 or more	92	88	93	94	90	100	79	93
Mean	$43,876	$103,625	$284,918	$242,256	$39,950	$62,871	$106,269	$198,045
Median	$25,000	$87,500	$67,852	$169,250	$25,000	$35,700	$30,000	$100,000
Responses	37	16	15	18	10	24	39	42
Benefits								
Health Insurance	61	71	79	97	60	67	65	89
Dental Insurance	28	32	48	87	15	24	32	64
Vision Program	24	26	41	67	15	21	26	48
Prescription Program	15	29	38	67	15	9	25	50
Life Insurance	37	32	52	73	35	21	34	64
Short Term Disability	13	10	21	53	20	9	9	34
Long Term Disability	12	16	31	53	20	6	12	38
Flex Spending	9	6	17	53	10	9	10	30
401 K	54	61	62	93	50	39	59	80
Paid Vacation Leave	82	87	93	100	65	88	90	96
Paid Sick Leave	61	71	90	77	40	73	71	81
Tuition Reimbursement	18	3	21	30	25	18	6	23
Training	46	42	55	53	15	45	47	48
Other	12	6	14	23	10	6	7	15
Responses	67	31	29	30	20	33	68	80

Q7. VP of Construction
(Percent of Respondents)

	Total	Region				2021 Dollar Volume				
		Northeast	Midwest	South	West	<$1M	$1M to $4.9M	$5M to $9.9M	$10M to $14.9M	$15M+
Does Position Exist?										
Yes, full time	50	36	47	50	57	26	32	56	46	76
Yes, part time	2		4	2	2	5	4	2	2	
No	48	64	49	48	41	68	64	42	54	24
Responses	239	14	49	122	54	19	76	52	28	63
Is it filled by a person(s) with experience in construction trades?										
Always	92		81	95	93		95	89	92	91
Sometimes	7		19	4	7		5	11	8	9
Never/Almost never	1			2						
Responses	111		21	55	30		22	28	12	45
Salary										
Less then $50,000	4		10	4			14	4	4	10
$50,000 to $99,999	34		48	35	25		76	41	33	
$100,000 or more	62		43	61	75		10	56	67	90
Mean	$113,007		$95,905	$110,598	$130,411		$69,429	$103,772	$116,250	$139,557
Median	$105,500		$85,000	$105,000	$122,500		$60,000	$100,000	$110,000	$125,000
Responses	102		21	49	28		21	27	12	41
Bonus/Commissions										
Yes	76		86	76	71		71	74	83	78
No	24		14	24	29		29	26	17	22
Responses	102		21	49	28		21	27	12	41
Bonus (among all with salary)										
Zero	24		14	24	29		29	26	17	22
$1,000 to $4,999	3		5	2	4		5	4		2
$5,000 to $9,999	5		10	2	7		14	4		2
$10,000 or more	69		71	71	61		52	67	83	73
Mean	$48,355		$35,429	$43,790	$69,733		$20,667	$31,611	$42,917	$73,164
Median	$25,000		$25,000	$25,000	$15,750		$10,000	$13,500	$25,000	$40,000
Responses	102		21	49	28		21	27	12	41

A-11

Q7. VP of Construction
(Percent of Respondents)

	2021 Single-Family Starts				Number of Employees			
	1 to 10	11 to 25	26 to 99	100+	0 to 2	3 to 4	5 to 9	10 or more
Does Position Exist?								
Yes, full time	30	53	72	80	25	29	52	68
Yes, part time	1	6			6	2		1
No	69	42	28	20	69	69	47	31
Responses	81	36	32	30	32	42	79	84
Is it filled by a person(s) with experience in construction trades?								
Always	90	90	95	100		80	95	93
Sometimes	10	10	5			20	3	7
Never/Almost never							3	
Responses	21	20	21	24		10	40	55
Salary								
Less then $50,000	5	11					7	
$50,000 to $99,999	73	33	19	9			41	20
$100,000 or more	23	56	81	91			51	80
Mean	$86,900	$92,559	$139,294	$142,121			$98,099	$133,633
Median	$75,000	$100,000	$125,000	$132,500			$100,000	$125,000
Responses	22	18	21	22			41	50
Bonus/Commissions								
Yes	77	67	76	82			76	78
No	23	33	24	18			24	22
Responses	22	18	21	22			41	50
Bonus (among all with salary)								
Zero	23	33	24	18			24	22
$1,000 to $4,999	5	6	10	5			5	2
$5,000 to $9,999	14						7	4
$10,000 or more	59	61	67	77			63	72
Mean	$22,886	$43,361	$35,691	$94,532			$38,195	$60,024
Median	$10,000	$15,000	$25,000	$65,000			$16,500	$28,000
Responses	22	18	21	22			41	50

Q7. VP of Construction - continued
(Percent of Respondents)

	Total	Region				2021 Dollar Volume				
		Northeast	Midwest	South	West	<$1M	$1M to $4.9M	$5M to $9.9M	$10M to $14.9M	$15M+
Bonus (among only those who actually got bonuses)										
$1,000 to $4,999	4		6	3	5		7	5		3
$5,000 to $9,999	6		11	3	10		20	5		3
$10,000 or more	90		83	95	85		73	90	100	94
Mean	$63,234		$41,333	$57,992	$97,626		$28,933	$42,675	$51,500	$93,741
Median	$33,000		$30,000	$40,000	$30,860		$15,000	$25,000	$27,500	$60,000
Responses	78		18	37	20		15	20	10	32
Benefits										
Health Insurance	77		68	74	89		53	67	83	93
Dental Insurance	51		47	49	56		29	30	67	68
Vision Program	43		32	43	52		24	30	67	53
Prescription Program	48		37	51	52		18	37	58	65
Life Insurance	42		21	45	52		18	30	50	58
Short Term Disability	24		16	23	30		*	15	33	38
Long Term Disability	24		11	21	37		*	15	25	38
Flex Spending	26		32	26	22		*	19	25	43
401 K	72		68	66	85		76	48	58	90
Paid Vacation Leave	95		84	96	100		76	100	100	98
Paid Sick Leave	86		79	89	93		59	89	100	90
Tuition Reimbursement	19		16	17	22		12	7	33	23
Training	49		47	47	59		29	48	67	53
Other	11		11	6	19		*	7	8	20
Responses	97		19	47	27		17	27	12	40

A-13

Q7. VP of Construction - continued
(Percent of Respondents)

	2021 Single-Family Starts				Number of Employees			
	1 to 10	11 to 25	26 to 99	100+	0 to 2	3 to 4	5 to 9	10 or more
Bonus (among only those who actually got bonuses)								
$1,000 to $4,999	6	8		6			6	3
$5,000 to $9,999	18		13				10	5
$10,000 or more	76	92	88	94			84	92
Mean	$29,618	$65,042	$46,845	$115,539			$50,516	$76,954
Median	$13,500	$27,500	$33,360	$72,500			$25,000	$50,000
Responses	17	12	16	18			31	39
Benefits								
Health Insurance	47	76	81	100			59	94
Dental Insurance	32	24	48	91			33	67
Vision Program	32	18	43	73			28	59
Prescription Program	21	35	43	82			36	65
Life Insurance	26	18	52	77			33	57
Short Term Disability	5	6	24	64			8	41
Long Term Disability	*	6	33	55			10	39
Flex Spending	5	6	19	64			10	41
401 K	63	59	67	100			64	84
Paid Vacation Leave	84	94	100	100			95	98
Paid Sick Leave	63	82	100	82			82	90
Tuition Reimbursement	16	*	19	41			8	29
Training	37	47	52	68			49	53
Other	11	12	10	23			5	18
Responses	19	17	21	22			39	49

Q7. CFO/Head of Finance
(Percent of Respondents)

	Total	Region				2021 Dollar Volume				
		Northeast	Midwest	South	West	<$1M	$1M to $4.9M	$5M to $9.9M	$10M to $14.9M	$15M+
Does Position Exist?										
Yes, full time	25	20	27	23	30	21	8	25	11	54
Yes, part time	7	13	6	5	11		9	12		6
No	68	67	67	72	59	79	83	63	89	40
Responses	240	15	49	122	54	19	77	52	28	63
Salary										
$50,000 to $99,999	33		33	39	21			46		18
$100,000 or more	67		67	61	79			54		82
Mean	$118,159		$110,127	$104,804	$151,721			$97,974		$137,391
Median	$115,000		$106,580	$100,000	$156,500			$100,000		$137,250
Responses	51		12	23	14			13		28
Bonus/Commissions										
Yes	65		58	57	86			46		79
No	35		42	43	14			54		21
Responses	51		12	23	14			13		28
Bonus (among all with salary)										
Zero	35		42	43	14			54		21
$1,000 to $4,999	2		8		7					4
$5,000 to $9,999	6				14					7
$10,000 or more	57		50	57	64			46		68
Mean	$32,871		$33,042	$30,609	$39,709			$21,808		$45,229
Median	$15,000		$8,250	$15,000	$23,750			$0		$29,000
Responses	51		12	23	14			13		28
Bonus (among only those who actually got bonuses)										
$1,000 to $4,999	3				8					5
$5,000 to $9,999	9				17					9
$10,000 or more	88			100	75					86
Mean	$50,801			$54,154	$46,327					$57,565
Median	$30,000			$28,000	$33,360					$38,360
Responses	33			13	12					22

Q7. CFO/Head of Finance
(Percent of Respondents)

	2021 Single-Family Starts				Number of Employees			
	1 to 10	11 to 25	26 to 99	100+	0 to 2	3 to 4	5 to 9	10 or more
Does Position Exist?								
Yes, full time	7	31	41	63	6	10	20	45
Yes, part time	12	3	6	3	3	5	8	9
No	80	67	53	33	91	86	72	46
Responses	82	36	32	30	32	42	79	85
Salary								
$50,000 to $99,999		70	17	12			50	25
$100,000 or more		30	83	88			50	75
Mean		$73,700	$148,983	$136,921			$99,844	$128,082
Median		$62,500	$155,000	$139,000			$95,000	$120,000
Responses		10	12	17			16	32
Bonus/Commissions								
Yes		30	75	82			44	72
No		70	25	18			56	28
Responses		10	12	17			16	32
Bonus (among all with salary)								
Zero		70	25	18			56	28
$1,000 to $4,999				6				3
$5,000 to $9,999			17				13	3
$10,000 or more		30	58	76			31	66
Mean		$15,500	$27,102	$62,424			$14,219	$40,279
Median		$0	$18,750	$50,000			$0	$20,000
Responses		10	12	17			16	32
Bonus (among only those who actually got bonuses)								
$1,000 to $4,999				7				4
$5,000 to $9,999								4
$10,000 or more				93				91
Mean				$75,800				$56,040
Median				$55,000				$36,720
Responses				14				23

A-16

Q7. CFO/Head of Finance - continued
(Percent of Respondents)

Benefits	Total	Region				2021 Dollar Volume				
		Northeast	Midwest	South	West	<$1M	$1M to $4.9M	$5M to $9.9M	$10M to $14.9M	$15M+
Health Insurance	89		80	100	86			100		86
Dental Insurance	72		60	86	64			70		75
Vision Program	57		40	62	64			70		57
Prescription Program	51		10	71	50			40		57
Life Insurance	70		60	67	86			50		75
Short Term Disability	34		50	33	29			30		43
Long Term Disability	38		40	29	57			30		46
Flex Spending	36		40	43	29			20		43
401 K	74		80	67	86			50		86
Paid Vacation Leave	98	100	100	100	93			100		96
Paid Sick Leave	85		80	86	93			100		86
Tuition Reimbursement	21		10	19	29			*		25
Training	53		60	38	64			40		54
Other	21		*	19	43			10		32
Responses	47	15	10	21	14			10		28

Q7. CIO/Head of IT
(Percent of Respondents)

Does Position Exist?	Total	Region				2021 Dollar Volume				
		Northeast	Midwest	South	West	<$1M	$1M to $4.9M	$5M to $9.9M	$10M to $14.9M	$15M+
Yes, full time	4		2	6	2	11	1	2	4	8
Yes, part time	1			2						2
No	95	100	98	93	98	89	99	98	96	90
Responses	239	15	49	122	53	19	77	52	28	62

Q7. CFO/Head of Finance - continued
(Percent of Respondents)

Benefits	2021 Single-Family Starts				Number of Employees			
	1 to 10	11 to 25	26 to 99	100+	0 to 2	3 to 4	5 to 9	10 or more
Health Insurance			75	94			93	87
Dental Insurance			58	94			64	74
Vision Program			50	65			57	58
Prescription Program			42	76			36	58
Life Insurance			83	82			71	74
Short Term Disability			25	59			21	42
Long Term Disability			33	59			21	48
Flex Spending			25	59			21	42
401 K			83	88			57	84
Paid Vacation Leave			92	100			100	97
Paid Sick Leave			92	82			93	81
Tuition Reimbursement			25	35			7	29
Training			58	53			50	58
Other			33	24			14	26
Responses			12	17			14	31

Q7. CIO/Head of IT
(Percent of Respondents)

	2021 Single-Family Starts				Number of Employees			
	1 to 10	11 to 25	26 to 99	100+	0 to 2	3 to 4	5 to 9	10 or more
Does Position Exist?								
Yes, full time	1	6		10	6	2	1	6
Yes, part time				3				2
No	99	94	100	86	94	98	99	92
Responses	82	36	32	29	32	42	79	84

A-18

Q7. Head/Director of Purchasing
(Percent of Respondents)

	Total	Region				2021 Dollar Volume				
		Northeast	Midwest	South	West	<$1M	$1M to $4.9M	$5M to $9.9M	$10M to $14.9M	$15M+
Does Position Exist?										
Yes, full time	21	27	24	19	22	11	6	15	14	51
Yes, part time	1	1		1	2		1			2
No	78	73	76	80	76	89	92	85	86	48
Responses	240	15	49	122	54	19	77	52	28	63
Is it filled by a person(s) with experience in construction trades?										
Always	79		55	86	90					84
Sometimes	17		36	9	10					13
Never/Almost never	4		9	5						3
Responses	47		11	22	10					31
Salary										
Less then $50,000	6		8	4						
$50,000 to $99,999	64		83	65	45					58
$100,000 or more	30		8	30	55					42
Mean	$86,601		$75,338	$85,748	$106,253					$94,674
Median	$82,000		$74,250	$80,000	$120,000					$90,000
Responses	50		12	23	11					31
Bonus/Commissions										
Yes	78		83	74	91					84
No	22		17	26	9					16
Responses	50		12	23	11					31
Bonus (among all with salary)										
Zero	22		17	26	9					16
$1,000 to $4,999	8		17	4	9					10
$5,000 to $9,999	16		17	13	18					6
$10,000 or more	54		50	57	64					68
Mean	$16,923		$13,325	$15,957	$26,116					$21,428
Median	$10,000		$9,450	$10,000	$17,304					$20,000
Responses	50		12	23	11					31

OPERATIONS JOBS

Q7. Head/Director of Purchasing
(Percent of Respondents)

	2021 Single-Family Starts				Number of Employees			
	1 to 10	11 to 25	26 to 99	100+	0 to 2	3 to 4	5 to 9	10 or more
Does Position Exist?								
Yes, full time	4	17	31	70			14	47
Yes, part time				3		2		1
No	96	83	69	27	100	98	86	52
Responses	82	36	32	30	32	42	79	85
Is it filled by a person(s) with experience in construction trades?								
Always				81				81
Sometimes				14				16
Never/Almost never				5				3
Responses				21				37
Salary								
Less then $50,000			10				18	3
$50,000 to $99,999			40	62			73	62
$100,000 or more			50	38			9	36
Mean			$93,110	$95,209			$72,741	$90,510
Median			$100,000	$90,000			$76,000	$86,520
Responses			10	21			11	39
Bonus/Commissions								
Yes			80	86			73	79
No			20	14			27	21
Responses			10	21			11	39
Bonus (among all with salary)								
Zero			20	14			27	21
$1,000 to $4,999			10					10
$5,000 to $9,999				10			36	10
$10,000 or more			70	76			36	59
Mean			$19,695	$26,015			$11,036	$18,584
Median			$20,000	$23,500			$5,000	$12,500
Responses			10	21			11	39

A-20

	Total	Region				2021 Dollar Volume				
		Northeast	Midwest	South	West	<$1M	$1M to $4.9M	$5M to $9.9M	$10M to $14.9M	$15M+
Bonus (among only those who actually got bonuses)										
$1,000 to $4,999	10		20	6	10					12
$5,000 to $9,999	21		20	18	20					8
$10,000 or more	69		60	76	70					81
Mean	$21,697		$15,990	$21,588	$28,727					$25,549
Median	$17,304		$11,250	$20,000	$18,652					$21,750
Responses	39		10	17	10					26
Benefits										
Health Insurance	88		92	86	91					94
Dental Insurance	69		58	77	73					74
Vision Program	59		33	64	73					58
Prescription Program	51		*	73	55					61
Life Insurance	53		42	55	64					65
Short Term Disability	41		33	45	45					52
Long Term Disability	43		33	41	64					52
Flex Spending	31		8	41	36					42
401 K	84		83	82	91					94
Paid Vacation Leave	96		100	95	91					97
Paid Sick Leave	76		58	91	82					74
Tuition Reimbursement	27		33	23	27					26
Training	49		42	55	45					45
Other	14		*	14	27					23
Responses	49		12	22	11					31

Q7. Head/Director of Purchasing - *continued*
(Percent of Respondents)

	2021 Single-Family Starts				Number of Employees			
	1 to 10	11 to 25	26 to 99	100+	0 to 2	3 to 4	5 to 9	10 or more
Bonus (among only those who actually got bonuses)								
$1,000 to $4,999				11				13
$5,000 to $9,999								13
$10,000 or more				89				74
Mean				$30,351				$23,380
Median				$26,000				$20,000
Responses				18				31
Benefits								
Health Insurance			80	95			80	90
Dental Insurance			60	90			60	72
Vision Program			50	76			60	59
Prescription Program			40	71			40	54
Life Insurance			50	71			30	59
Short Term Disability			30	62			30	44
Long Term Disability			50	57			30	46
Flex Spending			30	48			20	33
401 K			80	95			50	92
Paid Vacation Leave			80	100			90	97
Paid Sick Leave			90	71			90	72
Tuition Reimbursement			10	38			10	31
Training			50	57			60	46
Other			20	24			*	18
Responses			10	21			10	39

A-22

Q7. Head/Director of Land Acquisition
(Percent of Respondents)

	Total	Region				2021 Dollar Volume				
		Northeast	Midwest	South	West	<$1M	$1M to $4.9M	$5M to $9.9M	$10M to $14.9M	$15M+
Does Position Exist?										
Yes, full time	12	7	2	11	22	5	1	2	4	38
Yes, part time	1		2	2		5		2	4	
No	87	93	96	87	78	89	99	96	93	62
Responses	240	15	49	122	54	19	77	52	28	63
Is it filled by a person(s) with experience in construction trades?										
Always	73			71						74
Sometimes	27			29						26
Responses	26			14						19
Salary										
Less then $50,000	4			8						
$50,000 to $99,999	19			15	27					23
$100,000 or more	77			77	73					77
Mean	$127,210			$119,731	$134,404					$123,376
Median	$122,500			$117,000	$130,000					$118,500
Responses	26			13	11					22
Bonus/Commissions										
Yes	85			77	91					82
No	15			23	9					18
Responses	26			13	11					22
Bonus (among all with salary)										
Zero	15			23	9					18
$5,000 to $9,999	4			9	9					5
$10,000 or more	81			77	82					77
Mean	$54,418			$58,038	$53,124					$45,135
Median	$35,000			$35,000	$19,914					$27,457
Responses	26			13	11					22

Q7. *Head/Director of Land Acquisition*
(Percent of Respondents)

	2021 Single-Family Starts				Number of Employees			
	1 to 10	11 to 25	26 to 99	100+	0 to 2	3 to 4	5 to 9	10 or more
Does Position Exist?								
Yes, full time		6	19	57			5	28
Yes, part time	1	3	3		3		1	1
No	99	92	78	43	97	100	94	71
Responses	82	36	32	30	32	42	79	85
Is it filled by a person(s) with experience in construction trades?								
Always				67				73
Sometimes				33				27
Responses				15				22
Salary								
Less then $50,000								
$50,000 to $99,999				24				17
$100,000 or more				76				83
Mean				$124,263				$131,715
Median				$117,000				$125,000
Responses				17				23
Bonus/Commissions								
Yes				88				87
No				12				13
Responses				17				23
Bonus (among all with salary)								
Zero				12				13
$5,000 to $9,999				6				4
$10,000 or more				82				83
Mean				$48,568				$54,994
Median				$35,000				$35,000
Responses				17				23

A-24

Q7. *Head/Director of Land Acquisition - continued*
(Percent of Respondents)

	Total	Region				2021 Dollar Volume				
		NE	MW	SO	WE	<$1M	$1M to $4.9M	$5M to $9.9M	$10M to $14.9M	$15M+
Bonus (among only those who actually got bonuses)										
$5,000 to $9,999	5				10					6
$10,000 or more	95			100	90					94
Mean	$64,312			$75,450	$58,436					$55,165
Median	$40,000			$62,500	$29,957					$37,500
Responses	22			10	10					18
Benefits										
Health Insurance	92			85	100					95
Dental Insurance	88			77	100					91
Vision Program	65			62	73					68
Prescription Program	62			69	55					64
Life Insurance	69			69	64					73
Short Term Disability	58			54	55					59
Long Term Disability	62			46	73					59
Flex Spending	46			46	36					50
401 K	92			92	91					95
Paid Vacation Leave	100			100	100					100
Paid Sick Leave	85			85	91					82
Tuition Reimbursement	42			38	45					36
Training	58			69	45					50
Other	27			31	18					32
Responses	26			13	11					22

A-25

Q7. Head/Director of Land Acquisition - continued
(Percent of Respondents)

	2021 Single-Family Starts				Number of Employees			
	1 to 10	11 to 25	26 to 99	100+	0 to 2	3 to 4	5 to 9	10 or more
Bonus (among only those who actually got bonuses)								
$5,000 to $9,999				7				5
$10,000 or more				93				95
Mean				$55,044				$63,243
Median				$40,000				$37,500
Responses				15				20
Benefits								
Health Insurance				100				96
Dental Insurance				94				91
Vision Program				76				70
Prescription Program				76				70
Life Insurance				76				74
Short Term Disability				65				65
Long Term Disability				65				70
Flex Spending				53				52
401 K				100				96
Paid Vacation Leave				100				100
Paid Sick Leave				76				83
Tuition Reimbursement				41				43
Training				59				61
Other				29				26
Responses				17				23

A-26

Q7. Head/Director of Production
(Percent of Respondents)

	Total	Region				2021 Dollar Volume				
		NE	MW	SO	WE	<$1M	$1M to $4.9M	$5M to $9.9M	$10M to $14.9M	$15M+
Does Position Exist?										
Yes, full time	13	13	12	12	17	11	5	10	7	30
Yes, part time	1	7	1	1		5	1			
No	86	80	88	87	83	84	93	90	93	70
Responses	239	15	49	122	53	19	76	52	28	63
Is it filled by a person(s) with experience in construction trades?										
Always	86									92
Sometimes	14									8
Responses	22									12
Salary										
Less then $50,000	10			13						50
$50,000 to $99,999	52			47						50
$100,000 or more	39			40						
Mean	$92,406			$88,233						$101,616
Median	$90,000			$85,000						$95,000
Responses	31			15						18
Bonus/Commissions										
Yes	84			80						89
No	16			20						11
Responses	31			15						18
Bonus (among all with salary)										
Zero	16			20						11
$1,000 to $4,999	3			7						
$5,000 to $9,999	6			7						6
$10,000 or more	74			67						83
Mean	$27,824			$25,133						$29,530
Median	$20,000			$15,000						$24,500
Responses	31			15						18

A-27

Q7. Head/Director of Production
(Percent of Respondents)

	2021 Single-Family Starts				Number of Employees			
	1 to 10	11 to 25	26 to 99	100+	0 to 2	3 to 4	5 to 9	10 or more
Does Position Exist?								
Yes, full time	2	8	25	40			9	29
Yes, part time	1				3		1	
No	96	92	75	60	97	100	90	71
Responses	82	36	32	30	32	42	78	85
Is it filled by a person(s) with experience in construction trades?								
Always								81
Sometimes								19
Responses								16
Salary								
Less then $50,000				42				4
$50,000 to $99,999								54
$100,000 or more				58				42
Mean				$100,167				$98,316
Median				$100,000				$92,500
Responses				12				24
Bonus/Commissions								
Yes				92				83
No				8				17
Responses				12				24
Bonus (among all with salary)								
Zero				8				17
$1,000 to $4,999								8
$5,000 to $9,999								
$10,000 or more				92				75
Mean				$33,000				$27,898
Median				$25,000				$23,524
Responses				12				24

Q7. *Head/Director of Production - continued*
(Percent of Respondents)

	Total	Region				2021 Dollar Volume				
		NE	MW	SO	WE	<$1M	$1M to $4.9M	$5M to $9.9M	$10M to $14.9M	$15M+
Bonus (among only those who actually got bonuses)										
$1,000 to $4,999	4			8						6
$5,000 to $9,999	8			8						
$10,000 or more	88			83						94
Mean	$33,175			$31,417						$33,222
Median	$24,500			$22,000						$25,000
Responses	26			12						16
Benefits										
Health Insurance	84			73						94
Dental Insurance	61			60						78
Vision Program	58			47						67
Prescription Program	52			60						67
Life Insurance	39			47						44
Short Term Disability	29			33						39
Long Term Disability	29			27						33
Flex Spending	39			40						39
401 K	90			87						100
Paid Vacation Leave	100			100						100
Paid Sick Leave	84			80						89
Tuition Reimbursement	26			27						28
Training	52			60						56
Other	16			20						28
Responses	31			15						18

Q7. *Head/Director of Development and Training*
(Percent of Respondents)

	Total	Region				2021 Dollar Volume				
		NE	MW	SO	WE	<$1M	$1M to $4.9M	$5M to $9.9M	$10M to $14.9M	$15M+
Does Position Exist?										
Yes, full time	2		2	2	2		3		4	3
Yes, part time	*		2					2		
No	98	100	96	98	98	100	97	98	96	97
Responses	240	15	49	122	54	19	77	52	28	63

A-29

Q7. Head/Director of Production - continued
(Percent of Respondents)

	2021 Single-Family Starts				Number of Employees			
	1 to 10	11 to 25	26 to 99	100+	0 to 2	3 to 4	5 to 9	10 or more
Bonus (among only those who actually got bonuses)								
$1,000 to $4,999								
$5,000 to $9,999								10
$10,000 or more				100				90
Mean				$36,000				$33,477
Median				$25,000				$25,000
Responses				11				20
Benefits								
Health Insurance				100				88
Dental Insurance				92				67
Vision Program				75				63
Prescription Program				75				58
Life Insurance				58				42
Short Term Disability				50				33
Long Term Disability				42				33
Flex Spending				42				42
401 K				100				96
Paid Vacation Leave				100				100
Paid Sick Leave				83				88
Tuition Reimbursement				33				33
Training				58				50
Other				33				21
Responses				12				24

Q7. Head/Director of Development and Training
(Percent of Respondents)

	2021 Single-Family Starts				Number of Employees			
	1 to 10	11 to 25	26 to 99	100+	0 to 2	3 to 4	5 to 9	10 or more
Does Position Exist?								
Yes, full time	1	3		3			1	5
Yes, part time	1							1
No	98	97	100	97	100	100	99	94
Responses	82	36	32	30	32	42	79	85

Q7. *Head/Director of Sales & Marketing*
(Percent of Respondents)

	Total	Region				2021 Dollar Volume				
		NE	MW	SO	WE	<$1M	$1M to $4.9M	$5M to $9.9M	$10M to $14.9M	$15M+
Does Position Exist?										
Yes, full time	21	20	18	21	24	5	9	6	25	52
Yes, part time	5	20	4	4	6	16	4	10	4	2
No	73	60	78	75	70	79	87	85	71	46
Responses	240	15	49	122	54	19	77	52	28	63
Is it filled by a person(s) with experience in construction trades?										
Always	48			45	58					50
Sometimes	31			38	17					29
Never/Almost never	20			17	25					21
Responses	54			29	12					28
Salary										
Less then $50,000	5				18					7
$50,000 to $99,999	41			50	18					33
$100,000 or more	55			50	64					60
Mean	$101,913			$103,246	$105,590					$104,872
Median	$100,000			$92,500	$120,000					$102,500
Responses	44			22	11					30
Bonus/Commissions										
Yes	84			73	100					90
No	16			27						10
Responses	44			22	11					30
Bonus (among all with salary)										
Zero	16			27						10
$1,000 to $4,999	2				18					
$5,000 to $9,999	9			9						7
$10,000 or more	73			64	82					83
Mean	$44,377			$34,216	$74,132					$55,937
Median	$28,500			$20,000	$80,000					$45,000
Responses	44			22	11					30

A-31

Q7. Head/Director of Sales & Marketing
(Percent of Respondents)

	2021 Single-Family Starts				Number of Employees			
	1 to 10	11 to 25	26 to 99	100+	0 to 2	3 to 4	5 to 9	10 or more
Does Position Exist?								
Yes, full time	6	17	38	73	6	2	11	46
Yes, part time	7	6	6		3	5	5	7
No	87	78	56	27	91	93	84	47
Responses	82	36	32	30	32	42	79	85
Is it filled by a person(s) with experience in construction trades?								
Always			42	58			25	54
Sometimes			42	26			50	26
Never/Almost never			17	16			25	21
Responses			12	19			12	39
Salary								
Less then $50,000				5				5
$50,000 to $99,999			45	36				35
$100,000 or more			55	59				59
Mean			$109,522	$108,155				$106,599
Median			$100,000	$102,500				$105,000
Responses			11	22				37
Bonus/Commissions								
Yes			82	91				84
No			18	9				16
Responses			11	22				37
Bonus (among all with salary)								
Zero			18	9				16
$1,000 to $4,999				5				8
$5,000 to $9,999			18					
$10,000 or more			64	86				76
Mean			$46,187	$55,798				$49,341
Median			$15,000	$45,000				$32,000
Responses			11	22				37

A-32

Q7. Head/Director of Sales & Marketing - continued
(Percent of Respondents)

	Total	Region				2021 Dollar Volume				
		NE	MW	SO	WE	<1M	$1M to $4.9M	$5M to $9.9M	$10M to $14.9M	$15M+
Bonus (among only those who actually got bonuses)										
$1,000 to $4,999	3									
$5,000 to $9,999	11			13	18					7
$10,000 or more	86			88	82					93
Mean	$52,773			$47,047	$74,132					$62,152
Median	$40,000			$41,000	$80,000					$50,000
Responses	37			16	11					27
Benefits										
Health Insurance	89			91	91					93
Dental Insurance	77			82	64					80
Vision Program	61			59	73					63
Prescription Program	59			77	36					63
Life Insurance	61			64	64					67
Short Term Disability	43			45	36					53
Long Term Disability	41			36	55					50
Flex Spending	41			45	36					50
401 K	80			73	91					87
Paid Vacation Leave	95			95	91					97
Paid Sick Leave	86			91	91					83
Tuition Reimbursement	32			23	36					30
Training	64			59	64					57
Other	25			18	45					30
Responses	44			22	11					30

Q7. Head/Director of Sales & Marketing - continued
(Percent of Respondents)

	2021 Single-Family Starts				Number of Employees			
	1 to 10	11 to 25	26 to 99	100+	0 to 2	3 to 4	5 to 9	10 or more
Bonus (among only those who actually got bonuses)								
$1,000 to $4,999				5				10
$5,000 to $9,999				95				90
$10,000 or more								
Mean				$61,378				$58,890
Median				$50,000				$50,000
Responses				20				31
Benefits								
Health Insurance			73	100				92
Dental Insurance			55	95				81
Vision Program			36	82				65
Prescription Program			27	77				62
Life Insurance			45	77				65
Short Term Disability			18	64				49
Long Term Disability			27	59				46
Flex Spending			27	59				46
401 K			64	95				86
Paid Vacation Leave			82	100				97
Paid Sick Leave			91	82				84
Tuition Reimbursement			27	41				35
Training			64	59				62
Other			27	27				27
Responses			11	22				37

A-34

FINANCE JOBS

Q7. Controller
(Percent of Respondents)

	Total	Region				2021 Dollar Volume				
		NE	MW	SO	WE	<$1M	$1M to $4.9M	$5M to $9.9M	$10M to $14.9M	$15M+
Does Position Exist?										
Yes, full time	19	13	14	20	24	5	3	10	36	44
Yes, part time	3		4	3			1	6	4	2
No	78	87	82	77	76	95	96	85	61	54
Responses	240	15	49	122	54	19	77	52	28	63
Salary										
$50,000 to $99,999	72			82	46					61
$100,000 or more	28			18	54					39
Mean	$92,182			$87,159	$103,433					$97,547
Median	$88,500			$85,000	$100,000					$92,250
Responses	43			22	13					28
Bonus/Commissions										
Yes	86			82	100					89
No	14			18						11
Responses	43			22	13					28
Bonus (among all with salary)										
Zero	14			18						11
$1,000 to $4,999	2				8					4
$5,000 to $9,999	16			14	23					7
$10,000 or more	67			68	69					79
Mean	$20,344			$23,273	$19,985					$26,985
Median	$10,000			$10,000	$12,545					$14,250
Responses	43			22	13					28
Bonus (among only those who actually got bonuses)										
$1,000 to $4,999	3				8					4
$5,000 to $9,999	19			17	23					8
$10,000 or more	78			83	69					88
Mean	$23,643			$28,444	$19,985					$30,224
Median	$13,000			$14,000	$12,545					$15,000
Responses	37			18	13					25

FINANCE JOBS

Q7. Controller
(Percent of Respondents)

	2021 Single-Family Starts				Number of Employees			
	1 to 10	11 to 25	26 to 99	100+	0 to 2	3 to 4	5 to 9	10 or more
Does Position Exist?								
Yes, full time	2	22	22	73	6		11	41
Yes, part time	1	6	6				4	4
No	96	72	72	27	94	100	85	55
Responses	82	36	32	30	32	42	79	85
Salary								
$50,000 to $99,999				59				69
$100,000 or more				41				31
Mean				$97,242				$92,573
Median				$92,250				$90,000
Responses				22				35
Bonus/Commissions								
Yes				86				89
No				14				11
Responses				22				35
Bonus (among all with salary)								
Zero				14				11
$1,000 to $4,999								3
$5,000 to $9,999				5				14
$10,000 or more				82				71
Mean				$27,666				$21,351
Median				$13,250				$13,000
Responses				22				35
Bonus (among only those who actually got bonuses)								
$1,000 to $4,999				5				3
$5,000 to $9,999								16
$10,000 or more				95				81
Mean				$32,034				$24,106
Median				$15,000				$13,500
Responses				19				31

A-36

Q7. Controller - continued
(Percent of Respondents)

Benefits				
Health Insurance	90	90	100	100
Dental Insurance	76	86	77	85
Vision Program	57	67	62	63
Prescription Program	60	71	62	67
Life Insurance	57	57	54	74
Short Term Disability	45	43	46	56
Long Term Disability	43	33	62	56
Flex Spending	36	38	31	48
401 K	88	86	85	96
Paid Vacation Leave	98	95	100	100
Paid Sick Leave	83	86	92	78
Tuition Reimbursement	29	24	31	26
Training	43	43	38	44
Other	10	5	15	11
Responses	42	21	13	27

Q7. Controller - continued
(Percent of Respondents)

Benefits					
Health Insurance	100				89
Dental Insurance	95				77
Vision Program	73				57
Prescription Program	68				60
Life Insurance	73				60
Short Term Disability	55				51
Long Term Disability	55				49
Flex Spending	45				40
401 K	100				91
Paid Vacation Leave	100				100
Paid Sick Leave	77				83
Tuition Reimbursement	32				31
Training	50				43
Other	9				11
Responses	22				35

Q7. Payroll Manager
(Percent of Respondents)

	Total	Region				2021 Dollar Volume				
		NE	MW	SO	WE	<$1M	$1M to $4.9M	$5M to $9.9M	$10M to $14.9M	$15M+
Does Position Exist?										
Yes, full time	7	13	4	7	6	5	4	4	4	14
Yes, part time	5	7	4	3	7	5	5	8	4	3
No	89	80	92	89	87	95	91	88	93	83
Responses	240	15	49	122	54	19	77	52	28	63
Salary										
Less then $50,000	21									
$50,000 to $99,999	71									
$100,000 or more	7									
Mean	$64,763									
Median	$65,000									
Responses	14									
Bonus/Commissions										
Yes	50									
No	50									
Responses	14									
Bonus (among all with salary)										
Zero	50									
$1,000 to $4,999	14									
$10,000 or more	36									
Mean	$6,339									
Median	$500									
Responses	14									

A-39

	2021 Single-Family Starts				Number of Employees			
	1 to 10	11 to 25	26 to 99	100+	0 to 2	3 to 4	5 to 9	10 or more
Does Position Exist?								
Yes, full time	4	6	3	23	3		5	13
Yes, part time	4	8	3	3			9	5
No	93	86	94	73	97	100	86	82
Responses	82	36	32	30	32	42	79	85
Salary								
Less then $50,000								27
$50,000 to $99,999								64
$100,000 or more								9
Mean								$63,335
Median								$55,000
Responses								11
Bonus/Commissions								
Yes								55
No								45
Responses								11
Bonus (among all with salary)								
Zero								45
$1,000 to $4,999								18
$10,000 or more								36
Mean								$7,159
Median								$1,000
Responses								11

A-40

Q7. Payroll Manager - continued
(Percent of Respondents)

	Total	Region					2021 Dollar Volume				
		NE	MW	SO	WE	≤$1M	$1M to $4.9M	$5M to $9.9M	$10M to $14.9M	$15M+
Health Insurance	86									
Dental Insurance	64									
Vision Program	57									
Prescription Program	64									
Life Insurance	43									
Short Term Disability	29									
Long Term Disability	29									
Flex Spending	36									
401 K	86									
Paid Vacation Leave	100									
Paid Sick Leave	79									
Tuition Reimbursement	14									
Training	50									
Other	14									
Responses	14									

A-41

Q7. Payroll Manager - continued
(Percent of Respondents)

	2021 Single-Family Starts				Number of Employees			
	1 to 10	11 to 25	26 to 99	100+	0 to 2	3 to 4	5 to 9	10 or more
Health Insurance								91
Dental Insurance								82
Vision Program								73
Prescription Program								82
Life Insurance								55
Short Term Disability								36
Long Term Disability								36
Flex Spending								45
401 K								91
Paid Vacation Leave								100
Paid Sick Leave								73
Tuition Reimbursement								18
Training								55
Other								18
Responses								11

Q7. Staff Accountant
(Percent of Respondents)

	Total	Region				2021 Dollar Volume				
		NE	MW	SO	WE	<$1M	$1M to $4.9M	$5M to $9.9M	$10M to $14.9M	$15M+
Does Position Exist?										
Yes, full time	13	7	12	13	17	11	1	8	18	32
Yes, part time	3		4	3	2		3	4	4	3
No	84	93	84	84	81	89	96	88	79	65
Responses	240	15	49	122	54	19	77	52	28	63
Salary										
Less then $50,000	10			13						95
$50,000 to $99,999	83			73						
$100,000 or more	7			13						5
Mean	$67,488			$69,981						$69,097
Median	$61,050			$65,000						$63,550
Responses	30			15						20
Bonus/Commissions										
Yes	73			67						80
No	27			33						20
Responses	30			15						20
Bonus (among all with salary)										
Zero	27			33						20
$1,000 to $4,999	20			13						30
$5,000 to $9,999	23			13						25
$10,000 or more	30			40						25
Mean	$9,233			$8,507						$9,549
Median	$5,700			$6,000						$4,950
Responses	30			15						20
Bonus (among only those who actually got bonuses)										
$1,000 to $4,999	27			20						38
$5,000 to $9,999	32			20						31
$10,000 or more	41			60						31
Mean	$12,590			$12,760						$11,937
Median	$8,000			$10,000						$7,750
Responses	22			10						16

A-43

Q7. Staff Accountant
(Percent of Respondents)

	2021 Single-Family Starts				Number of Employees			
	1 to 10	11 to 25	26 to 99	100+	0 to 2	3 to 4	5 to 9	10 or more
Does Position Exist?								
Yes, full time	4	14	22	50	6	2	8	27
Yes, part time	1	6	6				4	5
No	95	81	72	50	94	98	89	68
Responses	82	36	32	30	32	42	79	85
Salary								
Less then $50,000				7				9
$50,000 to $99,999				93				91
$100,000 or more								
Mean				$65,764				$65,810
Median				$70,000				$65,000
Responses				15				23
Bonus/Commissions								
Yes				87				78
No				13				22
Responses				15				23
Bonus (among all with salary)								
Zero				13				22
$1,000 to $4,999				27				26
$5,000 to $9,999				33				30
$10,000 or more				27				22
Mean				$11,307				$9,652
Median				$6,000				$5,400
Responses				15				23
Bonus (among only those who actually got bonuses)								
$1,000 to $4,999				31				33
$5,000 to $9,999				38				39
$10,000 or more				31				28
Mean				$13,046				$12,333
Median				$7,500				$6,750
Responses				13				18

A-44

Q7. Staff Accountant - continued
(Percent of Respondents)

Benefits	Total	Region				2021 Dollar Volume				
		NE	MW	SO	WE	<$1M	$1M to $4.9M	$5M to $9.9M	$10M to $14.9M	$15M+
Benefits										
Health Insurance	86			79						95
Dental Insurance	83			71						95
Vision Program	66			64						75
Prescription Program	52			50						65
Life Insurance	62			50						80
Short Term Disability	45			36						55
Long Term Disability	48			29						55
Flex Spending	41			29						55
401 K	79			71						90
Paid Vacation Leave	100			100						100
Paid Sick Leave	86			86						80
Tuition Reimbursement	38			21						35
Training	59			57						50
Other	10			7						15
Responses	29			14						20

A-45

Q7. *Staff Accountant - continued*
(Percent of Respondents)

Benefits	2021 Single-Family Starts				Number of Employees			
	1 to 10	11 to 25	26 to 99	100+	0 to 2	3 to 4	5 to 9	10 or more
Health Insurance				100				100
Dental Insurance				100				100
Vision Program				73				78
Prescription Program				67				65
Life Insurance				80				74
Short Term Disability				60				52
Long Term Disability				60				57
Flex Spending				53				52
401 K				100				91
Paid Vacation Leave				100				100
Paid Sick Leave				73				83
Tuition Reimbursement				40				39
Training				53				57
Other				7				9
Responses				15				23

A-46

Q7. Bookkeeper
(Percent of Respondents)

	Total	Region				2021 Dollar Volume				
		NE	MW	SO	WE	<$1M	$1M to $4.9M	$5M to $9.9M	$10M to $14.9M	$15M+
Does Position Exist?										
Yes, full time	29	20	18	33	33	16	17	29	25	51
Yes, part time	16	40	18	16	7	16	25	25	7	2
No	55	40	63	52	59	68	58	46	68	48
Responses	240	15	49	122	54	19	77	52	28	63
Salary										
Less then $50,000	50			49	44		36	60		47
$50,000 to $99,999	50			51	56		64	40		53
Mean	$49,693			$51,388	$48,122		$52,189	$49,156		$50,440
Median	$49,250			$50,000	$50,000		$52,000	$47,840		$50,000
Responses	66			37	18		11	15		32
Bonus/Commissions										
Yes	61			62	56		73	60		63
No	39			38	44		27	40		38
Responses	66			37	18		11	15		32
Bonus (among all with salary)										
Zero	39			38	44		27	40		38
$1,000 to $4,999	24			16	28		36	20		28
$5,000 to $9,999	15			19	11		18	20		13
$10,000 or more	21			27	17		18	20		22
Mean	$5,858			$7,332	$4,761		$4,773	$4,293		$7,647
Median	$2,100			$3,200	$1,750		$1,000	$2,500		$3,750
Responses	66			37	18		11	15		32
Bonus (among only those who actually got bonuses)										
$1,000 to $4,999	40			26	50					45
$5,000 to $9,999	25			30	20					20
$10,000 or more	35			43	30					35
Mean	$9,665			$11,796	$8,570					$12,235
Median	$6,000			$8,000	$5,850					$5,000
Responses	40			23	10					20

A-47

Q7. Bookkeeper - continued
(Percent of Respondents)

	2021 Single-Family Starts				Number of Employees			
	1 to 10	11 to 25	26 to 99	100+	0 to 2	3 to 4	5 to 9	10 or more
Does Position Exist?								
Yes, full time	16	33	38	60	9	14	25	48
Yes, part time	18	22	6		19	17	23	8
No	66	44	56	40	72	69	52	44
Responses	82	36	32	30	32	42	79	85
Salary								
Less then $50,000	46	40	33	56			44	51
$50,000 to $99,999	54	60	67	44			56	49
Mean	$49,046	$52,882	$51,250	$48,386			$52,611	$49,151
Median	$50,000	$51,000	$51,000	$48,250			$50,000	$48,500
Responses	13	10	12	18			18	41
Bonus/Commissions								
Yes	54	60	67	67			56	63
No	46	40	33	33			44	37
Responses	13	10	12	18			18	41
Bonus (among all with salary)								
Zero	46	40	33	33			44	37
$1,000 to $4,999	38	10	25	28			17	29
$5,000 to $9,999	8	10	25	11			11	15
$10,000 or more	8	40	17	28			28	20
Mean	$1,938	$13,100	$3,975	$6,961			$8,772	$4,956
Median	$1,000	$4,250	$4,000	$4,050			$1,100	$3,500
Responses	13	10	12	18			18	41
Bonus (among only those who actually got bonuses)								
$1,000 to $4,999				42			30	46
$5,000 to $9,999				17			20	23
$10,000 or more				42			50	31
Mean				$10,442			$15,790	$7,815
Median				$7,500			$7,500	$6,000
Responses				12			10	26

Q7. Bookkeeper - continued
(Percent of Respondents)

| | Total | Region | | | | <$1M | 2021 Dollar Volume | | | |
		NE	MW	SO	WE		$1M to $4.9M	$5M to $9.9M	$10M to $14.9M	$15M+
Benefits										
Health Insurance	73			68	82		40	71		87
Dental Insurance	47			41	47		10	43		60
Vision Program	39			29	53		20	36		47
Prescription Program	34			32	35		20	7		50
Life Insurance	37			35	35		30	21		50
Short Term Disability	21			12	35		*	14		37
Long Term Disability	23			12	41		10	21		33
Flex Spending	16			12	24		*	14		23
401 K	73			62	82		70	64		80
Paid Vacation Leave	95			97	100		90	100		97
Paid Sick Leave	77			82	88		60	93		77
Tuition Reimbursement	19			12	29		10	14		27
Training	45			44	41		70	36		40
Other	3			3	6		10	*		3
Responses	62			34	17		10	14		30

A-49

Q7. Bookkeeper - continued
(Percent of Respondents)

Benefits	2021 Single-Family Starts				Number of Employees			
	1 to 10	11 to 25	26 to 99	100+	0 to 2	3 to 4	5 to 9	10 or more
Health Insurance	67	50	82	94			56	85
Dental Insurance	33	30	55	83			25	63
Vision Program	25	30	45	67			31	48
Prescription Program	17	20	45	56			25	43
Life Insurance	50	10	36	67			13	50
Short Term Disability	*	10	18	56			*	33
Long Term Disability	17	10	18	50			6	30
Flex Spending	*	10	27	33			*	25
401 K	83	60	64	94			56	80
Paid Vacation Leave	83	100	91	100			100	98
Paid Sick Leave	50	100	91	67			94	75
Tuition Reimbursement	17	10	18	39			*	30
Training	50	60	36	56			44	48
Other	8	*	*	6			*	5
Responses	12	10	11	18			16	40

HUMAN RESOURCES JOBS

Q7. Director of Human Resources
(Percent of Respondents)

	Total	Region				2021 Dollar Volume				
		NE	MW	SO	WE	<$1M	$1M to $4.9M	$5M to $9.9M	$10M to $14.9M	$15M+
Does Position Exist?										
Yes, full time	5		6	4	9	5		4	7	16
Yes, part time	2		2	2	2		1		7	
No	93	100	92	93	89	95	99	96	86	84
Responses	240	15	49	122	54	19	77	52	28	63
Salary										
$50,000 to $99,999	75									70
$100,000 or more	25									30
Mean	$89,567									$91,181
Median	$90,000									$90,000
Responses	12									10
Bonus/Commissions										
Yes	75									70
No	25									30
Responses	12									10
Bonus (among all with salary)										
Zero	25									30
$1,000 to $4,999	17									10
$5,000 to $9,999	8									10
$10,000 or more	50									50
Mean	$17,008									$16,660
Median	$12,000									$12,000
Responses	12									10

HUMAN RESOURCES JOBS

Q7. Director of Human Resources
(Percent of Respondents)

	2021 Single-Family Starts				Number of Employees			
	1 to 10	11 to 25	26 to 99	100+	0 to 2	3 to 4	5 to 9	10 or more
Does Position Exist?								
Yes, full time	1	3	6	30			1	15
Yes, part time	2							5
No	96	97	94	70	100	100	99	80
Responses	82	36	32	30	32	42	79	85
Salary								
$50,000 to $99,999								75
$100,000 or more								25
Mean								$89,567
Median								$90,000
Responses								12
Bonus/Commissions								
Yes								75
No								25
Responses								12
Bonus (among all with salary)								
Zero								25
$1,000 to $4,999								17
$5,000 to $9,999								8
$10,000 or more								50
Mean								$17,008
Median								$12,000
Responses								12

A-52

Q7. Director of Human Resources - continued
(Percent of Respondents)

	Total	Region				2021 Dollar Volume				
		NE	MW	SO	WE	<$1M	$1M to $4.9M	$5M to $9.9M	$10M to $14.9M	$15M+
Benefits										
Health Insurance	100									100
Dental Insurance	83									80
Vision Program	58									50
Prescription Program	75									70
Life Insurance	83									80
Short Term Disability	50									50
Long Term Disability	67									60
Flex Spending	50									50
401 K	92									90
Paid Vacation Leave	100									100
Paid Sick Leave	92									90
Tuition Reimbursement	42									30
Training	58									50
Other	8									10
Responses	12									10

Q7. *Director of Human Resources Benefits - continued*
(Percent of Respondents)

Benefits	2021 Single-Family Starts				Number of Employees			
	1 to 10	11 to 25	26 to 99	100+	0 to 2	3 to 4	5 to 9	10 or more
Benefits								
Health Insurance								100
Dental Insurance								83
Vision Program								58
Prescription Program								75
Life Insurance								83
Short Term Disability								50
Long Term Disability								67
Flex Spending								50
401 K								92
Paid Vacation Leave								100
Paid Sick Leave								92
Tuition Reimbursement								42
Training								58
Other								8
Responses								12

A-54

Q7. Recruiter
(Percent of Respondents)

Does Position Exist?	Total	Region				2021 Dollar Volume				
		NE	MW	SO	WE	<$1M	$1M to $4.9M	$5M to $9.9M	$10M to $14.9M	$15M+
Yes, full time	*	7								2
Yes, part time	1		2	1			1	2		
No	99	93	98	99	100	100	99	98	100	98
Responses	240	15	49	122	54	19	77	52	28	63

Q7. In-house legal counsel
(Percent of Respondents)

Does Position Exist?	Total	Region				2021 Dollar Volume				
		NE	MW	SO	WE	<$1M	$1M to $4.9M	$5M to $9.9M	$10M to $14.9M	$15M+
Yes, full time	2		2	1	7	5		2		5
Yes, part time	*									2
No	98	100	98	99	93	95	100	98	100	94
Responses	240	15	49	122	54	19	77	52	28	63

Q7. Recruiter
(Percent of Respondents)

Does Position Exist?	2021 Single-Family Starts				Number of Employees			
	1 to 10	11 to 25	26 to 99	100+	0 to 2	3 to 4	5 to 9	10 or more
Yes, full time				3				1
Yes, part time	2				3			1
No	98	100	100	97	97	100	100	98
Responses	82	36	32	30	32	42	79	85

Q7. In-house legal counsel
(Percent of Respondents)

Does Position Exist?	2021 Single-Family Starts				Number of Employees			
	1 to 10	11 to 25	26 to 99	100+	0 to 2	3 to 4	5 to 9	10 or more
Yes, full time				7		2		5
Yes, part time		3	3	3				1
No	100	97	97	90	100	98	100	94
Responses	82	36	32	30	32	42	79	85

A-56

Q7. Director of IT
(Percent of Respondents)

Does Position Exist?	Total	Region				2021 Dollar Volume				
		NE	MW	SO	WE	<$1M	$1M to $4.9M	$5M to $9.9M	$10M to $14.9M	$15M+
Yes, full time	3	7	2	4	2		1	2		10
Yes, part time	1		4	1			1	2	4	
No	95	93	94	95	98	100	97	96	96	90
Responses	240	15	49	122	54	19	77	52	28	63

Q7. Network Engineer
(Percent of Respondents)

Does Position Exist?	Total	Region				2021 Dollar Volume				
		NE	MW	SO	WE	<$1M	$1M to $4.9M	$5M to $9.9M	$10M to $14.9M	$15M+
Yes, full time	*				2					2
Yes, part time	*		2						4	
No	99	100	98	100	98	100	100	100	96	98
Responses	240	15	49	122	54	19	77	52	28	63

Q7. Web Design Specialist
(Percent of Respondents)

Does Position Exist?	Total	Region				2021 Dollar Volume				
		NE	MW	SO	WE	<$1M	$1M to $4.9M	$5M to $9.9M	$10M to $14.9M	$15M+
Yes, full time	1			2	2		1		4	3
Yes, part time	4	7	6	3	2			8	4	5
No	95	93	94	95	96	100	99	92	93	92
Responses	240	15	49	122	54	19	77	52	28	63

A-57

IT JOBS

Q7. Director of IT
(Percent of Respondents)

Does Position Exist?	2021 Single-Family Starts				Number of Employees			
	1 to 10	11 to 25	26 to 99	100+	0 to 2	3 to 4	5 to 9	10 or more
Yes, full time		3	3	13			3	7
Yes, part time	2							4
No	98	97	97	87	100	100	97	89
Responses	82	36	32	30	32	42	79	85

Q7. Network Engineer
(Percent of Respondents)

Does Position Exist?	2021 Single-Family Starts				Number of Employees			
	1 to 10	11 to 25	26 to 99	100+	0 to 2	3 to 4	5 to 9	10 or more
Yes, full time								1
Yes, part time	1							1
No	99	100	100	100	100	100	100	98
Responses	82	36	32	30	32	42	79	85

Q7. Web Design Specialist
(Percent of Respondents)

Does Position Exist?	2021 Single-Family Starts				Number of Employees			
	1 to 10	11 to 25	26 to 99	100+	0 to 2	3 to 4	5 to 9	10 or more
Yes, full time				10				4
Yes, part time	2	3	3	7			4	7
No	98	97	97	83	100	100	96	89
Responses	82	36	32	30	32	42	79	85

A-58

ADMINISTRATIVE JOBS

Q7. Executive Assistant
(Percent of Respondents)

	Total	Region				2021 Dollar Volume				
		NE	MW	SO	WE	<$1M	$1M to $4.9M	$5M to $9.9M	$10M to $14.9M	$15M+
Does Position Exist?										
Yes, full time	11	13	14	11	7		6	8	29	14
Yes, part time	1		2	1		5			4	
No	88	87	84	89	93	95	94	92	68	86
Responses	240	15	49	122	54	19	77	52	28	63
Salary										
Less then $50,000	42			54						
$50,000 to $99,999	58			46						
Mean	$49,394			$45,858						
Median	$50,000			$49,000						
Responses	26			13						
Bonus/Commissions										
Yes	50			38						
No	50			62						
Responses	26			13						
Bonus (among all with salary)										
Zero	50			62						
$1,000 to $4,999	23			15						
$5,000 to $9,999	8			8						
$10,000 or more	19			15						
Mean	$4,227			$4,646						
Median	$1,000			$0						
Responses	26			13						
Bonus (among only those who actually got bonuses)										
$1,000 to $4,999	46									
$5,000 to $9,999	15									
$10,000 or more	38									
Mean	$8,454									
Median	$5,000									
Responses	13									

A-59

ADMINISTRATIVE JOBS

Q7. Executive Assistant
(Percent of Respondents)

	2021 Single-Family Starts				Number of Employees			
	1 to 10	11 to 25	26 to 99	100+	0 to 2	3 to 4	5 to 9	10 or more
Does Position Exist?								
Yes, full time	6	11	16	20	3	2	9	20
Yes, part time	1	3					1	1
No	93	86	84	80	97	98	90	79
Responses	82	36	32	30	32	42	79	85
Salary								
Less then $50,000								35
$50,000 to $99,999								65
Mean								$50,979
Median								$50,000
Responses								17
Bonus/Commissions								
Yes								47
No								53
Responses								17
Bonus (among all with salary)								
Zero								53
$1,000 to $4,999								24
$5,000 to $9,999								6
$10,000 or more								18
Mean								$3,229
Median								$0
Responses								17
Bonus (among only those who actually got bonuses)								
$1,000 to $4,999								
$5,000 to $9,999								
$10,000 or more								
Mean								
Median								
Responses								

Q7. Executive Assistant - continued
(Percent of Respondents)

	Total	Region				2021 Dollar Volume				
		NE	MW	SO	WE	<$1M	$1M to $4.9M	$5M to $9.9M	$10M to $14.9M	$15M+
Benefits										
Health Insurance	79			62						
Dental Insurance	54			62						
Vision Program	50			54						
Prescription Program	33			54						
Life Insurance	46			46						
Short Term Disability	38			31						
Long Term Disability	42			31						
Flex Spending	42			46						
401 K	75			62						
Paid Vacation Leave	96			100						
Paid Sick Leave	75			85						
Tuition Reimbursement	38			46						
Training	67			77						
Other	17			8						
Responses	24			13						

A-61

Q7. Executive Assistant - continued
(Percent of Respondents)

Benefits	2021 Single-Family Starts				Number of Employees				
	1 to 10	11 to 25	26 to 99	100+	0 to 2	3 to 4	5 to 9	10 or more
Health Insurance								88
Dental Insurance								65
Vision Program								59
Prescription Program								41
Life Insurance								53
Short Term Disability								41
Long Term Disability								41
Flex Spending								47
401 K								88
Paid Vacation Leave								94
Paid Sick Leave								76
Tuition Reimbursement								41
Training								65
Other								18
Responses								17

A-62

Q7. Office Manager
(Percent of Respondents)

	Total	Region				2021 Dollar Volume				
		NE	MW	SO	WE	<$1M	$1M to $4.9M	$5M to $9.9M	$10M to $14.9M	$15M+
Does Position Exist?										
Yes, full time	14	13	18	13	13	5	8	19	7	24
Yes, part time	4	7	4	3	4		3	4		8
No	82	80	78	84	83	95	90	77	93	68
Responses	240	15	49	122	54	19	77	52	28	63
Salary										
Less then $50,000	30			33				50		13
$50,000 to $99,999	67			67				40		87
$100,000 or more	3							10		
Mean	$58,348			$54,640				$61,100		$59,767
Median	$55,000			$50,000				$52,200		$57,000
Responses	33			15				10		15
Bonus/Commissions										
Yes	64			53				70		60
No	36			47				30		40
Responses	33			15				10		15
Bonus (among all with salary)										
Zero	36			47				30		40
$1,000 to $4,999	15			7				30		7
$5,000 to $9,999	15			7				10		20
$10,000 or more	33			40				30		33
Mean	$6,220			$7,067				$4,276		$8,067
Median	$4,000			$3,000				$2,381		$5,000
Responses	33			15				10		15
Bonus (among only those who actually got bonuses)										
$1,000 to $4,999	24									
$5,000 to $9,999	24									
$10,000 or more	52									
Mean	$9,774									
Median	$10,000									
Responses	21									

Q7. Office Manager
(Percent of Respondents)

	2021 Single-Family Starts				Number of Employees			
	1 to 10	11 to 25	26 to 99	100+	0 to 2	3 to 4	5 to 9	10 or more
Does Position Exist?								
Yes, full time	10	8	25	33		7	15	22
Yes, part time	2		9				5	6
No	88	92	66	67	100	93	80	72
Responses	82	36	32	30	32	42	79	85
Salary								
Less then $50,000				10			33	22
$50,000 to $99,999				90			67	78
$100,000 or more								
Mean				$63,350			$52,133	$61,550
Median				$62,250			$52,500	$61,500
Responses				10			12	18
Bonus/Commissions								
Yes				60			67	67
No				40			33	33
Responses				10			12	18
Bonus (among all with salary)								
Zero				40			33	33
$1,000 to $4,999				10			17	17
$5,000 to $9,999				10			17	11
$10,000 or more				50			33	39
Mean				$10,500			$4,958	$7,820
Median				$7,500			$4,000	$4,500
Responses				10			12	18
Bonus (among only those who actually got bonuses)								
$1,000 to $4,999								25
$5,000 to $9,999								17
$10,000 or more								58
Mean								$11,730
Median								$10,000
Responses								12

A-64

Q7. Office Manager - continued
(Percent of Respondents)

| | Total | Region | | | | 2021 Dollar Volume | | | | |
		NE	MW	SO	WE	≤$1M	$1M to $4.9M	$5M to $9.9M	$10M to $14.9M	$15M+
Benefits										
Health Insurance	75			86				70		86
Dental Insurance	56			50				30		86
Vision Program	50			50				20		71
Prescription Program	47			50				30		79
Life Insurance	44			43				30		71
Short Term Disability	28			36				20		50
Long Term Disability	38			43				20		64
Flex Spending	28			36				20		50
401 K	72			64				60		86
Paid Vacation Leave	94			100				100		86
Paid Sick Leave	72			86				90		57
Tuition Reimbursement	16			14				10		21
Training	44			64				40		43
Other	6			*				*		14
Responses	32			14				10		14

Q7. Office Manager - continued
(Percent of Respondents)

Benefits	2021 Single-Family Starts				Number of Employees			
	1 to 10	11 to 25	26 to 99	100+	0 to 2	3 to 4	5 to 9	10 or more
Health Insurance				90			64	83
Dental Insurance				90			36	78
Vision Program				80			45	61
Prescription Program				80			18	72
Life Insurance				80			27	61
Short Term Disability				60			*	50
Long Term Disability				70			18	56
Flex Spending				70			9	44
401 K				80			55	83
Paid Vacation Leave				100			100	89
Paid Sick Leave				60			73	67
Tuition Reimbursement				30			*	28
Training				40			45	44
Other				10			*	11
Responses				10			11	18

Q7. Administrative Assistant
(Percent of Respondents)

	Total	Region				2021 Dollar Volume				
		NE	MW	SO	WE	<$1M	$1M to $4.9M	$5M to $9.9M	$10M to $14.9M	$15M+
Does Position Exist?										
Yes, full time	10	7	8	11	9	16	6	8	21	14
Yes, part time	6	7	8	6	6		4	4	7	8
No	84	87	84	83	85	84	90	88	71	78
Responses	240	15	49	122	54	19	77	52	28	63
Salary										
Less then $50,000	75			71						
$50,000 to $99,999	25			29						
Mean	$44,956			$45,614						
Median	$43,603			$42,600						
Responses	24			14						
Bonus/Commissions										
Yes	58			50						
No	42			50						
Responses	24			14						
Bonus (among all with salary)										
Zero	42			50						
$1 to $999	4									
$1,000 to $4,999	25			14						
$5,000 to $9,999	21			21						
$10,000 or more	8			14						
Mean	$2,708			$3,143						
Median	$1,288			$500						
Responses	24			14						
Bonus (among only those who actually got bonuses)										
$1 to $999	7									
$1,000 to $4,999	43									
$5,000 to $9,999	36									
$10,000 or more	14									
Mean	$4,642									
Median	$4,000									
Responses	14									

A-67

Q7. Administrative Assistant
(Percent of Respondents)

	2021 Single-Family Starts				Number of Employees			
	1 to 10	11 to 25	26 to 99	100+	0 to 2	3 to 4	5 to 9	10 or more
Does Position Exist?								
Yes, full time	5	11	9	23	6	2	11	16
Yes, part time	4	11	13			5	6	7
No	91	78	78	77	94	93	82	76
Responses	82	36	32	30	32	42	79	85
Salary								
Less then $50,000								79
$50,000 to $99,999								21
Mean								$43,788
Median								$44,569
Responses								14
Bonus/Commissions								
Yes								64
No								36
Responses								14
Bonus (among all with salary)								
Zero								36
$1 to $999								
$1,000 to $4,999								36
$5,000 to $9,999								21
$10,000 or more								7
Mean								$2,810
Median								$1,663
Responses								14
Bonus (among only those who actually got bonuses)								
$1 to $999								
$1,000 to $4,999								
$5,000 to $9,999								
$10,000 or more								
Mean								
Median								
Responses								

A-68

Q7. Administrative Assistant - continued
(Percent of Respondents)

	Total	Region				2021 Dollar Volume				
		NE	MW	SO	WE	<$1M	$1M to $4.9M	$5M to $9.9M	$10M to $14.9M	$15M+
Benefits										
Health Insurance	74			62						
Dental Insurance	48			46						
Vision Program	48			46						
Prescription Program	35			38						
Life Insurance	26			23						
Short Term Disability	26			31						
Long Term Disability	30			31						
Flex Spending	17			23						
401 K	70			46						
Paid Vacation Leave	100			100						
Paid Sick Leave	87			92						
Tuition Reimbursement	22			15						
Training	30			31						
Other	*			*						
Responses	23			13						

A-69

Q7. Administrative Assistant - continued
(Percent of Respondents)

| Benefits | 2021 Single-Family Starts | | | | | Number of Employees | | | |
	1 to 10	11 to 25	26 to 99	100+	0 to 2	3 to 4	5 to 9	10 or more
Health Insurance								86
Dental Insurance								64
Vision Program								57
Prescription Program								50
Life Insurance								43
Short Term Disability								36
Long Term Disability								43
Flex Spending								29
401 K								86
Paid Vacation Leave								100
Paid Sick Leave								86
Tuition Reimbursement								29
Training								29
Other								*
Responses								14

A-70

Q7. Receptionist
(Percent of Respondents)

	Total	Region				2021 Dollar Volume				
		NE	MW	SO	WE	<$1M	$1M to $4.9M	$5M to $9.9M	$10M to $14.9M	$15M+
Does Position Exist?										
Yes, full time	10	7	10	10	9		8	2		26
Yes, part time	4	13	8	2	2	5	3	8		5
No	86	80	82	88	89	95	90	90	100	69
Responses	239	15	49	122	53	19	77	52	28	62
Salary										
Less then $50,000	100									100
Mean	$35,971									$37,280
Median	$36,500									$37,500
Responses	18									15
Bonus/Commissions										
Yes	72									80
No	28									20
Responses	18									15
Bonus (among all with salary)										
Zero	28									20
$1,000 to $4,999	33									40
$5,000 to $9,999	28									27
$10,000 or more	11									13
Mean	$3,791									$4,216
Median	$2,250									$2,500
Responses	18									15
Bonus (among only those who actually got bonuses)										
$1,000 to $4,999	46									50
$5,000 to $9,999	38									33
$10,000 or more	15									17
Mean	$5,249									$5,270
Median	$5,000									$4,250
Responses	13									12

Q7. Receptionist
(Percent of Respondents)

	2021 Single-Family Starts				Number of Employees			
	1 to 10	11 to 25	26 to 99	100+	0 to 2	3 to 4	5 to 9	10 or more
Does Position Exist?								
Yes, full time	2	6	9	43	3	2	6	21
Yes, part time	2	6		7		2	4	6
No	95	89	91	50	97	98	90	73
Responses	82	35	32	30	32	42	79	84
Salary								
Less then $50,000				100				100
Mean				$37,152				$37,499
Median				$37,000				$37,500
Responses				13				15
Bonus/Commissions								
Yes				85				87
No				15				13
Responses				13				15
Bonus (among all with salary)								
Zero				15				13
$1,000 to $4,999				38				40
$5,000 to $9,999				31				33
$10,000 or more				15				13
Mean				$4,788				$4,549
Median				$3,500				$3,500
Responses				13				15
Bonus (among only those who actually got bonuses)								
$1,000 to $4,999				45				46
$5,000 to $9,999				36				38
$10,000 or more				18				15
Mean				$5,658				$5,249
Median				$5,000				$5,000
Responses				11				13

A-72

Q7. Receptionist - continued
(Percent of Respondents)

	Total	Region				2021 Dollar Volume				
		NE	MW	SO	WE	<$1M	$1M to $4.9M	$5M to $9.9M	$10M to $14.9M	$15M+
Benefits										
Health Insurance	82									93
Dental Insurance	88									93
Vision Program	65									64
Prescription Program	59									71
Life Insurance	53									64
Short Term Disability	47									57
Long Term Disability	41									50
Flex Spending	24									29
401 K	88									93
Paid Vacation Leave	100									100
Paid Sick Leave	94									93
Tuition Reimbursement	29									36
Training	53									57
Other	6									7
Responses	17									14

A-73

Q7. Receptionist - continued
(Percent of Respondents)

	2021 Single-Family Starts				Number of Employees			
	1 to 10	11 to 25	26 to 99	100+	0 to 2	3 to 4	5 to 9	10 or more
Benefits								
Health Insurance				100				100
Dental Insurance				100				100
Vision Program				67				71
Prescription Program				67				71
Life Insurance				75				64
Short Term Disability				58				57
Long Term Disability				50				50
Flex Spending				33				29
401 K				100				100
Paid Vacation Leave				100				100
Paid Sick Leave				92				93
Tuition Reimbursement				42				36
Training				50				57
Other				8				7
Responses				12				14

A-74

Q7. Settlement Coordinator
(Percent of Respondents)

	Total	Region				2021 Dollar Volume				
		NE	MW	SO	WE	<$1M	$1M to $4.9M	$5M to $9.9M	$10M to $14.9M	$15M+
Does Position Exist?										
Yes, full-time	8	13	2	8	9		3	2		24
Yes, part-time	*			1			1			
No	92	87	98	91	91	100	96	98	100	76
Responses	240	15	49	122	54	19	77	52	28	63
Salary										
Less then $50,000	22			30						27
$50,000 to $99,999	78			70						73
Mean	$56,838			$51,450						$52,843
Median	$53,750			$50,000						$50,000
Responses	18			10						15
Bonus/Commissions										
Yes	78			70						80
No	22			30						20
Responses	18			10						15
Bonus (among all with salary)										
Zero	22			30						20
$1,000 to $4,999	22			20						27
$5,000 to $9,999	22			10						13
$10,000 or more	33			40						40
Mean	$8,915			$8,780						$9,867
Median	$5,000			$4,500						$5,000
Responses	18			10						15
Bonus (among only those who actually got bonuses)										
$1,000 to $4,999	29									33
$5,000 to $9,999	29									17
$10,000 or more	43									50
Mean	$11,463									$12,333
Median	$6,239									$7,500
Responses	14									12

A-75

Q7. Settlement Coordinator
(Percent of Respondents)

	2021 Single-Family Starts				Number of Employees			
	1 to 10	11 to 25	26 to 99	100+	0 to 2	3 to 4	5 to 9	10 or more
Does Position Exist?								
Yes, full time	1	6	9	33			3	19
Yes, part time								1
No	99	94	91	67	100	100	97	80
Responses	82	36	32	30	32	42	79	85
Salary								
Less then $50,000				30				19
$50,000 to $99,999				70				81
Mean				$50,364				$57,506
Median				$50,000				$53,750
Responses				10				16
Bonus/Commissions								
Yes				70				81
No				30				19
Responses				10				16
Bonus (among all with salary)								
Zero				30				19
$1,000 to $4,999				30				25
$5,000 to $9,999								25
$10,000 or more				40				31
Mean				$10,420				$8,730
Median				$4,100				$5,000
Responses				10				16
Bonus (among only those who actually got bonuses)								
$1,000 to $4,999								31
$5,000 to $9,999								31
$10,000 or more								38
Mean								$10,744
Median								$5,000
Responses								13

Q7. Settlement Coordinator - continued
(Percent of Respondents)

Benefits	Total	Region				2021 Dollar Volume				
		NE	MW	SO	WE	<$1M	$1M to $4.9M	$5M to $9.9M	$10M to $14.9M	$15M+
Health Insurance	82									86
Dental Insurance	65									64
Vision Program	47									50
Prescription Program	53									50
Life Insurance	59									64
Short Term Disability	53									57
Long Term Disability	47									50
Flex Spending	35									43
401 K	82									86
Paid Vacation Leave	100									100
Paid Sick Leave	82									86
Tuition Reimbursement	41									36
Training	65									57
Other	12									14
Responses	17									14

Q7. Settlement Coordinator - continued
(Percent of Respondents)

| Benefits | 2021 Single-Family Starts | | | | Number of Employees | | | |
	1 to 10	11 to 25	26 to 99	100+	0 to 2	3 to 4	5 to 9	10 or more
Health Insurance				100				93
Dental Insurance				90				73
Vision Program				70				53
Prescription Program				60				60
Life Insurance				90				67
Short Term Disability				80				60
Long Term Disability				70				53
Flex Spending				60				40
401 K				100				93
Paid Vacation Leave				100				100
Paid Sick Leave				80				80
Tuition Reimbursement				50				47
Training				70				67
Other				10				13
Responses				10				15

A-78

PRODUCTION.JOBS

Q7. Production Manager
(Percent of Respondents)

	Total	Region NE	Region MW	Region SO	Region WE	2021 Dollar Volume <$1M	$1M to $4.9M	$5M to $9.9M	$10M to $14.9M	$15M+
Does Position Exist?										
Yes, full time	24	33	18	24	26	11	11	31	29	37
Yes, part time	*			1			1			
No	76	67	82	75	74	89	88	69	71	63
Responses	239	15	49	121	54	19	76	52	28	63
Is it filled by a person(s) with experience in construction trades?										
Always	90			93	82			87	87	90
Sometimes	10			7	18			13	13	10
Responses	51			28	11			15		20
Salary										
Less than $50,000	4			7	7					
$50,000 to $99,999	70			56	69			87		57
$100,000 or more	26			37	31			13		43
Mean	$80,842			$81,204	$89,099			$74,600		$93,259
Median	$80,000			$80,000	$92,272			$75,000		$95,200
Responses	54			27	13			15		21
Bonus/Commissions										
Yes	80			78	85			73		90
No	20			22	15			27		10
Responses	54			27	13			15		21
Bonus (among all with salary)										
Zero	20			22	15			27		10
$1,000 to $4,999	4			4	23			20		19
$5,000 to $9,999	22			19						
$10,000 or more	54			56	62			53		71
Mean	$18,050			$23,648	$16,862			$20,000		$21,319
Median	$10,000			$10,000	$14,553			$10,000		$18,000
Responses	54			27	13			15		21

A-79

Q7. Production Manager
(Percent of Respondents)

	2021 Single-Family Starts				Number of Employees			
	1 to 10	11 to 25	26 to 99	100+	0 to 2	3 to 4	5 to 9	10 or more
Does Position Exist?								
Yes, full time	15	31	31	50	9	17	29	29
Yes, part time						2		
No	85	69	69	50	91	81	71	71
Responses	82	36	32	30	32	42	79	84
Is it filled by a person(s) with experience in construction trades?								
Always	90			86			90	91
Sometimes	10			14			10	9
Responses	10			14			20	22
Salary								
Less then $50,000	8	9					4	
$50,000 to $99,999	75	73		53			74	64
$100,000 or more	17	18		47			22	36
Mean	$76,125	$70,182		$96,412			$75,957	$92,202
Median	$77,500	$65,000		$96,515			$73,000	$93,636
Responses	12	11		15			23	22
Bonus/Commissions								
Yes	67	82		87			74	86
No	33	18		13			26	14
Responses	12	11		15			23	22
Bonus (among all with salary)								
Zero	33	18		13			26	14
$1,000 to $4,999	8	27					4	18
$5,000 to $9,999	33	55		13			26	
$10,000 or more	25			73			43	68
Mean	$7,292	$38,273		$16,377			$18,522	$14,555
Median	$5,000	$10,000		$18,000			$6,500	$13,277
Responses	12	11		15			23	22

A-80

Q7. Production Manager
(Percent of Respondents)

| | Total | Region | | | | 2021 Dollar Volume | | | | |
		NE	MW	SO	WE	<$1M	$1M to $4.9M	$5M to $9.9M	$10M to $14.9M	$15M+
Bonus (among only those who actually got bonuses)										
$1,000 to $4,999	5			5						
$5,000 to $9,999	28			24	27					21
$10,000 or more	67			71	73					79
Mean	$22,668			$30,405	$19,928			$27,273		$23,563
Median	$12,500			$15,000	$20,000			$15,000		$20,000
Responses	43			21	11			11		19
Benefits										
Health Insurance	81			85	92			86		90
Dental Insurance	48			58	50			36		81
Vision Program	42			54	33			36		67
Prescription Program	40			62	17			43		67
Life Insurance	29			38	25			21		52
Short Term Disability	31			35	25			14		48
Long Term Disability	33			42	33			21		57
Flex Spending	27			31	17			36		38
401 K	69			62	92			57		90
Paid Vacation Leave	92			92	83			93		100
Paid Sick Leave	75			77	92			64		86
Tuition Reimbursement	19			23	17			7		24
Training	52			65	33			57		52
Other	10			12	8			7		19
Responses	52			26	12			14		21

Q7. Land Manager
(Percent of Respondents)

| | Total | Region | | | | 2021 Dollar Volume | | | | |
		NE	MW	SO	WE	<$1M	$1M to $4.9M	$5M to $9.9M	$10M to $14.9M	$15M+
Does Position Exist?										
Yes, full time	4	7	2	2	9	5				14
Yes, part time	*		2			5				
No	95	93	96	98	91	89	100	100	100	86
Responses	239	15	49	121	54	19	76	52	28	63

A-81

APPENDIX A **187**

Q7. Production Manager
(Percent of Respondents)

	2021 Single-Family Starts				Number of Employees			
	1 to 10	11 to 25	26 to 99	100+	0 to 2	3 to 4	5 to 9	10 or more
Bonus (among only those who actually got bonuses)								
$1,000 to $4,999							6	
$5,000 to $9,999				15			35	21
$10,000 or more				85			59	79
Mean				$18,896			$25,059	$16,853
Median				$20,000			$10,000	$18,000
Responses				13			17	19
Benefits								
Health Insurance	75	70		100			68	91
Dental Insurance	8	30		100			23	82
Vision Program	*	30		80			23	73
Prescription Program	8	40		73			27	64
Life Insurance	17	*		67			14	55
Short Term Disability	*	20		60			18	55
Long Term Disability	8	10		67			14	64
Flex Spending	8	10		53			14	50
401 K	58	30		93			59	86
Paid Vacation Leave	83	90		100			91	100
Paid Sick Leave	58	60		80			64	86
Tuition Reimbursement	25	10		33			9	23
Training	58	50		53			55	50
Other	8	*		20			*	18
Responses	12	10		15			22	22

Q7. Land Manager
(Percent of Respondents)

	2021 Single-Family Starts				Number of Employees			
	1 to 10	11 to 25	26 to 99	100+	0 to 2	3 to 4	5 to 9	10 or more
Does Position Exist?								
Yes, full time	1		13	20				12
Yes, part time					3			
No	99	100	88	80	97	100	100	88
Responses	82	36	32	30	32	42	79	84

A-82

Q7. Purchasing Manager
(Percent of Respondents)

	Total	Region				2021 Dollar Volume				
		NE	MW	SO	WE	<$1M	$1M to $4.9M	$5M to $9.9M	$10M to $14.9M	$15M+
Does Position Exist?										
Yes, full time	9	13	2	12	9		3	10	7	21
No	91	87	98	88	91	100	97	90	93	79
Responses	239	15	49	121	54	19	76	52	28	63
Is it filled by a person(s) with experience in construction trades?										
Always	76			67						
Sometimes	12			17						
Never/Almost never	12			17						
Responses	17			12						
Salary										
Less then $50,000	5			7						8
$50,000 to $99,999	86			86						92
$100,000 or more	10			7						
Mean	$69,567			$70,014						$65,075
Median	$70,000			$70,000						$67,500
Responses	21			14						12
Bonus/Commissions										
Yes	62			64						67
No	38			36						33
Responses	21			14						12
Bonus (among all with salary)										
Zero	38			36						33
$1,000 to $4,999	14			14						8
$5,000 to $9,999	14			14						17
$10,000 or more	33			36						42
Mean	$7,476			$8,250						$6,875
Median	$3,500			$4,000						$5,000
Responses	21			14						12

A-83

Q7. Purchasing Manager
(Percent of Respondents)

	2021 Single-Family Starts				Number of Employees			
	1 to 10	11 to 25	26 to 99	100+	0 to 2	3 to 4	5 to 9	10 or more
Does Position Exist?								
Yes, full time	1	14	6	33		2	9	17
No	99	86	94	67	100	98	91	83
Responses	82	36	32	30	32	42	79	84
Is it filled by a person(s) with experience in construction trades?								
Always								80
Sometimes								20
Never/Almost never								
Responses								10
Salary								
Less then $50,000								8
$50,000 to $99,999				100				92
$100,000 or more								
Mean				$67,090				$63,916
Median				$67,500				$65,000
Responses				10				13
Bonus/Commissions								
Yes				70				62
No				30				38
Responses				10				13
Bonus (among all with salary)								
Zero				30				38
$1,000 to $4,999				10				8
$5,000 to $9,999				10				15
$10,000 or more				50				38
Mean				$7,750				$6,346
Median				$7,500				$5,000
Responses				10				13

Q7. Purchasing Manager - continued
(Percent of Respondents)

| | Total | Region | | | | 2021 Dollar Volume | | | | |
		NE	MW	SO	WE	<$1M	$1M to $4.9M	$5M to $9.9M	$10M to $14.9M	$15M+
Bonus (among only those who actually got bonuses)										
$1,000 to $4,999	23									
$5,000 to $9,999	23									
$10,000 or more	54									
Mean	$12,077									
Median	$10,000									
Responses	13									
Benefits										
Health Insurance	84			92						100
Dental Insurance	79			92						92
Vision Program	84			92						100
Prescription Program	68			85						83
Life Insurance	42			46						58
Short Term Disability	47			54						67
Long Term Disability	47			54						67
Flex Spending	37			46						50
401 K	84			85						100
Paid Vacation Leave	100			100						100
Paid Sick Leave	84			92						75
Tuition Reimbursement	21			15						33
Training	53			54						58
Other	11			15						17
Responses	19			13						12

	2021 Single-Family Starts				Number of Employees			
	1 to 10	11 to 25	26 to 99	100+	0 to 2	3 to 4	5 to 9	10 or more
Bonus (among only those who actually got bonuses)								
$1,000 to $4,999								
$5,000 to $9,999								
$10,000 or more								
Mean								
Median								
Responses								
Benefits								
Health Insurance				100				92
Dental Insurance				90				85
Vision Program				100				92
Prescription Program				80				77
Life Insurance				60				54
Short Term Disability				60				62
Long Term Disability				60				62
Flex Spending				50				46
401 K				100				92
Paid Vacation Leave				100				100
Paid Sick Leave				70				77
Tuition Reimbursement				40				31
Training				60				62
Other				20				15
Responses				10				13

A-86

Q7. Home Services/Warranty Manager
(Percent of Respondents)

	Total	Region				2021 Dollar Volume				
		NE	MW	SO	WE	<$1M	$1M to $4.9M	$5M to $9.9M	$10M to $14.9M	$15M+
Does Position Exist?										
Yes, full time	20	7	20	17	30	5	1	4	18	62
Yes, part time	3	7		3	4			6	7	3
No	77	87	80	80	67	95	99	90	75	35
Responses	240	15	49	122	54	19	77	52	28	63
Salary										
Less then $50,000	21		30	19	20					18
$50,000 to $99,999	72		70	76	67					74
$100,000 or more	6			5	13					8
Mean	$64,239		$56,760	$61,708	$72,051					$67,377
Median	$60,000		$57,600	$56,000	$73,542					$63,682
Responses	47		10	21	15					38
Bonus/Commissions										
Yes	74		60	71	93					76
No	26		40	29	7					24
Responses	47		10	21	15					38
Bonus (among all with salary)										
Zero	26		40	29	7					24
$1,000 to $4,999	9			14	7					8
$5,000 to $9,999	23		40	14	27					18
$10,000 or more	43		20	43	60					50
Mean	$8,818		$4,800	$9,086	$11,710					$9,354
Median	$7,000		$5,500	$6,000	$11,627					$9,413
Responses	47		10	21	15					38
Bonus (among only those who actually got bonuses)										
$1,000 to $4,999	11			20	7					10
$5,000 to $9,999	31			20	29					24
$10,000 or more	57			60	64					66
Mean	$11,841			$12,720	$12,547					$12,257
Median	$10,000			$10,000	$13,314					$11,627
Responses	35			15	14					29

A-87

Q7. Home Services/Warranty Manager
(Percent of Respondents)

	2021 Single-Family Starts				Number of Employees			
	1 to 10	11 to 25	26 to 99	100+	0 to 2	3 to 4	5 to 9	10 or more
Does Position Exist?								
Yes, full time		3	28	83			10	47
Yes, part time	2		13			2	4	4
No	98	97	59	17	100	98	86	49
Responses	82	36	32	30	32	42	79	85
Salary								
Less then $50,000				16				18
$50,000 to $99,999				76				77
$100,000 or more				8				5
Mean				$69,503				$65,278
Median				$70,000				$60,000
Responses				25				39
Bonus/Commissions								
Yes				84				77
No				16				23
Responses				25				39
Bonus (among all with salary)								
Zero				16				23
$1,000 to $4,999				4				10
$5,000 to $9,999				32				26
$10,000 or more				48				41
Mean				$9,921				$8,576
Median				$8,825				$7,000
Responses				25				39
Bonus (among only those who actually got bonuses)								
$1,000 to $4,999				5				13
$5,000 to $9,999				38				33
$10,000 or more				57				53
Mean				$11,811				$11,148
Median				$10,000				$10,000
Responses				21				30

A-88

Q7. Home Services/Warranty Manager - continued
(Percent of Respondents)

	Total	Region				2021 Dollar Volume				
		NE	MW	SO	WE	<$1M	$1M to $4.9M	$5M to $9.9M	$10M to $14.9M	$15M+
Benefits										
Health Insurance	89		90	86	93					89
Dental Insurance	64		40	71	67					66
Vision Program	55		40	57	60					53
Prescription Program	55		20	62	67					58
Life Insurance	53		40	57	53					55
Short Term Disability	34		20	43	27					37
Long Term Disability	40		20	38	53					42
Flex Spending	34		30	43	20					34
401 K	87		80	86	93					87
Paid Vacation Leave	100		100	100	100					100
Paid Sick Leave	85		70	90	93					84
Tuition Reimbursement	34		20	38	40					29
Training	47		40	57	40					39
Other	13		*	14	13					16
Responses	47	15	10	21	15					38

Q7. Contract Manager
(Percent of Respondents)

	Total	Region				2021 Dollar Volume				
		NE	MW	SO	WE	<$1M	$1M to $4.9M	$5M to $9.9M	$10M to $14.9M	$15M+
Does Position Exist?										
Yes, full time	4			4	7		1	2		11
No	96	100	100	96	93	100	99	98	100	89
Responses	240	15	49	122	54	19	77	52	28	63

Q7. Home Services/Warranty Manager - continued
(Percent of Respondents)

Benefits	2021 Single-Family Starts				Number of Employees			
	1 to 10	11 to 25	26 to 99	100+	0 to 2	3 to 4	5 to 9	10 or more
Health Insurance				100				95
Dental Insurance				92				74
Vision Program				72				59
Prescription Program				68				64
Life Insurance				72				62
Short Term Disability				56				41
Long Term Disability				56				46
Flex Spending				48				41
401 K				100				92
Paid Vacation Leave				100				100
Paid Sick Leave				80				85
Tuition Reimbursement				44				38
Training				56				49
Other				20				15
Responses				25				39

Q7. Contract Manager
(Percent of Respondents)

Does Position Exist?	2021 Single-Family Starts				Number of Employees			
	1 to 10	11 to 25	26 to 99	100+	0 to 2	3 to 4	5 to 9	10 or more
Yes, full-time			3	17			1	9
No	100	100	97	83	100	100	99	91
Responses	82	36	32	30	32	42	79	85

A-90

Q7. Project Manager
(Percent of Respondents)

	Total	Region				2021 Dollar Volume				
		NE	MW	SO	WE	<$1M	$1M to $4.9M	$5M to $9.9M	$10M to $14.9M	$15M+
Does Position Exist?										
Yes, full time	34	13	35	36	35	11	16	60	39	41
Yes, part time	1		2	1			1			2
No	65	87	63	63	65	89	83	40	61	57
Responses	240	15	49	122	54	19	77	52	28	63
Salary										
Less then $50,000	12		18	10	11		8	23		4
$50,000 to $99,999	69		71	71	67		75	57	80	79
$100,000 or more	19		12	20	22		17	20	20	17
Mean	$78,294		$69,882	$81,489	$76,827		$80,312	$75,313	$79,900	$79,783
Median	$73,900		$70,000	$75,000	$72,400		$73,500	$71,400	$67,500	$79,000
Responses	78		17	41	18		12	30	10	24
Bonus/Commissions										
Yes	77		76	68	94		67	70	90	88
No	23		24	32	6		33	30	10	13
Responses	78		17	41	18		12	30	10	24
Bonus (among all with salary)										
Zero	23		24	32	6		33	30	10	13
$1,000 to $4,999	9		18	2	11		25	7	10	4
$5,000 to $9,999	18		12	12	39		8	20	10	25
$10,000 or more	50		47	54	44		33	43	70	58
Mean	$13,724		$9,750	$14,280	$15,347		$8,083	$13,817	$12,850	$16,500
Median	$9,750		$9,000	$10,000	$7,750		$2,500	$6,000	$10,000	$10,000
Responses	78		17	41	18		12	30	10	24
Bonus (among only those who actually got bonuses)										
$1,000 to $4,999	12		23	4	12			10		5
$5,000 to $9,999	23		15	18	41			29		29
$10,000 or more	65		62	79	47			62		67
Mean	$17,842		$12,750	$20,911	$16,250			$19,738		$18,857
Median	$10,000		$10,000	$16,500	$9,500			$12,000		$10,000
Responses	60		13	28	17			21		21

A-91

Q7. Project Manager
(Percent of Respondents)

	2021 Single-Family Starts				Number of Employees			
	1 to 10	11 to 25	26 to 99	100+	0 to 2	3 to 4	5 to 9	10 or more
Does Position Exist?								
Yes, full time	29	42	44	43	3	31	32	51
Yes, part time	1		3	3		2		1
No	70	58	53	57	97	67	68	48
Responses	82	36	32	30	32	42	79	85
Salary								
Less then $50,000		46	14	8		8	22	7
$50,000 to $99,999	70	46	79	77		67	65	74
$100,000 or more	30	8	7	15		25	13	19
Mean	$89,084	$62,062	$68,520	$80,608		$79,417	$75,804	$78,820
Median	$75,000	$55,000	$62,700	$75,000		$73,500	$70,000	$73,900
Responses	23	13	14	13		12	23	42
Bonus/Commissions								
Yes	61	77	93	92		67	61	90
No	39	23	7	8		33	39	10
Responses	23	13	14	13		12	23	42
Bonus (among all with salary)								
Zero	39	23	7	8		33	39	10
$1,000 to $4,999	17		7			17	4	10
$5,000 to $9,999	9	23	36	23		17	17	19
$10,000 or more	35	54	50	69		33	39	62
Mean	$10,978	$11,269	$15,786	$21,577		$8,625	$9,391	$17,881
Median	$3,000	$10,000	$8,500	$15,000		$5,000	$5,000	$10,000
Responses	23	13	14	13		12	23	42
Bonus (among only those who actually got bonuses)								
$1,000 to $4,999	29		8				7	11
$5,000 to $9,999	14	30	38	25			29	21
$10,000 or more	57	70	54	75			64	68
Mean	$18,036	$14,650	$17,000	$23,375			$15,429	$19,763
Median	$10,000	$11,000	$10,000	$16,000			$12,750	$10,000
Responses	14	10	13	12			14	38

Q7. Project Manager - continued
(Percent of Respondents)

Benefits	Total	Region				2021 Dollar Volume				
		NE	MW	SO	WE	≤$1M	$1M to $4.9M	$5M to $9.9M	$10M to $14.9M	$15M+
Health Insurance	76		88	73	76		50	74		96
Dental Insurance	50		63	49	41		30	41		71
Vision Program	43		56	41	35		20	37		54
Prescription Program	36		25	43	29		10	26		58
Life Insurance	35		44	30	35		30	26		50
Short Term Disability	25		38	22	24		10	19		38
Long Term Disability	22		25	19	29		*	15		38
Flex Spending	18		19	19	18		*	15		29
401 K	69		94	51	82		50	59		92
Paid Vacation Leave	96		100	97	88		80	100		96
Paid Sick Leave	79		75	78	88		40	93		79
Tuition Reimbursement	22		25	22	18		10	22		21
Training	61		56	68	53		60	59		63
Other	13		6	11	24		10	4		25
Responses	72		16	37	17		10	27		24

A-93

Q7. Project Manager - continued
(Percent of Respondents)

	2021 Single-Family Starts				Number of Employees			
Benefits	1 to 10	11 to 25	26 to 99	100+	0 to 2	3 to 4	5 to 9	10 or more
Health Insurance	57	55	85	100		50	65	88
Dental Insurance	33	27	54	100		20	35	64
Vision Program	33	9	54	77		10	30	57
Prescription Program	19	18	46	77		10	25	48
Life Insurance	38	18	23	69		*	25	48
Short Term Disability	14	18	23	54		10	10	36
Long Term Disability	10	9	31	54		*	10	33
Flex Spending	5	9	15	46		10	10	24
401 K	62	64	69	100		20	55	88
Paid Vacation Leave	95	100	92	100		90	95	98
Paid Sick Leave	71	82	92	77		80	70	83
Tuition Reimbursement	19	27	23	31		*	25	26
Training	62	64	54	69		50	65	62
Other	14	9	15	23		*	*	21
Responses	21	11	13	13		10	20	42

A-94

Q7. Architect
(Percent of Respondents)

	Total	Region				2021 Dollar Volume				
		NE	MW	SO	WE	<$1M	$1M to $4.9M	$5M to $9.9M	$10M to $14.9M	$15M+
Does Position Exist?										
Yes, full time	8	7	10	6	13	5	5	2	4	21
Yes, part time	2		4	2			5	2	2	
No	90	93	86	92	87	95	90	96	96	79
Responses	240	15	49	122	54	19	77	52	28	63
Salary										
Less then $50,000	15									8
$50,000 to $99,999	55									54
$100,000 or more	30									38
Mean	$81,618									$86,908
Median	$67,500									$75,400
Responses	20									13
Bonus/Commissions										
Yes	75									69
No	25									31
Responses	20									13
Bonus (among all with salary)										
Zero	25									31
$1,000 to $4,999	15									15
$5,000 to $9,999	25									23
$10,000 or more	35									31
Mean	$14,835									$9,669
Median	$6,250									$5,000
Responses	20									13
Bonus (among only those who actually got bonuses)										
$1,000 to $4,999	20									
$5,000 to $9,999	33									
$10,000 or more	47									
Mean	$19,779									
Median	$9,000									
Responses	15									

	2021 Single-Family Starts				Number of Employees			
	1 to 10	11 to 25	26 to 99	100+	0 to 2	3 to 4	5 to 9	10 or more
Does Position Exist?								
Yes, full-time	4	6	16	23	3	5	3	19
Yes, part-time	5					5	1	1
No	91	94	84	77	97	90	96	80
Responses	82	36	32	30	32	42	79	85
Salary								
Less then $50,000								6
$50,000 to $99,999								56
$100,000 or more								38
Mean								$87,835
Median								$72,700
Responses								16
Bonus/Commissions								
Yes								75
No								25
Responses								16
Bonus (among all with salary)								
Zero								25
$1,000 to $4,999								13
$5,000 to $9,999								31
$10,000 or more								31
Mean								$14,668
Median								$6,250
Responses								16
Bonus (among only those who actually got bonuses)								
$1,000 to $4,999								17
$5,000 to $9,999								42
$10,000 or more								42
Mean								$19,558
Median								$8,250
Responses								12

A-96

Q7. Architect - continued
(Percent of Respondents)

| | Total | Region | | | | 2021 Dollar Volume | | | | |
		NE	MW	SO	WE	≤$1M	$1M to $4.9M	$5M to $9.9M	$10M to $14.9M	$15M+
Benefits										
Health Insurance	78									92
Dental Insurance	61									67
Vision Program	50									50
Prescription Program	39									50
Life Insurance	50									58
Short Term Disability	44									58
Long Term Disability	39									42
Flex Spending	17									17
401 K	78									92
Paid Vacation Leave	94									92
Paid Sick Leave	83									75
Tuition Reimbursement	22									17
Training	67									67
Other	28									42
Responses	18									12

Q7. Architect - continued
(Percent of Respondents)

Benefits	2021 Single-Family Starts				Number of Employees			
	1 to 10	11 to 25	26 to 99	100+	0 to 2	3 to 4	5 to 9	10 or more
Health Insurance								87
Dental Insurance								67
Vision Program								53
Prescription Program								47
Life Insurance								53
Short Term Disability								47
Long Term Disability								40
Flex Spending								13
401 K								87
Paid Vacation Leave								93
Paid Sick Leave								80
Tuition Reimbursement								27
Training								67
Other								33
Responses								15

A-98

Q7. Estimator
(Percent of Respondents)

	Total	Region				2021 Dollar Volume				
		NE	MW	SO	WE	<$1M	$1M to $4.9M	$5M to $9.9M	$10M to $14.9M	$15M+
Does Position Exist?										
Yes, full time	15	20	16	16	11		4	23	14	29
Yes, part time	1		2	1			1			2
No	84	80	82	83	89	100	95	77	86	70
Responses	240	15	49	122	54	19	77	52	28	63
Salary										
Less then $50,000	14			20				18	18	18
$50,000 to $99,999	83			75				82	82	76
$100,000 or more	3			5						6
Mean	$62,155			$59,992				$60,727		$61,172
Median	$60,000			$56,500				$65,000		$58,000
Responses	35			20				11	11	17
Bonus/Commissions										
Yes	71			65				73		71
No	29			35				27		29
Responses	35			20				11		17
Bonus (among all with salary)										
Zero	29			35				27		29
$1,000 to $4,999	17			15				18		18
$5,000 to $9,999	14			10				18		6
$10,000 or more	40			40				36		47
Mean	$9,295			$7,617				$11,909		$8,373
Median	$6,000			$5,750				$7,500		$6,000
Responses	35			20				11		17
Bonus (among only those who actually got bonuses)										
$1,000 to $4,999	24			23						25
$5,000 to $9,999	20			15						8
$10,000 or more	56			62						67
Mean	$13,014			$11,718						$11,862
Median	$10,000			$10,000						$10,750
Responses	25			13						12

A-99

Q7. Estimator
(Percent of Respondents)

	2021 Single-Family Starts				Number of Employees			
	1 to 10	11 to 25	26 to 99	100+	0 to 2	3 to 4	5 to 9	10 or more
Does Position Exist?								
Yes, full time	11	11	13	47	3	3	5	38
Yes, part time	1		3		3			1
No	88	89	84	53	94	100	95	61
Responses	82	36	32	30	32	42	79	85
Salary								
Less then $50,000				7				10
$50,000 to $99,999				86				87
$100,000 or more				7				3
Mean				$64,093				$63,948
Median				$59,000				$63,500
Responses				14				30
Bonus/Commissions								
Yes				79				77
No				21				23
Responses				14				30
Bonus (among all with salary)								
Zero				21				23
$1,000 to $4,999				7				20
$5,000 to $9,999				14				13
$10,000 or more				57				43
Mean				$10,539				$9,745
Median				$10,000				$6,750
Responses				14				30
Bonus (among only those who actually got bonuses)								
$1,000 to $4,999				9				26
$5,000 to $9,999				18				17
$10,000 or more				73				57
Mean				$13,413				$12,710
Median				$11,500				$10,000
Responses				11				23

A-100

Q7. Estimator - continued
(Percent of Respondents)

	Total	Region				2021 Dollar Volume				
		NE	MW	SO	WE	<1M	$1M to $4.9M	$5M to $9.9M	$10M to $14.9M	$15M+
Benefits										
Health Insurance	88			89				73		100
Dental Insurance	68			68				55		88
Vision Program	53			53				36		71
Prescription Program	47			53				18		71
Life Insurance	50			47				36		65
Short Term Disability	35			26				27		53
Long Term Disability	26			21				9		47
Flex Spending	24			21				9		41
401 K	88			84				82		100
Paid Vacation Leave	100			100				100		100
Paid Sick Leave	79			79				91		76
Tuition Reimbursement	35			26				45		29
Training	56			53				64		59
Other	15			21				*		18
Responses	34			19				11		17

Q7. Estimator - continued
(Percent of Respondents)

| Benefits | 2021 Single-Family Starts | | | | Number of Employees | | | |
	1 to 10	11 to 25	26 to 99	100+	0 to 2	3 to 4	5 to 9	10 or more
Benefits								
Health Insurance				100				90
Dental Insurance				93				73
Vision Program				71				60
Prescription Program				64				50
Life Insurance				71				53
Short Term Disability				64				37
Long Term Disability				50				30
Flex Spending				43				27
401 K				100				90
Paid Vacation Leave				100				100
Paid Sick Leave				71				77
Tuition Reimbursement				36				30
Training				64				57
Other				21				13
Responses				14				30

Q7. Superintendent
(Percent of Respondents)

	Total	Region				2021 Dollar Volume				
		NE	MW	SO	WE	<$1M	$1M to $4.9M	$5M to $9.9M	$10M to $14.9M	$15M+
Does Position Exist?										
Yes, full time	47	40	35	48	57	21	25	42	68	77
Yes, part time	1		4	1			3	2		
No	52	60	60	52	43	79	73	56	32	23
Responses	239	15	48	122	54	19	77	52	28	62
Salary										
Less then $50,000	8		12	9	7		21	5	5	4
$50,000 to $99,999	86		88	86	83		79	95	89	87
$100,000 or more	5			5	10				5	9
Mean	$69,361		$68,109	$67,093	$76,992		$56,545	$71,497	$71,060	$73,545
Median	$65,000		$70,000	$65,000	$75,000		$55,000	$69,250	$65,000	$70,000
Responses	111		17	58	30		19	22	19	47
Bonus/Commissions										
Yes	74		65	74	83		37	86	84	81
No	26		35	26	17		63	14	16	19
Responses	111		17	58	30		19	22	19	47
Bonus (among all with salary)										
Zero	26		35	26	17		63	14	16	19
$1,000 to $4,999	10			10	17		11	9	11	9
$5,000 to $9,999	17		41	14	13		5	27	26	15
$10,000 or more	47		24	50	53		21	50	47	57
Mean	$11,045		$6,088	$11,862	$13,149		$2,816	$12,750	$8,658	$14,669
Median	$8,000		$6,000	$9,500	$10,000		$0	$9,500	$8,000	$10,000
Responses	111		17	58	30		19	22	19	47
Bonus (among only those who actually got bonuses)										
$1,000 to $4,999	13			14	20			11	13	11
$5,000 to $9,999	23		64	19	16			32	31	18
$10,000 or more	63		36	67	64			58	56	71
Mean	$14,951		$9,409	$16,000	$15,779			$14,763	$10,281	$18,144
Median	$10,000		$8,000	$12,000	$10,000			$10,000	$10,000	$15,000
Responses	82		11	43	25			19	16	38

A-103

Q7. Superintendent
(Percent of Respondents)

	2021 Single-Family Starts				Number of Employees			
	1 to 10	11 to 25	26 to 99	100+	0 to 2	3 to 4	5 to 9	10 or more
Does Position Exist?								
Yes, full time	30	44	77	77	6	24	48	74
Yes, part time	2	3			3	5		
No	67	53	23	23	91	71	52	26
Responses	82	36	31	30	32	42	79	84
Salary								
Less then $50,000	4	6	13	4		20	11	5
$50,000 to $99,999	96	88	79	96		80	82	90
$100,000 or more		6	8				8	5
Mean	$65,580	$69,909	$70,648	$68,108		$55,050	$70,757	$71,308
Median	$65,000	$69,250	$65,000	$69,092		$55,000	$65,000	$69,092
Responses	25	16	24	23		10	38	61
Bonus/Commissions								
Yes	52	81	83	87		50	68	82
No	48	19	17	13		50	32	18
Responses	25	16	24	23		10	38	61
Bonus (among all with salary)								
Zero	48	19	17	13		50	32	18
$1,000 to $4,999	8	13	17				5	13
$5,000 to $9,999	16	25	21	17		10	16	20
$10,000 or more	28	44	46	70		40	47	49
Mean	$7,940	$13,719	$9,840	$14,514		$6,050	$11,829	$11,680
Median	$1,000	$7,750	$7,750	$15,500		$2,750	$8,000	$9,000
Responses	25	16	24	23		10	38	61
Bonus (among only those who actually got bonuses)								
$1,000 to $4,999	15	15	20				8	16
$5,000 to $9,999	31	31	25	20			23	24
$10,000 or more	54	54	55	80			69	60
Mean	$15,269	$16,885	$11,807	$16,691			$17,288	$14,249
Median	$10,000	$10,000	$10,000	$16,500			$10,000	$11,000
Responses	13	13	20	20			26	50

A-104

Q7. Superintendent - continued
(Percent of Respondents)

Benefits	Total	Region				2021 Dollar Volume				
		NE	MW	SO	WE	<$1M	$1M to $4.9M	$5M to $9.9M	$10M to $14.9M	$15M+
Health Insurance	79		81	76	86		65	73	82	89
Dental Insurance	49		38	54	54		18	45	53	64
Vision Program	42		31	43	50		24	36	47	52
Prescription Program	38		19	44	36		6	23	41	57
Life Insurance	37		31	39	36		18	32	29	50
Short Term Disability	30		31	28	32		12	27	35	39
Long Term Disability	27		19	24	36		6	23	24	39
Flex Spending	22		19	24	18		6	14	24	34
401 K	65		69	61	79		29	55	76	84
Paid Vacation Leave	98		100	98	96		94	100	100	98
Paid Sick Leave	81		81	80	86		53	86	94	84
Tuition Reimbursement	26		19	24	32		12	23	41	27
Training	54		44	56	57		59	59	53	50
Other	13		6	11	21		12	5	12	20
Responses	104		16	54	28		17	22	17	44

Q7. Superintendent - continued
(Percent of Respondents)

Benefits	2021 Single-Family Starts				Number of Employees				
	1 to 10	11 to 25	26 to 99	100+	0 to 2	3 to 4	5 to 9	10 or more
Benefits								
Health Insurance	68	69	73	96			74	86
Dental Insurance	27	31	50	87			37	63
Vision Program	23	25	45	74			34	53
Prescription Program	14	19	41	70			23	51
Life Insurance	32	19	32	70			23	49
Short Term Disability	14	31	23	61			14	41
Long Term Disability	9	19	32	52			11	39
Flex Spending	9	6	18	52			6	34
401 K	45	56	68	91			54	80
Paid Vacation Leave	95	100	95	100			97	98
Paid Sick Leave	59	94	91	78			74	83
Tuition Reimbursement	23	13	36	39			17	32
Training	64	44	59	57			54	54
Other	18	6	18	22			9	19
Responses	22	16	22	23			35	59

A-106

SALES & MARKETING JOBS

Q7. Sales Manager
(Percent of Respondents)

	Total	Region				2021 Dollar Volume				
		NE	MW	SO	WE	≤$1M	$1M to $4.9M	$5M to $9.9M	$10M to $14.9M	$15M+
Does Position Exist?										
Yes, full time	15	13	14	16	15		6	6	4	40
Yes, part time	1			2	2		1	1	4	
No	84	87	86	83	83	100	94	92	82	60
Responses	240	15	49	122	54	19	77	52	28	63
Is it filled by a person(s) with experience in construction trades?										
Always	47			42						48
Sometimes	31			32						33
Never/Almost never	22			26						19
Responses	32			19						21
Salary										
Less then $50,000	33			35						17
$50,000 to $99,999	36			30						42
$100,000 or more	31			35						42
Mean	$69,133			$67,850						$82,333
Median	$62,500			$70,000						$82,500
Responses	36			20						24
Bonus/Commissions										
Yes	86			90						88
No	14			10						13
Responses	36			20						24
Bonus (among all with salary)										
Zero	14			10						13
$1 to $999	3			5						4
$1,000 to $4,999	3									4
$5,000 to $9,999	14			5						13
$10,000 or more	67			80						67
Mean	$46,847			$56,703						$51,312
Median	$30,000			$50,000						$30,500
Responses	36			20						24

SALES & MARKETING JOBS
Q7. Sales Manager
(Percent of Respondents)

	2021 Single-Family Starts				Number of Employees			
	1 to 10	11 to 25	26 to 99	100+	0 to 2	3 to 4	5 to 9	10 or more
Does Position Exist?								
Yes, full time	2	11	31	50	3	2	13	29
Yes, part time	1	3						2
No	96	86	69	50	97	98	87	68
Responses	82	36	32	30	32	42	79	85
Is it filled by a person(s) with experience in construction trades?								
Always				54				59
Sometimes				31				32
Never/Almost never				15				9
Responses				13				22
Salary								
Less then $50,000			40	13			70	17
$50,000 to $99,999			30	47			20	42
$100,000 or more			30	40			10	42
Mean			$61,580	$87,547			$42,280	$84,000
Median			$50,000	$85,000			$41,000	$82,500
Responses			10	15			10	24
Bonus/Commissions								
Yes			90	100			80	92
No			10				20	8
Responses			10	15			10	24
Bonus (among all with salary)								
Zero			10				20	8
$1 to $999				7				4
$1,000 to $4,999				7				4
$5,000 to $9,999				20			20	13
$10,000 or more			90	67			60	71
Mean			$71,223	$43,417			$51,500	$45,062
Median			$50,000	$31,000			$27,500	$30,000
Responses			10	15			10	24

A-108

Q7. Sales Manager - continued
(Percent of Respondents)

	Total	Region				2021 Dollar Volume				
		NE	MW	SO	WE	<$1M	$1M to $4.9M	$5M to $9.9M	$10M to $14.9M	$15M+
Bonus (among only those who actually got bonuses)										
$1 to $999	3			6						5
$1,000 to $4,999	3									5
$5,000 to $9,999	16			6						14
$10,000 or more	77			89						76
Mean	$54,403			$63,003						$58,642
Median	$40,000			$62,500						$50,000
Responses	31			18						21
Benefits										
Health Insurance	91			94						96
Dental Insurance	73			72						83
Vision Program	58			56						65
Prescription Program	48			61						61
Life Insurance	48			44						61
Short Term Disability	30			33						43
Long Term Disability	30			28						43
Flex Spending	27			28						39
401 K	73			61						83
Paid Vacation Leave	100			100						100
Paid Sick Leave	82			89						83
Tuition Reimbursement	30			28						30
Training	36			33						35
Other	15			22						17
Responses	33			18						23

Q7. Model Home Host
(Percent of Respondents)

	Total	Region				2021 Dollar Volume				
		NE	MW	SO	WE	<$1M	$1M to $4.9M	$5M to $9.9M	$10M to $14.9M	$15M+
Does Position Exist?										
Yes, full time	3		2	3	2				4	8
Yes, part time	3		8	2						10
No	95	100	90	95	98	100	100	100	96	83
Responses	240	15	49	122	54	19	77	52	28	63

A-109

Q7. Sales Manager – continued
(Percent of Respondents)

	2021 Single-Family Starts				Number of Employees			
	1 to 10	11 to 25	26 to 99	100+	0 to 2	3 to 4	5 to 9	10 or more
Bonus (among only those who actually got bonuses)								
$1 to $999				7				5
$1,000 to $4,999				7				5
$5,000 to $9,999				20				14
$10,000 or more				67				77
Mean				$43,417				$49,158
Median				$31,000				$30,500
Responses				15				22
Benefits								
Health Insurance				100				96
Dental Insurance				93				80
Vision Program				80				64
Prescription Program				73				56
Life Insurance				67				56
Short Term Disability				53				40
Long Term Disability				53				40
Flex Spending				47				36
401 K				100				80
Paid Vacation Leave				100				100
Paid Sick Leave				80				80
Tuition Reimbursement				40				28
Training				47				40
Other				27				16
Responses				15				25

Q7. Model Home Host
(Percent of Respondents)

	2021 Single-Family Starts				Number of Employees			
	1 to 10	11 to 25	26 to 99	100+	0 to 2	3 to 4	5 to 9	10 or more
Does Position Exist?								
Yes, full time			6	13				7
Yes, part time			3	7				7
No	100	100	91	80	100	100	100	86
Responses	82	36	32	30	32	42	79	85

A-110

Q7. Salesperson
(Percent of Respondents)

	Total	Region				2021 Dollar Volume				
		NE	MW	SO	WE	<$1M	$1M to $4.9M	$5M to $9.9M	$10M to $14.9M	$15M+
Does Position Exist?										
Yes, full time	16	20	16	17	13	5	5	6	11	44
Yes, part time	1	7	2	1			4			
No	83	73	82	82	87	95	91	94	89	56
Responses	240	15	49	122	54	19	77	52	28	63
Salary										
Less then $50,000	70			80						78
$50,000 to $99,999	19			15						11
$100,000 or more	11			5						11
Mean	$36,199			$28,416						$30,355
Median	$25,500			$25,250						$24,000
Responses	37			20						27
Bonus/Commissions										
Yes	78			90						85
No	22			10						15
Responses	37			20						27
Bonus (among all with salary)										
Zero	22			10						15
$10,000 or more	78			90						85
Mean	$95,928			$94,750						$114,946
Median	$84,000			$90,000						$100,000
Responses	37			20						27
Bonus (among only those who actually got bonuses)										
$10,000 or more	100			100						100
Mean	$122,391			$105,278						$134,936
Median	$110,000			$100,000						$120,000
Responses	29			18						23

A-111

Q7. Salesperson
(Percent of Respondents)

	2021 Single-Family Starts				Number of Employees			
	1 to 10	11 to 25	26 to 99	100+	0 to 2	3 to 4	5 to 9	10 or more
Does Position Exist?								
Yes, full time	2	14	13	67	3		9	36
Yes, part time	1	3					3	1
No	96	83	88	33	97	100	89	62
Responses	82	36	32	30	32	42	79	85
Salary								
Less then $50,000				75				73
$50,000 to $99,999				10				13
$100,000 or more				15				13
Mean				$33,726				$35,469
Median				$24,750				$25,250
Responses				20				30
Bonus/Commissions								
Yes				85				83
No				15				17
Responses				20				30
Bonus (among all with salary)								
Zero				15				17
$10,000 or more				85				83
Mean				$108,450				$107,618
Median				$92,500				$92,500
Responses				20				30
Bonus (among only those who actually got bonuses)								
$10,000 or more				100				100
Mean				$127,588				$129,142
Median				$120,000				$110,000
Responses				17				25

A-112

Q7. Salesperson - continued
(Percent of Respondents)

| | Total | Region | | | | 2021 Dollar Volume | | | | |
		NE	MW	SO	WE	<$1M	$1M to $4.9M	$5M to $9.9M	$10M to $14.9M	$15M+
Benefits										
Health Insurance	81			89						92
Dental Insurance	67			74						84
Vision Program	56			58						68
Prescription Program	56			68						68
Life Insurance	56			53						68
Short Term Disability	47			53						60
Long Term Disability	47			47						60
Flex Spending	36			37						44
401 K	78			79						88
Paid Vacation Leave	92			100						96
Paid Sick Leave	64			84						68
Tuition Reimbursement	22			21						24
Training	50			53						48
Other	8			11						12
Responses	36			19						25

A-113

Q7. Salesperson - continued
(Percent of Respondents)

Benefits	2021 Single-Family Starts				Number of Employees			
	1 to 10	11 to 25	26 to 99	100+	0 to 2	3 to 4	5 to 9	10 or more
Health Insurance				94				93
Dental Insurance				94				79
Vision Program				78				66
Prescription Program				72				66
Life Insurance				83				66
Short Term Disability				72				55
Long Term Disability				67				55
Flex Spending				50				45
401 K				89				83
Paid Vacation Leave				94				97
Paid Sick Leave				67				66
Tuition Reimbursement				39				28
Training				61				48
Other				11				10
Responses				18				29

A-114

Q7. Design Center Manager
(Percent of Respondents)

	Total	Region				2021 Dollar Volume				
		NE	MW	SO	WE	<$1M	$1M to $4.9M	$5M to $9.9M	$10M to $14.9M	$15M+
Does Position Exist?										
Yes, full time	8		8	10	6		3	2	4	24
Yes, part time	*			1			1			
No	92	100	92	89	94	100	96	98	96	76
Responses	240	15	49	122	54	19	77	52	28	63
Salary										
$50,000 to $99,999	100			100						100
Mean	$65,819			$66,636						$66,936
Median	$65,850			$65,000						$68,350
Responses	16			11						14
Bonus/Commissions										
Yes	69			64						71
No	31			36						29
Responses	16			11						14
Bonus (among all with salary)										
Zero	31			36						29
$5,000 to $9,999	19			9						21
$10,000 or more	50			55						50
Mean	$17,630			$20,223						$15,723
Median	$9,000			$10,000						$9,000
Responses	16			11						14
Bonus (among only those who actually got bonuses)										
$5,000 to $9,999	27									30
$10,000 or more	73									70
Mean	$25,643									$22,013
Median	$11,627									$10,814
Responses	11									10

A-115

Q7. Design Center Manager
(Percent of Respondents)

	2021 Single-Family Starts				Number of Employees			
	1 to 10	11 to 25	26 to 99	100+	0 to 2	3 to 4	5 to 9	10 or more
Does Position Exist?								
Yes, full time	2	6	3	40		2	3	19
Yes, part time								1
No	98	94	97	60	100	98	97	80
Responses	82	36	32	30	32	42	79	85
Salary								
$50,000 to $99,999				100				100
Mean				$67,392				$66,936
Median				$68,350				$68,350
Responses				12				14
Bonus/Commissions								
Yes				75				71
No				25				29
Responses				12				14
Bonus (among all with salary)								
Zero				25				29
$5,000 to $9,999				25				21
$10,000 or more				50				50
Mean				$17,375				$15,723
Median				$9,000				$9,000
Responses				12				14
Bonus (among only those who actually got bonuses)								
$5,000 to $9,999				30				30
$10,000 or more				70				70
Mean				$22,013				$22,013
Median				$10,814				$10,814
Responses				10				10

Q7. Design Center Manager - continued
(Percent of Respondents)

Benefits	Total	Region				2021 Dollar Volume				
		NE	MW	SO	WE	<$1M	$1M to $4.9M	$5M to $9.9M	$10M to $14.9M	$15M+
Benefits										
Health Insurance	93			90						100
Dental Insurance	87			90						92
Vision Program	67			70						77
Prescription Program	67			80						77
Life Insurance	67			60						77
Short Term Disability	60			50						69
Long Term Disability	60			50						69
Flex Spending	53			50						62
401 K	93			90						100
Paid Vacation Leave	93			100						92
Paid Sick Leave	80			90						77
Tuition Reimbursement	53			50						54
Training	80			80						77
Other	33			30						31
Responses	15			10						13

A-117

Q7. Design Center Manager - continued
(Percent of Respondents)

Benefits	2021 Single-Family Starts					Number of Employees			
	1 to 10	11 to 25	26 to 99	100+	0 to 2	3 to 4	5 to 9	10 or more
Health Insurance				100				100
Dental Insurance				100				92
Vision Program				82				77
Prescription Program				82				77
Life Insurance				82				77
Short Term Disability				73				69
Long Term Disability				73				69
Flex Spending				64				62
401 K				100				100
Paid Vacation Leave				91				92
Paid Sick Leave				73				77
Tuition Reimbursement				64				54
Training				82				77
Other				27				31
Responses				11				13

A-118

Q7. Selections Coordinator
(Percent of Respondents)

	Total	Region				2021 Dollar Volume				
		NE	MW	SO	WE	<$1M	$1M to $4.9M	$5M to $9.9M	$10M to $14.9M	$15M+
Does Position Exist?										
Yes, full time	14	13	10	17	11		5	17	11	29
Yes, part time	1			2			1			2
No	85	87	90	81	89	100	94	83	89	70
Responses	240	15	49	122	54	19	77	52	28	63
Salary										
Less then $50,000	42			43						41
$50,000 to $99,999	55			52						53
$100,000 or more	3			5						6
Mean	$53,930			$55,083						$54,879
Median	$50,000			$50,000						$50,000
Responses	33			21						17
Bonus/Commissions										
Yes	73			62						76
No	27			38						24
Responses	33			21						17
Bonus (among all with salary)										
Zero	27			38						24
$1,000 to $4,999	30			24						35
$5,000 to $9,999	12			10						6
$10,000 or more	30			29						35
Mean	$8,585			$7,705						$7,088
Median	$4,000			$3,000						$4,000
Responses	33			21						17
Bonus (among only those who actually got bonuses)										
$1,000 to $4,999	42			38						46
$5,000 to $9,999	17			15						8
$10,000 or more	42			46						46
Mean	$11,804			$12,446						$9,269
Median	$5,250			$9,000						$5,500
Responses	24			13						13

Q7. Selections Coordinator
(Percent of Respondents)

	2021 Single-Family Starts				Number of Employees			
	1 to 10	11 to 25	26 to 99	100+	0 to 2	3 to 4	5 to 9	10 or more
Does Position Exist?								
Yes, full time	9	8	13	47	3	2	6	32
Yes, part time							1	1
No	91	92	88	53	97	98	92	67
Responses	82	36	32	30	32	42	79	85
Salary								
Less then $50,000				43				38
$50,000 to $99,999				50				58
$100,000 or more				7				4
Mean				$56,246				$55,450
Median				$50,000				$50,000
Responses				14				26
Bonus/Commissions								
Yes				79				81
No				21				19
Responses				14				26
Bonus (among all with salary)								
Zero				21				19
$1,000 to $4,999				29				35
$5,000 to $9,999				14				15
$10,000 or more				36				31
Mean				$7,929				$8,473
Median				$4,750				$4,400
Responses				14				26
Bonus (among only those who actually got bonuses)								
$1,000 to $4,999				36				43
$5,000 to $9,999				18				19
$10,000 or more				45				38
Mean				$10,091				$10,490
Median				$9,000				$5,000
Responses				11				21

Q7. *Selections Coordinator - continued*
(Percent of Respondents)

| | Total | Region | | | | 2021 Dollar Volume | | | | |
		NE	MW	SO	WE	<1M	$1M to $4.9M	$5M to $9.9M	$10M to $14.9M	$15M+
Benefits										
Health Insurance	77			74						94
Dental Insurance	65			58						88
Vision Program	52			42						63
Prescription Program	39			42						63
Life Insurance	45			47						63
Short Term Disability	32			32						56
Long Term Disability	26			21						44
Flex Spending	23			26						31
401 K	74			63						94
Paid Vacation Leave	94			100						88
Paid Sick Leave	68			68						69
Tuition Reimbursement	26			26						25
Training	55			58						50
Other	13			16						19
Responses	31			19						16

Q7. Selections Coordinator - continued
(Percent of Respondents)

Benefits	2021 Single-Family Starts				Number of Employees			
	1 to 10	11 to 25	26 to 99	100+	0 to 2	3 to 4	5 to 9	10 or more
Benefits								
Health Insurance				100				83
Dental Insurance				100				79
Vision Program				77				58
Prescription Program				69				46
Life Insurance				69				54
Short Term Disability				69				42
Long Term Disability				54				33
Flex Spending				38				25
401 K				100				88
Paid Vacation Leave				92				92
Paid Sick Leave				69				71
Tuition Reimbursement				31				29
Training				46				54
Other				15				17
Responses				13				24

Q7. *Customer service Manager*
(Percent of Respondents)

	Total	Region				2021 Dollar Volume				
		NE	MW	SO	WE	<$1M	$1M to $4.9M	$5M to $9.9M	$10M to $14.9M	$15M+
Does Position Exist?										
Yes, full time	5	7	4	7	2		1	2	4	14
Yes, part time	1				2			2		2
No	94	93	96	93	96	100	99	96	96	84
Responses	240	15	49	122	54	19	77	52	28	63
Salary										
Less then $50,000	64									
$50,000 to $99,999	36									
Mean	$47,109									
Median	$41,600									
Responses	11									
Bonus/Commissions										
Yes	55									
No	45									
Responses	11									
Bonus (among all with salary)										
Zero	45									
$1,000 to $4,999	9									
$5,000 to $9,999	27									
$10,000 or more	18									
Mean	$5,309									
Median	$4,000									
Responses	11									

A-123

Q7. Customer service Manager
(Percent of Respondents)

	2021 Single-Family Starts				Number of Employees			
	1 to 10	11 to 25	26 to 99	100+	0 to 2	3 to 4	5 to 9	10 or more
Does Position Exist?								
Yes, full time	1	3	6	27			3	12
Yes, part time								2
No	99	97	94	73	100	100	97	86
Responses	82	36	32	30	32	42	79	85
Salary								
Less then $50,000								
$50,000 to $99,999								
Mean								
Median								
Responses								
Bonus/Commissions								
Yes								
No								
Responses								
Bonus (among all with salary)								
Zero								
$1,000 to $4,999								
$5,000 to $9,999								
$10,000 or more								
Mean								
Median								
Responses								

Q7. Customer service Manager - continued
(Percent of Respondents)

| Benefits | Total | Region | | | | 2021 Dollar Volume | | | | |
		NE	MW	SO	WE	<$1M	$1M to $4.9M	$5M to $9.9M	$10M to $14.9M	$15M+
Health Insurance	91									
Dental Insurance	91									
Vision Program	91									
Prescription Program	64									
Life Insurance	36									
Short Term Disability	36									
Long Term Disability	36									
Flex Spending	36									
401 K	82									
Paid Vacation Leave	91									
Paid Sick Leave	82									
Tuition Reimbursement	27									
Training	55									
Other	27									
Responses	11									

Q7. Customer service Manager - continued
(Percent of Respondents)

Benefits	2021 Single-Family Starts				Number of Employees			
	1 to 10	11 to 25	26 to 99	100+	0 to 2	3 to 4	5 to 9	10 or more
Health Insurance								
Dental Insurance								
Vision Program								
Prescription Program								
Life Insurance								
Short Term Disability								
Long Term Disability								
Flex Spending								
401 K								
Paid Vacation Leave								
Paid Sick Leave								
Tuition Reimbursement								
Training								
Other								
Responses								

A-126

Average Total Compensation for 39 Jobs

	Percent Who Have Full-Time Position (A)	Average Salary (B)	Average Bonus (among all with salary) (C)	Average Total Compensation (D=A+B)	Average Bonus (among only those who acutally got bonuses) (E)
EXECUTIVE JOBS					
President/CEO	94	$150,426	$68,432	$218,858	$124,963
VP of Construction	50	$113,007	$48,355	$161,362	$63,234
CFO/Head of Finance	25	$118,159	$32,871	$151,030	$50,801
CIO/Head of IT	4				
OPERATIONS JOBS					
Head/Director of Purchasing	21	$86,601	$16,923	$103,524	$21,697
Head/Director of Land Acquisition	12	$127,210	$54,418	$181,628	$64,312
Head/Director of Production	13	$92,406	$27,824	$120,230	$33,175
Head/Director of Development and	2				
Head/Director of Sales & Marketing	21	$101,913	$44,377	$146,290	$52,773
FINANCE JOBS					
Controller	19	$92,182	$20,344	$112,526	$23,643
Payroll Manager	7	$64,763	$6,339	$71,102	
Staff Accountant	13	$67,488	$9,233	$76,721	$12,590
Bookkeeper	29	$49,693	$5,858	$55,551	$9,665
HUMAN RESOURCES					
Director of Human Resources	5	$89,567	$17,008	$106,575	
Recruiter	*				
In-house legal counsel	2				
IT JOBS					
Director of IT	3				
Network Engineer	*				
Web Design Specialist	1				
ADMINISTRATIVE JOBS					
Executive Assistant	11	$49,394	$4,227	$53,621	$8,454
Office Manager	14	$58,348	$6,220	$64,568	$9,774
Administrative Assistant	10	$44,956	$2,708	$47,664	$4,642
Receptionist	10	$35,971	$3,791	$39,762	$5,249
Settlement Coordinator	8	$56,838	$8,915	$65,753	$11,463
PRODUCTION JOBS					
Production Manager	24	$80,842	$18,050	$98,892	$22,668
Land Manager	4				
Purchasing Manager	9	$69,567	$7,476	$77,043	$12,077
Home Services/Warranty Manager	20	$64,239	$8,818	$73,057	$11,841
Contract Manager	4				
Project Manager	34	$78,294	$13,724	$92,018	$17,842
Architect	8	$81,618	$14,835	$96,453	$19,779
Estimator	15	$62,155	$9,295	$71,450	$13,014
Superintendent	47	$69,361	$11,045	$80,406	$14,951
SALES & MARKETING JOBS					
Sales Manager	15	$69,133	$46,847	$115,980	$54,403
Model Home Host	3				
Salesperson	16	$36,199	$95,928	$132,127	$122,391
Design Center Manager	8	$65,819	$17,630	$83,449	$25,643
Selections Coordinator	14	$53,930	$8,585	$62,515	$11,804
Customer Service Manager	5	$47,109	$5,309	$52,418	

* Less than 0.5%.   B-1

Appendix C

Compensation and Benefits by Job Category

Executive Jobs
(Percent of Respondents)

	President/CEO	VP of Construction	CFO/Head of Finance	CIO/Head of IT
Does this Position Exist?				
Yes, full time	94	50	25	4
Yes, part time	3	2	7	1
No	3	48	68	95
Responses	*240*	*239*	*240*	*239*
Is it filled by a person(s) with experience in construction trades?				
Always	90	92		
Sometimes	6	7		
Never/Almost never	4	1		
Responses	*216*	*111*		
Salary				
Less then $50,000	6	4		
$50,000 to $99,999	27	34	33	
$100,000 or more	67	62	67	
Mean	$150,426	$113,007	$118,159	
Responses	*210*	*102*	*51*	
Bonus/Commissions				
Yes	55	76	65	
No	45	24	35	
Responses	*210*	*102*	*51*	
Bonus (among all with salary)				
Zero	45	24	35	
$1,000 to $4,999	1	3	2	
$5,000 to $9,999	4	5	6	
$10,000 or more	49	69	57	
Mean	$68,432	$48,355	$32,871	
Responses	*210*	*102*	*51*	
Bonus (among only those who actually got bonuses)				
$1,000 to $4,999	3	4	3	
$5,000 to $9,999	8	6	9	
$10,000 or more	90	90	88	
Mean	$124,963	$63,234	$50,801	
Responses	*115*	*78*	*33*	
Benefits				
Health Insurance	74	77	89	
Dental Insurance	42	51	72	
Vision Program	33	43	57	
Prescription Program	31	48	51	
Life Insurance	44	42	70	
Short Term Disability	20	24	34	
Long Term Disability	22	24	38	
Flex Spending	18	26	36	
401 K	63	72	74	
Paid Vacation Leave	90	95	98	
Paid Sick Leave	72	86	85	
Tuition Reimbursement	16	19	21	
Training	44	49	53	
Other	10	11	21	
Responses	*202*	*97*	*47*	

C-1

Operations Jobs
(Percent of Respondents)

	Head/Director of Purchasing	Head/Director of Land Acquisition	Head/Director of Production	Head/Director of Development and Training	Head/Director of Sales & Marketing
Does this Position Exist?					
Yes, full time	21	12	13	2	21
Yes, part time	1	1	1	*	5
No	78	87	86	98	73
Responses	*240*	*240*	*239*	*240*	*240*
Is it filled by person(s) with experience in construction trades?					
Always	79	73	86		48
Sometimes	17	27	14		31
Never/Almost never	4				20
Responses	*47*	*26*	*22*		*54*
Salary					
Less then $50,000	6	4	10		5
$50,000 to $99,999	64	19	52		41
$100,000 or more	30	77	39		55
Mean	$86,601	$127,210	$92,406		$101,913
Responses	*50*	*26*	*31*		*44*
Bonus/Commissions					
Yes	78	85	84		84
No	22	15	16		16
Responses	*50*	*26*	*31*		*44*
Bonus (among all with salary)					
Zero	22	15	16		16
$1,000 to $4,999	8	3	3		2
$5,000 to $9,999	16	4	6		9
$10,000 or more	54	81	74		73
Mean	$16,923	$54,418	$27,824		$44,377
Responses	*50*	*26*	*31*		*44*
Bonus (among only those who actually got bonuses)					
$1,000 to $4,999	10		4		3
$5,000 to $9,999	21	5	8		11
$10,000 or more	69	95	88		86
Mean	$21,697	$64,312	$33,175		$52,773
Responses	*39*	*22*	*26*		*37*
Benefits					
Health Insurance	88	92	84		89
Dental Insurance	69	88	61		77
Vision Program	59	65	58		61
Prescription Program	51	62	52		59
Life Insurance	53	69	39		61
Short Term Disability	41	58	29		43
Long Term Disability	43	62	29		41
Flex Spending	31	46	39		41
401 K	84	92	90		80
Paid Vacation Leave	96	100	100		95
Paid Sick Leave	76	85	84		86
Tuition Reimbursement	27	42	26		32
Training	49	58	52		64
Other	14	27	16		25
Responses	*49*	*22*	*31*		*44*

* Less than 0.5%.

C-2

Finance Jobs

(Percent of Respondents)

	Controller	Payroll Manager	Staff Accountant	Bookkeeper
Does this Position Exist?				
Yes, full time	19	7	13	29
Yes, part time	3	5	3	16
No	78	89	84	55
Responses	*240*	*240*	*240*	*240*
Salary				
Less then $50,000		21	10	50
$50,000 to $99,999	72	71	83	50
$100,000 or more	28	7	7	
Mean	$92,182	$64,763	$67,488	$49,693
Responses	*43*	*14*	*30*	*66*
Bonus/Commissions				
Yes	86	50	73	61
No	14	50	27	39
Responses	*43*	*14*	*30*	*66*
Bonus (among all with salary)				
Zero	14	50	27	39
$1,000 to $4,999	2	14	20	24
$5,000 to $9,999	16		23	15
$10,000 or more	67	36	30	21
Mean	$20,344	$6,339	$9,233	$5,858
Responses	*43*	*14*	*30*	*66*
Bonus (among only those who actually got bonuses)				
$1,000 to $4,999	3		27	40
$5,000 to $9,999	19		32	25
$10,000 or more	78		41	35
Mean	$23,643		$12,590	$9,665
Responses	*37*		*22*	*40*
Benefits				
Health Insurance	90	86	86	73
Dental Insurance	76	64	83	47
Vision Program	57	57	66	39
Prescription Program	60	64	52	34
Life Insurance	57	43	62	37
Short Term Disability	45	29	45	21
Long Term Disability	43	29	48	23
Flex Spending	36	36	41	16
401 K	88	86	79	73
Paid Vacation Leave	98	100	100	95
Paid Sick Leave	83	79	86	77
Tuition Reimbursement	29	14	38	19
Training	43	50	59	45
Other	10	14	10	3
Responses	*42*	*14*	*29*	*62*

C-3

Human Resources Jobs

(Percent of Respondents)

	Director of Human Resources	Recruiter	In-house legal counsel
Does this Position Exist?			
Yes, full time	5	*	2
Yes, part time	2	1	*
No	93	99	98
Responses	*240*	*240*	*240*
Salary			
Less then $50,000			
$50,000 to $99,999	75		
$100,000 or more	25		
Mean	$89,567		
Responses	*12*		
Bonus/Commissions			
Yes	75		
No	25		
Responses	*12*		
Bonus (among all with salary)			
Zero	25		
$1,000 to $4,999	17		
$5,000 to $9,999	8		
$10,000 or more	50		
Mean	$17,008		
Responses	*12*		
Bonus (among only those who actually got bonuses)			
$1,000 to $4,999			
$5,000 to $9,999			
$10,000 or more			
Mean			
Responses			
Benefits			
Health Insurance	100		
Dental Insurance	83		
Vision Program	58		
Prescription Program	75		
Life Insurance	83		
Short Term Disability	50		
Long Term Disability	67		
Flex Spending	50		
401 K	92		
Paid Vacation Leave	100		
Paid Sick Leave	92		
Tuition Reimbursement	42		
Training	58		
Other	8		
Responses	*12*		

* Less than 0.5%.

C-4

IT Jobs

(Percent of Respondents)

	Director of IT	Network Engineer	Web Design Specialist
Does this Position Exist?			
Yes, full time	3	*	1
Yes, part time	1	*	4
No	95	99	95
Responses	*240*	*240*	*240*
Salary			
Less then $50,000			
$50,000 to $99,999			
$100,000 or more			
Mean			
Responses			
Bonus/Commissions			
Yes			
No			
Responses			
Bonus (among all with salary)			
Zero			
$1,000 to $4,999			
$5,000 to $9,999			
$10,000 or more			
Mean			
Responses			
Bonus (among only those who actually got bonuses)			
$1,000 to $4,999			
$5,000 to $9,999			
$10,000 or more			
Mean			
Responses			
Benefits			
Health Insurance			
Dental Insurance			
Vision Program			
Prescription Program			
Life Insurance			
Short Term Disability			
Long Term Disability			
Flex Spending			
401 K			
Paid Vacation Leave			
Paid Sick Leave			
Tuition Reimbursement			
Training			
Other			
Responses			

* Less than 0.5%.

C-5

Administrative Jobs

(Percent of Respondents)

	Executive Assistant	Office Manager	Administrative Assistant	Receptionist	Settlement Coordinator
Does this Position Exist?					
Yes, full time	11	14	10	10	8
Yes, part time	1	4	6	4	*
No	88	82	84	86	92
Responses	*240*	*240*	*240*	*239*	*240*
Salary					
Less then $50,000	42	30	75	100	22
$50,000 to $99,999	58	67	25		78
$100,000 or more		3			
Mean	$49,394	$58,348	$44,956	$35,971	$56,838
Responses	*26*	*33*	*24*	*18*	*18*
Bonus/Commissions					
Yes	50	64	58	72	78
No	50	36	42	28	22
Responses	*26*	*33*	*24*	*18*	*18*
Bonus (among all with salary)					
Zero	50	36	42	28	22
$1 to $999			4		
$1,000 to $4,999	23	15	25	33	22
$5,000 to $9,999	8	15	21	28	22
$10,000 or more	19	33	8	11	33
Mean	$4,227	$6,220	$2,708	$3,791	$8,915
Responses	*26*	*33*	*24*	*18*	*18*
Bonus (among only those who actually got bonuses)					
$1 to $999			7		
$1,000 to $4,999	46	24	43	46	29
$5,000 to $9,999	15	24	36	38	29
$10,000 or more	38	52	14	15	43
Mean	$8,454	$9,774	$4,642	$5,249	$11,463
Responses	*13*	*21*	*14*	*13*	*14*
Benefits					
Health Insurance	79	75	74	82	82
Dental Insurance	54	56	48	88	65
Vision Program	50	50	48	65	47
Prescription Program	33	47	35	59	53
Life Insurance	46	44	26	53	59
Short Term Disability	38	28	26	47	53
Long Term Disability	42	38	30	41	47
Flex Spending	42	28	17	24	35
401 K	75	72	70	88	82
Paid Vacation Leave	96	94	100	100	100
Paid Sick Leave	75	72	87	94	82
Tuition Reimbursement	38	16	22	29	41
Training	67	44	30	53	65
Other	17	6	*	6	12
Responses	*24*	*32*	*23*	*17*	*17*

C-6

Production Jobs
(Percent of Respondents)

	Production Manager	Land Manager	Purchasing Manager	Home Services/ Warranty Manager	Contract Manager	Project Manager	Architect	Estimator	Superintendent
Does this Position Exist?									
Yes, full time	24	4	9	20	4	34	8	15	47
Yes, part time	*	*		3		1	2	1	1
No	76	95	91	77	96	65	90	84	52
Responses	*239*	*239*	*239*	*240*	*240*	*240*	*240*	*240*	*239*
Is it filled by a person(s) with experience in construction trades?									
Always	90		76						
Sometimes	10		12						
Never/Almost never			12						
Responses	*51*		*17*						
Salary									
Less then $50,000	4		5	21		12	15	14	8
$50,000 to $99,999	70		86	72		69	55	83	86
$100,000 or more	26		10	6		19	30	3	5
Mean	$80,842		$69,567	$64,239		$78,294	$81,618	$62,155	$69,361
Responses	*54*		*21*	*47*		*78*	*20*	*35*	*111*
Bonus/Commissions									
Yes	80		62	74		77	75	71	74
No	20		38	26		23	25	29	26
Responses	*54*		*21*	*47*		*78*	*20*	*35*	*111*
Bonus (among all with salary)									
Zero	20		38	26		23	25	29	26
$1,000 to $4,999	4		14	9		9	15	17	10
$5,000 to $9,999	22		14	23		18	25	14	17
$10,000 or more	54		33	43		50	35	40	47
Mean	$18,050		$7,476	$8,818		$13,724	$14,835	$9,295	$11,045
Responses	*54*		*21*	*47*		*78*	*20*	*35*	*111*
Bonus (among only those who actually got bonuses)									
$1,000 to $4,999	5		23	11		12	20	24	13
$5,000 to $9,999	28		23	31		23	33	20	23
$10,000 or more	67		54	57		65	47	56	63
Mean	$22,668		$12,077	$11,841		$17,842	$19,779	$13,014	$14,951
Responses	*43*		*13*	*35*		*60*	*15*	*25*	*82*
Benefits									
Health Insurance	81		84	89		76	78	88	79
Dental Insurance	48		79	64		50	61	68	49
Vision Program	42		84	55		43	50	53	42
Prescription Program	40		68	55		36	39	47	38
Life Insurance	29		42	53		35	50	50	37
Short Term Disability	31		47	34		25	44	35	30
Long Term Disability	33		47	40		22	39	26	27
Flex Spending	27		37	34		18	17	24	22
401 K	69		84	87		69	78	88	65
Paid Vacation Leave	92		100	100		96	94	100	98
Paid Sick Leave	75		84	85		79	83	79	81
Tuition Reimbursement	19		21	34		22	22	35	26
Training	52		53	47		61	67	56	54
Other	10		11	13		13	28	15	13
Responses	*52*		*19*	*47*		*72*	*18*	*34*	*104*

* Less than 0.5%.

C-7

Sales & Marketing Jobs
(Percent of Respondents)

	Sales Manager	Model Home Host	Salesperson	Design Center Manager	Selections Coordinator	Customer Service Manager
Does this Position Exist?						
Yes, full time	15	3	16	8	14	5
Yes, part time	1	3	1	*	1	1
No	84	95	83	92	85	94
Responses	*240*	*240*	*240*	*240*	*240*	*240*
Is it filled by a person(s) with experience in construction trades?						
Always	47					
Sometimes	31					
Never/Almost never	22					
Responses	*32*					
Salary						
Less then $50,000	33		70		42	64
$50,000 to $99,999	36		19	100	55	36
$100,000 or more	31		11		3	
Mean	$69,133		$36,199	$65,819	$53,930	$47,109
Responses	*36*		*37*	*16*	*33*	*11*
Bonus/Commissions						
Yes	86		78	69	73	55
No	14		22	31	27	45
Responses	*36*		*37*	*16*	*33*	*11*
Bonus (among all with salary)						
Zero	14		22	31	27	45
$1 to $999	3					
$1,000 to $4,999	3				30	9
$5,000 to $9,999	14			19	12	27
$10,000 or more	67		78	50	30	18
Mean	$46,847		$95,928	$17,630	$8,585	$5,309
Responses	*36*		*37*	*16*	*33*	*11*
Bonus (among only those who actually got bonuses)						
$1 to $999	3					
$1,000 to $4,999	3				42	
$5,000 to $9,999	16			27	17	
$10,000 or more	77		100	73	42	
Mean	$54,403		$122,391	$25,643	$11,804	
Responses	*31*		*29*	*11*	*24*	
Benefits						
Health Insurance	91		81	93	77	91
Dental Insurance	73		67	87	65	91
Vision Program	58		56	67	52	91
Prescription Program	48		56	67	39	64
Life Insurance	48		56	67	45	36
Short Term Disability	30		47	60	32	36
Long Term Disability	30		47	60	26	36
Flex Spending	27		36	53	23	36
401 K	73		78	93	74	82
Paid Vacation Leave	100		92	93	94	91
Paid Sick Leave	82		64	80	68	82
Tuition Reimbursement	30		22	53	26	27
Training	36		50	80	55	55
Other	15		8	33	13	27
Responses	*33*		*36*	*15*	*31*	*11*

C-8

Positions and Compensation by Single-Family Starts in 2021

	1-10 Starts		11-25 Starts		26-99 Starts		100 + Starts	
	% With Full-time Position	Average Total Compensation	% With Full-time Position	Average Total Compensation	% With Full-time Position	Average Total Compensation	% With Full-time Position	Average Total Compensation
EXECUTIVE JOBS								
President/CEO	95	$132,160	89	$174,646	91	$358,491	100	$437,149
VP of Construction	30	$109,786	53	$135,920	72	$174,985	80	$236,653
CFO/Head of Finance	7	--	31	$89,200	41	$176,085	63	$199,345
CIO/Head of IT	1	--	6	--	0	--	10	--
OPERATIONS JOBS								
Head/Director of Purchasing	4	--	17	--	31	$112,805	70	$121,224
Head/Director of Land Acquisition	0	--	6	--	19	--	57	$172,831
Head/Director of Production	2	--	8	--	25	--	40	$133,167
Head/Director of Development & Training	1	--	3	--	0	--	3	--
Head/Director of Sales & Marketing	6	--	17	--	38	$155,709	73	$163,953
FINANCE JOBS								
Controller	2	--	22	--	22	--	73	$124,908
Payroll Manager	4	--	6	--	3	--	23	--
Staff Accountant	4	--	14	--	22	--	50	$77,071
Bookkeeper	16	$50,984	33	$65,982	38	$55,225	60	$55,347
HUMAN RESOURCES								
Director of Human Resources	1	--	0	--	6	--	30	--
Recruiter	0	--	0	--	0	--	3	--
In-house legal counsel	0	--	3	--	3	--	7	--
IT JOBS								
Director of IT	0	--	3	--	3	--	13	--
Network Engineer	0	--	0	--	0	--	0	--
Web Design Specialist	0	--	0	--	0	--	10	--
ADMINISTRATIVE JOBS								
Executive Assistant	6	--	11	--	16	--	20	--
Office Manager	10	--	8	--	25	--	33	$73,850
Administrative Assistant	5	--	11	--	9	--	23	--
Receptionist	2	--	6	--	9	--	43	$41,940
Settlement Coordinator	1	--	6	--	9	--	33	$60,784
PRODUCTION JOBS								
Production Manager	15	$83,417	31	$108,455	31	--	50	$112,789
Land Manager	0	--	0	--	13	--	20	--
Purchasing Manager	1	--	14	--	6	--	33	$74,840
Home Services/Warranty Manager	0	--	3	--	28	--	83	$79,424
Contract Manager	0	--	0	--	3	--	17	--
Project Manager	29	$100,062	42	$73,331	44	$84,306	43	$102,185
Architect	4	--	6	--	16	--	23	--
Estimator	11	--	11	--	13	--	47	$74,632
Superintendent	30	$73,520	44	$83,628	77	$80,488	77	$82,622
SALES & MARKETING JOBS								
Sales Manager	2	--	11	--	31	$132,803	50	$130,964
Model Home Host	0	--	0	--	6	--	13	--
Salesperson	2	--	14	--	13	--	67	$142,176
Design Center Manager	2	--	6	--	3	--	40	$84,767
Selections Coordinator	9	--	8	--	13	--	47	$64,175
Customer service Manager	1	--	3	--	6	--	27	--

Other Fringe Benefits by Job Category

EXECUTIVE JOBS

President/CEO
* Cell phone
* Charity/Volunteer Week Off
* Company Funded HSA
* Health Savings Account
* Holiday Pay
* IRA (2)
* Matching 401k
* Misc Benefit
* Paid Holidays
* Paid Parental Leave
* "Phone, Vehicle, Gas"
* Profit Sharing (3)
* "Profit Sharing, 401K"
* SIMPLE IRA
* "SIMPLE, Paid Holidays"
* Vehicle (3)
* Vehicle Allowance

VP of Construction
* Cell Phone
* Charity/Volunteer Week Off
* Company Funded HSA
* Health Savings Account
* Holiday Pay
* IRA (2)
* Matching 401k
* Misc Benefit
* Paid Holidays
* Paid Parental Leave
* "Phone, Vehicle, Gas "
* Profit Sharing (3)
* Profit Sharing 401K
* SIMPLE IRA

* "SIMPLE, Paid Holidays"
* Vehicle (3)
* Vehicle Allowance

CFO/Head of Finance
* Cell Phone
* Charity/Volunteer Week Off
* Company Funded HSA
* Health Savings Account
* Holiday Pay
* IRA (2)
* Matching 401k
* Misc Benefit
* Paid Holidays
* Paid Parental Leave
* "Phone, Vehicle, Gas"
* Profit Sharing (3)
* Profit Sharing 401K
* SIMPLE IRA
* "SIMPLE, Paid Holidays"
* Vehicle (3)
* Vehicle Allowance

CFO/Head of IT
* Cell Phone
* Charity/Volunteer Week Off
* Company Funded HSA
* Health Savings Account
* Holiday Pay
* IRA (2)
* Matching 401k
* Misc Benefit
* Paid Holidays
* Paid Parental Leave
* "Phone, Vehicle, Gas"
* Profit Sharing (3)

* Profit Sharing 401K
* SIMPLE IRA
* "SIMPLE, Paid Holidays"
* Vehicle (3)
* Vehicle Allowance

OPERATIONS JOBS

Head/Director of Purchasing
* Childcare
* Company Car
* Gas Allowance
* Health Savings Account
* Holiday Pay
* Mileage
* Paid Parental Leave
* Profit Sharing (2)
* Profit Sharing 401K
* Vehicle
* Vehicle Allowance
* Volunteer Work Week Off

Head/Director of Land Acquisition
* Childcare
* Company Car
* Gas Allowance
* Health Savings Account
* Holiday Pay
* Mileage
* Paid Parental Leave
* Profit Sharing (2)
* Profit Sharing 401K
* Vehicle
* Vehicle Allowance
* Volunteer Work Week Off

Head/Director of Production
* Childcare
* Company Car
* Gas allowance
* Health Savings Account
* Holiday pay
* Mileage
* Paid Parental Leave
* Profit sharing (2)

* Profit Sharing 401K
* Vehicle
* Vehicle Allowance
* Volunteer work week off

Head/Director of Development and Training
* Childcare
* Company Car
* Gas Allowance
* Health Savings Account
* Holiday Pay
* Mileage
* Paid Parental Leave
* Profit Sharing (2)
* Profit Sharing 401K
* Vehicle
* Vehicle Allowance
* Volunteer Work Week Off

Head/Director of Sales & Marketing
* Childcare
* Company Car
* Gas Allowance
* Health Savings Account
* Holiday Pay
* Mileage
* Paid Parental Leave
* Profit Sharing (2)
* Profit Sharing 401K
* Vehicle
* Vehicle Allowance
* Volunteer Work Week Off

FINANCE JOBS

Controller
* Fuel Reimbursement and Vehicle Maintenance
* Paid Holidays
* Paid Parental Leave
* Profit sharing
* "Profit Sharing, 401K"
* Volunteer Work Week Off

Payroll Manager
* Fuel Reimbursement and Vehicle Maintenance
* Paid Holidays
* Paid Parental Leave
* Profit Sharing
* "Profit Sharing, 401K"
* Volunteer Work Week Off

Staff Accountant
* Fuel Reimbursement and Vehicle Maintenance
* Paid Holidays
* Paid Parental Leave
* Profit sharing
* "Profit Sharing, 401K"
* Volunteer Work Week Off

Bookkeeper
* Fuel Reimbursement and Vehicle Maintenance
* Paid Holidays
* Paid Parental Leave
* Profit Sharing
* "Profit Sharing, 401K"
* Volunteer Work Week Off

HUMAN RESOURCES JOBS

Director of Human Resources
* Volunteer Work Week Off

Recruiter
* Volunteer Work Week Off

In-house Legal Counsel
* Volunteer Work Week Off

In-house Legal Counsel
* Volunteer Work Week Off

IT JOBS

Director of IT
* Vehicle

Network Engineer
* Vehicle

Web Design Specialist
* Vehicle

ADMINISTRATIVE JOBS

Executive Assistant
* Health Savings Account
* Holiday Pay
* IRA
* Matching 401k
* Profit Sharing
* "SIMPLE, Paid Holidays"
* Vehicle Allowance
* Volunteer Work Week Off

Office Manager
* Health Savings Account
* Holiday Pay
* IRA
* Matching 401k
* Profit Sharing
* "SIMPLE, Paid Holidays"
* Vehicle Allowance
* Volunteer Work Week Off

Administrative Assistant
* Health Savings Account
* Holiday Pay
* IRA
* Matching 401k
* Profit Sharing
* "SIMPLE, Paid Holidays"
* Vehicle Allowance
* Volunteer Work Week Off

Receptionist
* Health Savings Account
* Holiday Pay
* IRA
* Matching 401k
* Profit Sharing
* "SIMPLE, Paid Holidays"
* Vehicle Allowance
* Volunteer Work Week Off

Settlement Coordinator
* Health Savings Account
* Holiday Pay
* IRA
* Matching 401k
* Profit Sharing
* "SIMPLE, Paid Holidays"
* Vehicle Allowance
* Volunteer Work Week Off

PRODUCTION JOBS

Production Manager
* Auto Reimbursement
* Gas Allowance
* Paid Parental Leave
* Profit Sharing
* Vehicle Allowance
* Volunteer Work Week Off

Land Manager
* Auto Reimbursement
* Gas Allowance
* Paid Parental Leave
* Profit Sharing
* Vehicle Allowance
* Volunteer Work Week Off

Purchasing Manager
* Auto Reimbursement
* Gas Allowance
* Paid Parental Leave
* Profit Sharing
* Vehicle Allowance
* Volunteer Work Week Off

Home Services/ Warranty Manager
* Co Funded HSA
* Gas Allowance
* Health Savings Account
* Holiday Pay
* IRA (2)
* Matching 401k
* Mileage
* Paid Holidays
* Paid Parental Leave
* Profit Sharing (2)
* Profit Sharing 401K
* "SIMPLE, Paid Holidays"
* Vehicle
* Vehicle Allowance
* Volunteer Work Week Off

Contract Manager
* Co Funded HSA
* Gas Allowance
* Health Savings Account
* Holiday Pay
* IRA (2)
* Matching 401k
* Mileage
* Paid Holidays
* Paid Parental Leave
* Profit Sharing (2)
* Profit Sharing 401K
* "SIMPLE, Paid Holidays"
* Vehicle
* Vehicle Allowance
* Volunteer Work Week Off

Project Manager
* Co Funded HSA
* Gas Allowance
* Health Savings Account
* Holiday Pay
* IRA (2)
* Matching 401k
* Mileage
* Paid Holidays
* Paid Parental Leave
* Profit Sharing (2)
* Profit Sharing 401K

* "SIMPLE, Paid Holidays"
* Vehicle
* Vehicle Allowance
* Volunteer Work Week Off

Architect
* Co Funded HSA
* Gas Allowance
* Health Savings Account
* Holiday Pay
* IRA (2)
* Matching 401k
* Mileage
* Paid Holidays
* Paid Parental Leave
* Profit Sharing (2)
* Profit Sharing 401K
* "SIMPLE, Paid Holidays"
* Vehicle
* Vehicle Allowance
* Volunteer Work Week Off

Estimator
* Co Funded HSA
* Gas Allowance
* Health Savings Account
* Holiday Pay
* IRA (2)
* Matching 401k
* Mileage
* Paid Holidays
* Paid Parental Leave
* Profit Sharing (2)
* Profit Sharing 401K
* "SIMPLE, Paid Holidays"
* Vehicle
* Vehicle Allowance
* Volunteer Work Week Off

Superintendent
* Co Funded HSA
* Gas Allowance
* Health Savings Account
* Holiday Pay
* IRA (2)
* Matching 401k

* Mileage
* Paid Holidays
* Paid Parental Leave
* Profit Sharing (2)
* Profit Sharing 401K
* "SIMPLE, Paid Holidays"
* Vehicle
* Vehicle Allowance
* Volunteer Work Week Off

SALES AND MARKETING JOBS

Sales Manager
* Gas Allowance
* Vehicle
* Vehicle Allowance

Model Home Host
* Automobile Reimbursement
* Holiday Pay
* Paid Holidays
* Paid Parental Leave
* Profit Sharing
* "Profit Sharing, 401K"
* Vehicle
* Volunteer Work Week Off

Salesperson
* Automobile Reimbursement
* Holiday Pay
* Paid Holidays
* Paid Parental Leave
* Profit Sharing
* "Profit Sharing, 401K"
* Vehicle
* Volunteer Work Week Off

Design Center Manager
* Automobile reimbursement
* Holiday Pay
* Paid Holidays
* Paid Parental Leave
* Profit Sharing
* "Profit Sharing, 401K"
* Vehicle
* Volunteer Work Week Off

Selections Coordinator

* Automobile Reimbursement
* Holiday Pay
* Paid Holidays
* Paid Parental Leave
* Profit Sharing
* "Profit Sharing, 401K"
* Vehicle
* Volunteer Work Week Off

Customer Service Manager

* Automobile Reimbursement
* Holiday Pay
* Paid Holidays
* Paid Parental Leave
* Profit Sharing
* "Profit Sharing, 401K"
* Vehicle
* Volunteer Work Week Off

2021 Single-Family Builder Compensation Survey

1. What is your company's principal operation? *[If not a single-family builder, end survey].*

☐☐ Single-Family Spec/Tract Builder
☐☐ Single-Family Custom Builder
☐☐ Single-Family General Contractor
☐☐ Other

2. How many <u>single-family units</u> does your company expect to start in 2021? _____

3. Approximately, what will be the company's total <u>dollar volume</u> of business in <u>2021</u>?

☐ Under $500,000
☐ $500,000 - $999,999
☐ $1 million - $4,999,999
☐ $5 million - $9,999,999

☐ $10 million - $14,999,999
☐ $15 million or over
☐ No business activity

4. How many years has your company been in the home building business? _____ Years

**5. How many employees were on your payroll as of September 30, 2021?
(Include Owner/President/CEO).** _____

**6. What was your total payroll as of September 30, 2021?
(Include Owner/President/CEO).** $ _____

7. **Please indicate whether each of the following positions exists in your company, its current annual salary, bonus/commission, and any fringe benefits currently offered.**
   - For positions with only one employee, report the actual salary/bonus/commission.
   - For positions with multiple employees, report the average of all salaries in that position. If a person does more than one job, report job that takes most of his/her time.
   - If job titles do not exactly match those in your company, please respond by matching job descriptions.
   - For some positions, report if job is filled by a person(s) with hands-on experience in construction trades.

	EXECUTIVE JOBS			
	President/CEO *(Owner, leader, senior manager of the company)*	**VP of Construction** *(Lead decision maker about company's construction practices and policies)*	**CFO/Head of Finance** *(Lead decision maker about company's finances. Provides financial analysis, budgets, and*	**CIO/Head of IT** *(Lead decision maker about company's information technology needs)*
Does position exist?	☐ Yes, full-time ☐ Yes, part-time ☐ No	☐ Yes, full-time ☐ Yes, part-time ☐ No	☐ Yes, full-time ☐ Yes, part-time ☐ No	☐ Yes, full-time ☐ Yes, part-time ☐ No
Is it filled by person(s) with experience in construction trades?	☐ Always ☐ Sometimes ☐ Never/Almost never	☐ Always ☐ Sometimes ☐ Never/Almost never		
Annual salary	$_____	$_____	$_____	$_____
Bonus/ Commissions	☐ Yes ☐ No $_____	☐ Yes ☐ No $_____	☐ Yes ☐ No $_____	☐ Yes ☐ No $_____
Fringe Benefits	☐ Health Insurance ☐ Dental Insurance ☐ Vision Program ☐ Prescription Program ☐ Life Insurance ☐ Short Term Disability ☐ Long Term Disability ☐ Flex Spending ☐ 401 K ☐ Paid vacation ☐ Paid sick leave ☐ Tuition Reimbursement ☐ Training ☐ Other (specify):___	☐ Health Insurance ☐ Dental Insurance ☐ Vision Program ☐ Prescription Program ☐ Life Insurance ☐ Short Term Disability ☐ Long Term Disability ☐ Flex Spending ☐ 401 K ☐ Paid vacation leave ☐ Paid sick leave ☐ Tuition Reimbursement ☐ Training ☐ Other (specify):___	☐ Health Insurance ☐ Dental Insurance ☐ Vision Program ☐ Prescription Program ☐ Life Insurance ☐ Short Term Disability ☐ Long Term Disability ☐ Flex Spending ☐ 401 K ☐ Paid vacation leave ☐ Paid sick leave ☐ Tuition Reimbursement ☐ Training ☐ Other (specify):___	☐ Health Insurance ☐ Dental Insurance ☐ Vision Program ☐ Prescription Program ☐ Life Insurance ☐ Short Term Disability ☐ Long Term Disability ☐ Flex Spending ☐ 401 K ☐ Paid vacation leave ☐ Paid sick leave ☐ Tuition Reimbursement ☐ Training ☐ Other (specify):___

F-2

	OPERATIONS JOBS			
	Head /Director of Purchasing *(in charge of ordering and negotiating building materials)*	**Head /Director of Land Acquisition** *(in charge of land acquisition, development, and zoning issues)*	**Head /Director of Production** *(manages engineers, production managers and implements company's production policies)*	**Head /Director of Development and Training** *(in charge of developing all in-house or external training)*
Does position exist?	☐ Yes, full-time ☐ Yes, part-time ☐ No	☐ Yes, full-time ☐ Yes, part-time ☐ No	☐ Yes, full-time ☐ Yes, part-time ☐ No	☐ Yes, full-time ☐ Yes, part-time ☐ No
Is it filled by person(s) with experience in construction trades?	☐ Always ☐ Sometimes ☐ Never/Almost never	☐ Always ☐ Sometimes ☐ Never/Almost never	☐ Always ☐ Sometimes ☐ Never/Almost never	☐ Always ☐ Sometimes ☐ Never/Almost never
Annual salary	$_____	$_____	$_____	$_____
Bonus/ Commissions	☐ Yes ☐ No $_____	☐ Yes ☐ No $_____	☐ Yes ☐ No $_____	☐ Yes ☐ No $_____
Fringe Benefits	☐ Health Insurance ☐ Dental Insurance ☐ Vision Program ☐ Prescription Program ☐ Life Insurance ☐ Short Term Disability ☐ Long Term Disability ☐ Flex Spending ☐ 401 K ☐ Paid vacation ☐ Paid sick leave ☐ Tuition Reimbursement ☐ Training ☐ Other (specify):___	☐ Health Insurance ☐ Dental Insurance ☐ Vision Program ☐ Prescription Program ☐ Life Insurance ☐ Short Term Disability ☐ Long Term Disability ☐ Flex Spending ☐ 401 K ☐ Paid vacation ☐ Paid sick leave ☐ Tuition Reimbursement ☐ Training ☐ Other (specify):___	☐ Health Insurance ☐ Dental Insurance ☐ Vision Program ☐ Prescription Program ☐ Life Insurance ☐ Short Term Disability ☐ Long Term Disability ☐ Flex Spending ☐ 401 K ☐ Paid vacation leave ☐ Paid sick leave ☐ Tuition Reimbursement ☐ Training ☐ Other (specify):___	☐ Health Insurance ☐ Dental Insurance ☐ Vision Program ☐ Prescription Program ☐ Life Insurance ☐ Short Term Disability ☐ Long Term Disability ☐ Flex Spending ☐ 401 K ☐ Paid vacation leave ☐ Paid sick leave ☐ Tuition Reimbursement ☐ Training ☐ Other (specify):___

F-3

OPERATIONS JOBS		FINANCE JOBS		
	Head /Director of Sales & Marketing *(in charge of marketing strategy to promote the company and product)*	**Controller** *(plans, organizes, and controls accounting system)*	**Payroll Manager** *(manages payroll process)*	**Staff Accountant** *(Assembles and analyzes accounting data to prepare financial statements)*
Does position exist?	☐ Yes, full-time ☐ Yes, part-time ☐ No	☐ Yes, full-time ☐ Yes, part-time ☐ No	☐ Yes, full-time ☐ Yes, part-time ☐ No	☐ Yes, full-time ☐ Yes, part-time ☐ No
Is it filled by person(s) with experience in construction trades?	☐ Always ☐ Sometimes ☐ Never/Almost never			
Annual salary	$_____	$_____	$_____	$_____
Bonus/ Commissions	☐ Yes ☐ No $_____	☐ Yes ☐ No $_____	☐ Yes ☐ No $_____	☐ Yes ☐ No $_____
Fringe Benefits	☐ Health Insurance ☐ Dental Insurance ☐ Vision Program ☐ Prescription Program ☐ Life Insurance ☐ Short Term Disability ☐ Long Term Disability ☐ Flex Spending ☐ 401 K ☐ Paid vacation ☐ Paid sick leave ☐ Tuition Reimbursement ☐ Training ☐ Other (specify):___	☐ Health Insurance ☐ Dental Insurance ☐ Vision Program ☐ Prescription Program ☐ Life Insurance ☐ Short Term Disability ☐ Long Term Disability ☐ Flex Spending ☐ 401 K ☐ Paid vacation ☐ Paid sick leave ☐ Tuition Reimbursement ☐ Training ☐ Other (specify):___	☐ Health Insurance ☐ Dental Insurance ☐ Vision Program ☐ Prescription Program ☐ Life Insurance ☐ Short Term Disability ☐ Long Term Disability ☐ Flex Spending ☐ 401 K ☐ Paid vacation leave ☐ Paid sick leave ☐ Tuition Reimbursement ☐ Training ☐ Other (specify):___	☐ Health Insurance ☐ Dental Insurance ☐ Vision Program ☐ Prescription Program ☐ Life Insurance ☐ Short Term Disability ☐ Long Term Disability ☐ Flex Spending ☐ 401 K ☐ Paid vacation leave ☐ Paid sick leave ☐ Tuition Reimbursement ☐ Training ☐ Other (specify):___

F-4

	FINANCE JOBS	HUMAN RESOURCES JOBS		
	Bookkeeper *(processes accounts payable and enters accounting data)*	**Director of Human Resources** *(manages all functions related to recruiting and retaining employees)*	**Recruiter** *(handles all functions related to recruiting employees)*	**In-house Legal Counsel** *(lead internal attorney for company)*
Does position exist?	☐ Yes, full-time ☐ Yes, part-time ☐ No	☐ Yes, full-time ☐ Yes, part-time ☐ No	☐ Yes, full-time ☐ Yes, part-time ☐ No	☐ Yes, full-time ☐ Yes, part-time ☐ No
Annual salary	$_____	$_____	$_____	$_____
Bonus/ Commissions	☐ Yes ☐ No $_____	☐ Yes ☐ No $_____	☐ Yes ☐ No $_____	☐ Yes ☐ No $_____
Fringe	☐ Health Insurance ☐ Dental Insurance ☐ Vision Program ☐ Prescription Program ☐ Life Insurance ☐ Short Term Disability ☐ Long Term Disability ☐ Flex Spending ☐ 401 K ☐ Paid vacation ☐ Paid sick leave ☐ Tuition Reimbursement ☐ Training ☐ Other (specify):___	☐ Health Insurance ☐ Dental Insurance ☐ Vision Program ☐ Prescription Program ☐ Life Insurance ☐ Short Term Disability ☐ Long Term Disability ☐ Flex Spending ☐ 401 K ☐ Paid vacation ☐ Paid sick leave ☐ Tuition Reimbursement ☐ Training ☐ Other (specify):___	☐ Health Insurance ☐ Dental Insurance ☐ Vision Program ☐ Prescription Program ☐ Life Insurance ☐ Short Term Disability ☐ Long Term Disability ☐ Flex Spending ☐ 401 K ☐ Paid vacation leave ☐ Paid sick leave ☐ Tuition Reimbursement ☐ Training ☐ Other (specify):___	☐ Health Insurance ☐ Dental Insurance ☐ Vision Program ☐ Prescription Program ☐ Life Insurance ☐ Short Term Disability ☐ Long Term Disability ☐ Flex Spending ☐ 401 K ☐ Paid vacation leave ☐ Paid sick leave ☐ Tuition Reimbursement ☐ Training ☐ Other (specify):___

F-5

	IT JOBS			ADMINISTRATIVE JOBS
	Director of IT *(directly manages company's networks, computer resources, and website)*	**Network Engineer** *(installs software, maintains network and computer inventory)*	**Web Design Specialist** *(designs, monitors, and updates company's website)*	**Executive Assistant** *(provides administrative and clerical support to company's executives)*
Does position exist?	☐ Yes, full-time ☐ Yes, part-time ☐ No	☐ Yes, full-time ☐ Yes, part-time ☐ No	☐ Yes, full-time ☐ Yes, part-time ☐ No	☐ Yes, full-time ☐ Yes, part-time ☐ No
Annual salary	$_____	$_____	$_____	$_____
Bonus/ Commissions	☐ Yes ☐ No $_____	☐ Yes ☐ No $_____	☐ Yes ☐ No $_____	☐ Yes ☐ No $_____
Fringe benefits	☐ Health Insurance ☐ Dental Insurance ☐ Vision Program ☐ Prescription Program ☐ Life Insurance ☐ Short Term Disability ☐ Long Term Disability ☐ Flex Spending ☐ 401 K ☐ Paid vacation ☐ Paid sick leave ☐ Tuition Reimbursement ☐ Training ☐ Other (specify):___	☐ Health Insurance ☐ Dental Insurance ☐ Vision Program ☐ Prescription Program ☐ Life Insurance ☐ Short Term Disability ☐ Long Term Disability ☐ Flex Spending ☐ 401 K ☐ Paid vacation leave ☐ Paid sick leave ☐ Tuition Reimbursement ☐ Training ☐ Other (specify):___	☐ Health Insurance ☐ Dental Insurance ☐ Vision Program ☐ Prescription Program ☐ Life Insurance ☐ Short Term Disability ☐ Long Term Disability ☐ Flex Spending ☐ 401 K ☐ Paid vacation leave ☐ Paid sick leave ☐ Tuition Reimbursement ☐ Training ☐ Other (specify):___	☐ Health Insurance ☐ Dental Insurance ☐ Vision Program ☐ Prescription Program ☐ Life Insurance ☐ Short Term Disability ☐ Long Term Disability ☐ Flex Spending ☐ 401 K ☐ Paid vacation leave ☐ Paid sick leave ☐ Tuition Reimbursement ☐ Training ☐ Other (specify):___

F-6

	ADMINISTRATIVE JOBS			
	Office Manager *(manages administrative office staff)*	**Administrative Assistant** *(handles office administrative duties, typing, filing)*	**Receptionist** *(receives and routes incoming calls and visitors, performs clerical duties)*	**Settlement Coordinator** *(serves as liaison between customers and the rest of the company)*
Does position exist?	☐ Yes, full-time ☐ Yes, part-time ☐ No	☐ Yes, full-time ☐ Yes, part-time ☐ No	☐ Yes, full-time ☐ Yes, part-time ☐ No	☐ Yes, full-time ☐ Yes, part-time ☐ No
Annual salary	$_____	$_____	$_____	$_____
Bonus/ Commissions	☐ Yes ☐ No $_____	☐ Yes ☐ No $_____	☐ Yes ☐ No $_____	☐ Yes ☐ No $_____
Fringe benefits	☐ Health Insurance ☐ Dental Insurance ☐ Vision Program ☐ Prescription Program ☐ Life Insurance ☐ Short Term Disability ☐ Long Term Disability ☐ Flex Spending ☐ 401 K ☐ Paid vacation ☐ Paid sick leave ☐ Tuition Reimbursement ☐ Training ☐ Other (specify):___	☐ Health Insurance ☐ Dental Insurance ☐ Vision Program ☐ Prescription Program ☐ Life Insurance ☐ Short Term Disability ☐ Long Term Disability ☐ Flex Spending ☐ 401 K ☐ Paid vacation ☐ Paid sick leave ☐ Tuition Reimbursement ☐ Training ☐ Other (specify):___	☐ Health Insurance ☐ Dental Insurance ☐ Vision Program ☐ Prescription Program ☐ Life Insurance ☐ Short Term Disability ☐ Long Term Disability ☐ Flex Spending ☐ 401 K ☐ Paid vacation leave ☐ Paid sick leave ☐ Tuition Reimbursement ☐ Training ☐ Other (specify):___	☐ Health Insurance ☐ Dental Insurance ☐ Vision Program ☐ Prescription Program ☐ Life Insurance ☐ Short Term Disability ☐ Long Term Disability ☐ Flex Spending ☐ 401 K ☐ Paid vacation leave ☐ Paid sick leave ☐ Tuition Reimbursement ☐ Training ☐ Other (specify):___

F-7

	Production Manager (responsible for field operations, including budgeting and cost controls at the divisional level or for smaller company)	**Land Manager** (responsible for land acquisition/development at the divisional level or for smaller company)	**Purchasing Manager** (orders and negotiates for building products at the divisional level or for smaller company)	**Home Services/ Warranty Manager** (maintains quality assurance and provides warranty service to homeowners after closing)
PRODUCTION JOBS				
Does position exist?	☐ Yes, full-time ☐ Yes, part-time ☐ No	☐ Yes, full-time ☐ Yes, part-time ☐ No	☐ Yes, full-time ☐ Yes, part-time ☐ No	☐ Yes, full-time ☐ Yes, part-time ☐ No
Is it filled by person(s) with experience in construction trades?	☐ Always ☐ Sometimes ☐ Never/Almost never	☐ Always ☐ Sometimes ☐ Never/Almost never	☐ Always ☐ Sometimes ☐ Never/Almost never	
Annual salary	$_____	$_____	$_____	$_____
Bonus/ Commissions	☐ Yes ☐ No $_____	☐ Yes ☐ No $_____	☐ Yes ☐ No $_____	☐ Yes ☐ No $_____
Fringe benefits	☐ Health Insurance ☐ Dental Insurance ☐ Vision Program ☐ Prescription Program ☐ Life Insurance ☐ Short Term Disability ☐ Long Term Disability ☐ Flex Spending ☐ 401 K ☐ Paid vacation leave ☐ Paid sick leave ☐ Tuition Reimbursement ☐ Training ☐ Other (specify):___	☐ Health Insurance ☐ Dental Insurance ☐ Vision Program ☐ Prescription Program ☐ Life Insurance ☐ Short Term Disability ☐ Long Term Disability ☐ Flex Spending ☐ 401 K ☐ Paid vacation leave ☐ Paid sick leave ☐ Tuition Reimbursement ☐ Training ☐ Other (specify):___	☐ Health Insurance ☐ Dental Insurance ☐ Vision Program ☐ Prescription Program ☐ Life Insurance ☐ Short Term Disability ☐ Long Term Disability ☐ Flex Spending ☐ 401 K ☐ Paid vacation leave ☐ Paid sick leave ☐ Tuition Reimbursement ☐ Training ☐ Other (specify):___	☐ Health Insurance ☐ Dental Insurance ☐ Vision Program ☐ Prescription Program ☐ Life Insurance ☐ Short Term Disability ☐ Long Term Disability ☐ Flex Spending ☐ 401 K ☐ Paid vacation leave ☐ Paid sick leave ☐ Tuition Reimbursement ☐ Training ☐ Other (specify):___

F-8

	PRODUCTION JOBS			
	Contract Manager *(responsible for producing and monitoring sales contracts)*	**Project Manager** *(monitors production schedules and ensures that homes are completed on time and meet quality and profit levels as well as client needs)*	**Architect** *(responsible for architectural and structural design aspects of the home building process)*	**Estimator** *(ensures accuracy of house take-offs)*
Does position exist?	☐ Yes, full-time ☐ Yes, part-time ☐ No	☐ Yes, full-time ☐ Yes, part-time ☐ No	☐ Yes, full-time ☐ Yes, part-time ☐ No	☐ Yes, full-time ☐ Yes, part-time ☐ No
Annual salary	$_____	$_____	$_____	$_____
Bonus/ Commissions	☐ Yes ☐ No $_____	☐ Yes ☐ No $_____	☐ Yes ☐ No $_____	☐ Yes ☐ No $_____
Fringe benefits	☐ Health Insurance ☐ Dental Insurance ☐ Vision Program ☐ Prescription Program ☐ Life Insurance ☐ Short Term Disability ☐ Long Term Disability ☐ Flex Spending ☐ 401 K ☐ Paid vacation ☐ Paid sick leave ☐ Tuition Reimbursement ☐ Training ☐ Other (specify):_	☐ Health Insurance ☐ Dental Insurance ☐ Vision Program ☐ Prescription Program ☐ Life Insurance ☐ Short Term Disability ☐ Long Term Disability ☐ Flex Spending ☐ 401 K ☐ Paid vacation leave ☐ Paid sick leave ☐ Tuition Reimbursement ☐ Training ☐ Other (specify):___	☐ Health Insurance ☐ Dental Insurance ☐ Vision Program ☐ Prescription Program ☐ Life Insurance ☐ Short Term Disability ☐ Long Term Disability ☐ Flex Spending ☐ 401 K ☐ Paid vacation ☐ Paid sick leave ☐ Tuition Reimbursement ☐ Training ☐ Other (specify):___	☐ Health Insurance ☐ Dental Insurance ☐ Vision Program ☐ Prescription Program ☐ Life Insurance ☐ Short Term Disability ☐ Long Term Disability ☐ Flex Spending ☐ 401 K ☐ Paid vacation ☐ Paid sick leave ☐ Tuition Reimbursement ☐ Training ☐ Other (specify):___

F-9

PRODUCTION JOBS		SALES & MARKETING JOBS		
	Superintendent *(manages daily construction activities)*	**Sales Manager** *(manages sales functions and personnel, establishes procedures for doing sales presentations and qualifying prospects)*	**Model Home Host** *(meets and greets public, collects customer registration cards)*	**Salesperson** *(conducts sales presentation for prospective customers, prepares home purchase agreements, follow up with clients about construction, design, financing)*
Does position exist?	☐ Yes, full-time ☐ Yes, part-time ☐ No	☐ Yes, full-time ☐ Yes, part-time ☐ No	☐ Yes, full-time ☐ Yes, part-time ☐ No	☐ Yes, full-time ☐ Yes, part-time ☐ No
Is it filled by person(s) with experience in construction trades?		☐ Always ☐ Sometimes ☐ Never/Almost never		
Annual salary	$_____	$_____	$_____	$_____
Bonus/ Commissions	☐ Yes ☐ No $_____	☐ Yes ☐ No $_____	☐ Yes ☐ No $_____	☐ Yes ☐ No $_____
Fringe benefits	☐ Health Insurance ☐ Dental Insurance ☐ Vision Program ☐ Prescription Program ☐ Life Insurance ☐ Short Term Disability ☐ Long Term Disability ☐ Flex Spending ☐ 401 K ☐ Paid vacation ☐ Paid sick leave ☐ Tuition Reimbursement ☐ Training ☐ Other (specify):_	☐ Health Insurance ☐ Dental Insurance ☐ Vision Program ☐ Prescription Program ☐ Life Insurance ☐ Short Term Disability ☐ Long Term Disability ☐ Flex Spending ☐ 401 K ☐ Paid vacation leave ☐ Paid sick leave ☐ Tuition Reimbursement ☐ Training ☐ Other (specify):__	☐ Health Insurance ☐ Dental Insurance ☐ Vision Program ☐ Prescription Program ☐ Life Insurance ☐ Short Term Disability ☐ Long Term Disability ☐ Flex Spending ☐ 401 K ☐ Paid vacation ☐ Paid sick leave ☐ Tuition Reimbursement ☐ Training ☐ Other (specify):___	☐ Health Insurance ☐ Dental Insurance ☐ Vision Program ☐ Prescription Program ☐ Life Insurance ☐ Short Term Disability ☐ Long Term Disability ☐ Flex Spending ☐ 401 K ☐ Paid vacation leave ☐ Paid sick leave ☐ Tuition Reimbursement ☐ Training ☐ Other (specify):___

F-10

	Design Center Manager (manages company's design center)	Selections Coordinator (helps customers make finish selections in company's design center)	Customer Service Manager (manages customer service at the divisional level or for a smaller company)
SALES & MARKETING JOBS			
Does position exist?	☐ Yes, full-time ☐ Yes, part-time ☐ No	☐ Yes, full-time ☐ Yes, part-time ☐ No	☐ Yes, full-time ☐ Yes, part-time ☐ No
Annual salary	$_____	$_____	$_____
Bonus/ Commissions	☐ Yes ☐ No $_____	☐ Yes ☐ No $_____	☐ Yes ☐ No $_____
Fringe benefits	☐ Health Insurance ☐ Dental Insurance ☐ Vision Program ☐ Prescription Program ☐ Life Insurance ☐ Short Term Disability ☐ Long Term Disability ☐ Flex Spending ☐ 401 K ☐ Paid vacation leave ☐ Paid sick leave ☐ Tuition Reimbursement ☐ Training ☐ Other (specify):___	☐ Health Insurance ☐ Dental Insurance ☐ Vision Program ☐ Prescription Program ☐ Life Insurance ☐ Short Term Disability ☐ Long Term Disability ☐ Flex Spending ☐ 401 K ☐ Paid vacation leave ☐ Paid sick leave ☐ Tuition Reimbursement ☐ Training ☐ Other (specify):___	☐ Health Insurance ☐ Dental Insurance ☐ Vision Program ☐ Prescription Program ☐ Life Insurance ☐ Short Term Disability ☐ Long Term Disability ☐ Flex Spending ☐ 401 K ☐ Paid vacation leave ☐ Paid sick leave ☐ Tuition Reimbursement ☐ Training ☐ Other (specify):___

8. If there are other position(s) in your company not listed above, please provide title and a description of duties.

_____

_____

_____

F-11